52

HF5415.3 .K36 1998

Kautz, Gerhard, 1938-

Developing international
markets : shaping your
c1998.

D1540481

SENECA
NEWNHAM
COLLEGE LIBRARY

AEY 1090   170201

WITHDRAWN

Developing International Markets

Shaping Your Global Presence

Gerhard Kautz

The Oasis Press® / PSI Research
Grants Pass, Oregon

PROPERTY OF
SENECA COLLEGE
LIBRARIES
MARKHAM CAMPUS

Published by The Oasis Press
© 1998 by Gerhard Kautz

All rights reserved. No part of this publication may be reproduced or used in any form
or by any means, graphic, electronic or mechanical, including photocopying, recording,
taping, or information storage and retrieval systems without written permission of the
publishers.

This publication is designed to provide accurate and authoritative information in regard
to the subject matter covered. It is sold with the understanding that the publisher is not
engaged in rendering legal, accounting, or other professional service. If legal advice or
other expert assistance is required, the services of a competent professional person
should be sought.
> — *from a declaration of principles jointly adopted by a committee of
> the American Bar Association and a committee of publishers.*

Editor and Book Designer: Constance C. Dickinson
Assistant Editor: Janelle Davidson
Compositor: Jan Olsson
Cover Designer: Steven Burns

Please direct any comments, questions, or suggestions regarding this book to
The Oasis Press®/PSI Research:

Editorial Department
P.O. Box 3727
Central Point, OR 97502
(541) 479-9464
info@psi-research.com *email*

The Oasis Press® is a Registered Trademark of Publishing Services, Inc.,
an Oregon corporation doing business as PSI Research.

Kautz, Gerhard, 1938–
    Developing international markets : shaping your global presence /
Gerhard Kautz.
       p.   cm. -- (PSI successful business library)
    Includes index.
    ISBN 1-55571-433-1 (pbk.)
    1. Market surveys.   2. Marketing research.   3. Motivation research
(Marketing)   4. Strategic planning.   I. Title. II. Series.
HF5415.3.K36 1998
658.8'3--dc21   98-24902

Printed in the United States of America
First Edition 10 9 8 7 6 5 4 3 2 1

 Printed on recycled paper when available.

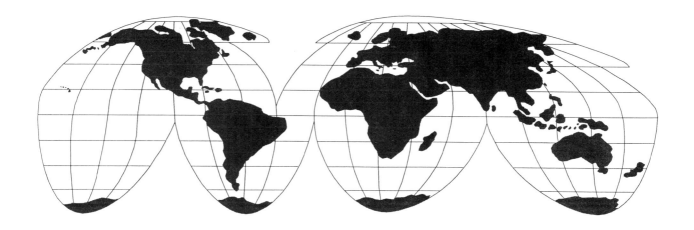

Table of Contents

Preface

Exporting your products can be a very profitable business; for many companies it is their only business. However, entering the international market is a challenging activity for the uninitiated. It's a different world. Its inhabitants not only speak differently but have different lifestyles and do business differently. How you sell in New York may not be the way to sell in Bangkok and vice versa.

Many companies have attempted the international market and discovered it is not as easy as they thought it would be. It is fraught with problems that can be costly and time consuming to solve. However, if this market is approached in a methodical way, one in which the major risks are addressed before too many company resources are committed, the resulting sales can be very rewarding. This book provides the guidance and information to help you get those rewards, and hopefully, it will help you expand your business into a global enterprise.

The book is aimed at small to medium-sized companies that are successful in their domestic market and are considering entering the international market. It also applies to larger companies and companies already in the international market that are considering marketing a new product internationally.

The products considered throughout the book and used as examples are primarily goods varying from mass-marketed commodities to sophisticated, integrated systems. However, the book can also be applied to service type products, such as consulting services.

The author would like to thank Alternative Heating Systems Incorporated for acting as the test company and test product for this book. Even though the information in the book is based on the author's experiences in marketing to over forty countries, it was beneficial to use an actual company to reaffirm the procedures presented.

How to Use this Book

The book takes a six-step approach toward identifying and exploring the most appropriate international market location for your product. It begins by helping you select the most profitable international market for your particular product. An actual example company and its product are used to emphasize the process. Decision gates at critical stages in the preparation process progressively narrow down the international market until you can identify the most cost-effective target countries for your product. Then you will continue through the process of how to exploit your chosen market. This is done from a practical point of view, with many anecdotal examples of how and how not to carry out international marketing.

Step 1, Assess Your Export Possibilities, will assist you through a general assessment of your company's products to see if they are suitable for, and competitive in, the international market.

Step 2, Identify Potential International Customers, uses a somewhat standard market evaluation process but with an international market in mind. Through this process you will be able to gauge your products' viability in the international market and identify country markets with the most potential.

Step 3, Select the Best Country for Your Product, will help you assess your products' marketability in the countries identified in Step 2 and develop a market entry strategy for each country. It will then guide you through the process of developing a marketing plan and some realistic cost estimates associated with the marketing plan. You will be able to do an overall marketing cost versus potential profit assessment, so you will be able to make a final market entry decision.

Step 4, Prepare to Visit Your Target Country, discusses the practical aspects of making that first marketing visit to your target country. The all-important process of selecting and contracting with local marketing agents is discussed in Step 5, Selecting a Marketing Agent.

Step 6, Determine Your Promotion and Pricing, addresses methods of promoting the product in a foreign market and pricing it. It discusses the many, but often overlooked, issues that must be considered in the pricing process, including the difficult and delicate subject of payoffs which are often required in international marketing.

Step 7, Meet the Sales Challenges, covers many additional practical issues of the international marketplace.

The Glossary lists most of the international marketing terms you will encounter, and there are two appendices that provide additional assistance and information. Appendix A contains two marketing trip check-off lists to assist your preparation. Appendix B has market related information on 120 countries which will be useful in the market selection process and as a reference for future marketing activities.

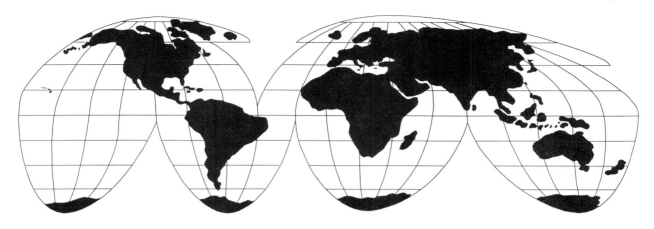

Assess Your Export Possibilities

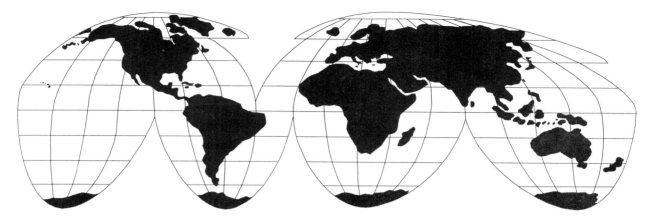

Chapter 1

Identifying the Export Product

You may find it hard to believe, but a lot of companies really do not definitively know what their products are. This is particularly true with technical products that have developed in response to the requirements of various customers. Your company may have a unique technology and a number of related products, but do you have anything specific that can be marketed to a new customer base? This is the first question that you must answer when assessing the international market.

Your aim is to come up with a tightly defined description of what the product is. Your product description must be one that can be easily understood by someone who has never seen the product. Even if you are confident that your proposed export product is well defined, you may still find it useful to go through the steps of confirming that definition.

Initial Product Definition

There are many ways to describe a product, and they will depend on the product itself. However, you should at least identify it by:

- Category

- Technology
- Basic type
- Uses

The category of a product is important because it relates to the customer base, the marketing effort, and the type of marketing required. It may be difficult to categorize some products, but in general, most products fall into the following categories.

- Systems incorporating a number of high-level components, such as electrical power generating plants. This category of product requires a lot of marketing effort and is usually the realm of the large, multinational companies.
- High-level products, such as specialized vehicles and computer systems. Companies with this category of product are usually small to medium-sized and are most likely to benefit from the process and information in this book.
- Commodity products, such as radios, clocks, and toothpaste. This category is also dominated by the big, multinational companies, which rely on large volume sales at low unit prices.
- Services, such as training, architectural design, maintenance, and data processing. These are also the products of small to medium-sized companies.

Identifying the technology is usually straightforward, unless it combines more than one technology. In general most product technologies can be described quite simply as electronic, mechanical, biochemical, and so forth. The technology of a product is useful in assessing the competition because sometimes the competition may be a different technology.

The basic type of product usually pertains to products other than complete systems and is often related to the technology used in it. For example, a type of electronic product may be a radio or a CD player, and a type of mechanical product may be a high-volume pump. The type of product often relates directly to the customer base as well as the competition. Also, most industrial product coding and government data bases are listed by product type, so if you want to use these effectively, you will have to identify your product type correctly.

Identifying the uses of the product usually gives it the most detailed definition, but this is sometimes the hardest thing to do. Designers want to be able to include all possible uses for their product, no matter how improbable it is that a customer will buy it for that reason. Resist this tendency as much as possible. Consider only the most prevalent uses of a product and disregard the rest, unless of course you think there may be a significant export market for those other uses. For example, a fiber optic link used for high data rate video transmission will, in all likelihood, also handle ordinary telephone line communication; however, there are much less costly links for telephone use. The high data rate video link should be described as for that use and not have its capability and value diluted by saying it can act as a telephone link.

You might be surprised, when you go through this exercise of defining your product, to discover what you really should be concentrating on in your domestic market before you attempt the international market. You may discover that you are squandering resources on variations of a basic technology, while if you focused on only one or two of the related products, your overhead would come down and your profit go up. This situation can be described by the following example.

Alternative Heating Systems Incorporated (AHSI) is a small mid-western company with a somewhat unique technology. They produce chemically treated elements encapsulated in fiberglass reinforced plastic forms that emit an infra-red heating wave when electricity is applied. The wave heats whatever it hits within about ten feet of the emitter, and the heated object in turn warms the surrounding air, much like how the sun heats the earth and the earth heats the surrounding air.

In the early stages of the company, they would design and manufacture heating products based on customer requests. As a result they ended up with heaters in many shapes and forms and for many purposes ranging from roof deicing heaters to floorboard heaters for trucks. Even though they were generating revenue, their overhead was extremely high, and they were operating at a loss.

They decided to analyze their products and identify what they really were. They discovered they had a commodity product that used infra-red technology and was a heater. When they looked at the users of the product, the company realized they were trying to be all things to all people. This was why they were getting into trouble. They quickly discovered that their most popular product variation was a heater, two foot by two foot square and about one inch thick, that mounted as a panel in suspended ceilings. This would be easy to produce on a larger scale and would appeal to a wide customer base. They decided to concentrate on this product, and thus the Heat-R-Tile was born.

Current Customers

The next step in identifying your product for the export market is to analyze who your current customers are. This will point you in the direction you should be investigating in the export market. Some of the questions to ask yourself about your product are:

- Is it used by a broad group of customers, or is it limited to definable groups?
- If limited to certain groups, what are they?
- Is it more popular with certain groups, such as a particular age group?
- Is it considered a necessity or a luxury?
- Is it affected by climate?
- What customer group has the largest demand?

AHSI took a look at their current customers and discovered that in the main they were homeowners with disposable income living in cold or occasionally cool climates. This narrowed down their North American market a bit, but, more importantly, it cut out a large portion of the international market. For example, they would obviously not find an export market in the slums of any country or in southern India or any equatorial country.

Customer Applications

Having identified the customers that currently use your product, the next question is how do they use it? Start by determining what they use it for in a broad sense, then list the particular applications. Don't just list the most popular ones because an application that is only occasionally useful in your domestic market could be a big seller in a foreign market. Once you have identified the applications, try to get as much information as possible about them, such as:

- Is the application constant or cyclical?
- How often do the customers actually use the product?
- Can they get by with a simpler solution to the application?
- Do they use the product in conjunction with other products?

The answers to some of these questions may cause you to consider an alteration to your product that could make it more appealing to an export market or even to your domestic market. But make sure the potential market is large enough before you go to the expense of redesigning your product. Many companies have gone off on tangents like this only to discover that the spin-off market was very limited, so they ended up losing money. On the other hand, a detailed analysis of how your customers apply your product could end up providing you with a new product line.

When AHSI investigated how their customers were applying the Heat-R-Tiles, they discovered some interesting applications. An auto body shop was using them to speed up the drying of paint, a family was using a Heat-R-Tile to heat an outside dog house, and some people were using them as the primary or only heat source in their house. However, by far the most popular use was for augmented heat in hard-to-heat areas of homes, such as basement recreation rooms, cold bedrooms, and drafty entrance ways. So the company began concentrating more on this domestic market.

Another interesting application they ran across was a hog farmer who had installed the Heat-R-Tile on the floor of a stall to keep baby pigs warm without the danger of being smothered by their mother. He had put a piece of plywood over the Heat-R-Tile to reduce the heat and to protect the pig's feet. AHSI knew that hog farming was big business in their area. Upon investigation they learned that keeping new born pigs warm was a major problem. They reduced the heat output of the Heat-R-Tiles by adjusting the chemically treated element, increased the durability of the fiberglass plastic case using the same molds, and created a new product, the Hog Hearth.

When AHSI considered entering the export market, they reassessed the customer applications of their two major products and came to the conclusion that:

- *The Heat-R-Tiles could be a big seller in areas that needed occasional, augmented heat, but that the customers would have to be able to afford them.*
- *The Hog Hearth could be a big seller in Europe, Russia, and those parts of Asia where there are large hog farms that must heat young piglets. There would be no Hog Hearth market in the Middle East or other equatorial countries.*

Product Considerations Associated With Export

Once you have identified the product you are planning to market internationally, listed the broad customer traits and applications, and generally concluded that there is a market out there for you, you must consider other aspects of your product that will affect its export. These will vary with the product, but the following are general considerations associated with export.

- Are there special shipping requirements for the product, or can it be delivered by the most economical means? There is quite a difference in the shipping costs by air versus by sea, and refrigerated transit can quickly render the product too expensive.

- Does the product require special installation or assembly skills? If so, you must select potential markets where these skills are readily available or be prepared to arrange for them.

- Does it need special training to operate? If so, where will you do the training, and how will it affect the cost?

- Are there associated equipment or services required to use the product? For example, will the buyer need a special water supply or refrigeration that may not be readily available?

- Is there a shelf life? This will affect the mode of transportation to your potential market or the method of distribution once there.

- How will after-sale maintenance and repair be done? Can you contract this function to a local company?

- Are there special regulatory or safety standards in the country you are considering that will affect the price and delivery of the product? For example, will the local government have to test the product prior to allowing it to be marketed?

- Are there special labeling requirements for the product, such as listing the contents in a particular format? Labeling requirements are a major issue in many foreign markets.

- Are there modifications to the product required to enable it to work in the foreign market? Electrical requirements are usually the issue, with many parts of the world operating on 220 or 240 volts, rather than the 120 volt supply in the United States, and at 50 cycles per second frequency, rather than 60 cycles or hertz.

- Will the label on the product have to be translated? In many countries this is not only a customer requirement, it is the law.

- Will the name of the product itself be acceptable to the foreign customers? There are many stories of American products being rejected because the name had a totally different meaning in another country.

- Will the instructions for your product have to be translated into the language of the country, and if so how will you validate the translation?

- Is the product aesthetically appealing in the foreign market? This is a hard one to judge, because it depends very much on the customs of the country involved. An example of this is how Americans buy kettles to boil water on a stove, while Canadians generally use electric kettles to heat water for cooking, coffee, and tea.

- Is the product or the potential foreign market under U.S. government export control? For many years it was against U.S. law to sell computer equipment to the U.S.S.R. and its associated countries.

Some of these considerations may cause you to rethink or even forget about entering the export market. However, there are solutions to most of the export problems you will face, but in all likelihood they will cost you money. This whole area of export considerations and costs are covered in more detail in chapters 2, 9, and 25. At this stage in your decision-making process you should just be aware of them, to make sure there are none significant enough to prevent you from entering the export market. It is better to make that decision now than later, after you have invested considerable resources in the venture.

AHSI went through the list of export considerations, and the first thing they discovered is that they would have to cater to a 220 or 240-volt electrical power supply in most of the world. This was not a problem because their Heat-R-Tiles and Hog Hearths already allowed for a 240-volt supply. The electrical frequency change was also not a problem.

Government regulations and product testing appeared to be a lengthy and expensive procedure for most of the European countries and Australia. Most other countries accept the American certification that is given by the Underwriters Laboratory, so they decided to avoid Europe and Australia, at least initially.

Potential Variations For Export Market

In the process of identifying the product or products you want to export, you will probably have noticed that there could be other applications of your product that would appeal to an export market. For example, a modularly constructed, portable building normally used at construction sites might have an application as a school or hospital in the remote areas of a developing country.

You also may have noticed that, with a slight alteration of the product, it could be offered to wider markets. This may look appealing, but be very cautious. Slight changes to the product that would incur very little extra cost may be worth pursuing; however, be careful about going through a major redesign without fully substantiating the new market.

AHSI realized that their Heat-R-Tile product could not be used in suspended ceilings in the export market because suspended ceilings are not used much outside North America. The company was particularly interested in the Middle East market for the Heat-R-Tiles because there is a need for augmented heat during the evenings in the winter and the potential customers could easily afford the product. However, most of the houses have very high ceilings, and Heat-R-Tiles

mounted on the ceilings would not work well. AHSI decided on a sim-
ple, yet decorative, addition to the Hear-R-Tile comprised of a brass
chain hanger that would lower the tiles to an eight-foot height over the
area to be heated. The additional cost of the hanger was only a few
dollars and could easily be included in the export price.

Export Business Arrangements

Another major issue you must consider about your export product is what
kind of export business arrangement will be most effective. These arrangements may vary from country to country, but the most advantageous
arrangement should be established at the same time the export product is
being identified. In some ways the export product considerations listed
above will drive the business arrangement, because with certain arrangements the onus to sort out local regulations will be on your in-country
associate. Some of the more popular export business arrangements are discussed.

Direct Exporting

You deal directly with your foreign customer, usually with the help of a
local marketing agent. The marketing agent is only responsible for finding
the customer and helping you make the sale. They normally do this for a
fee based on a percentage of the sale. However, you are responsible for all
the other aspects of the marketing activity, including obtaining local certification, installation, training, and after-sales service. So even though direct
exporting is the most common method of addressing the export market, it
is not suitable for all products.

Indirect Exporting

Here you use a company that purchases your products then resells them
in the local market. The most common arrangement of this kind is a distributorship. The distributor buys the products from you, stocks them if
required, and also maintains and repairs them if required. You get an
agreed price for the products from the distributor, then they sell them at
whatever price they can get.

This arrangement is less risky for you, provided you get paid for what
you sell to the distributor. You do not have to deal directly with the customers nor do you have to worry about activities such as obtaining local
certification, installation, training, and after-sales service. You lose control
of the pricing, however, which could affect you in other markets if it is too

low. If it is too high, you will be missing out on some of the profit the distributor is getting. Nevertheless, depending on the product, this is a good way to enter a foreign market.

Franchising

Franchising is a popular method of selling a proven product such as fast food and automobiles, but it can also be used effectively for other products. The advantages are similar to those of a distributorship, plus you control the standardization of the product marketing and you get income from the concept as well as the products. The disadvantage is that, in order to set up franchises, the product must be well known or fairly unique.

License Manufacturing

You grant the rights to a local company to manufacture all or part of your product and to sell it locally. The advantages are that you get income without having to manufacture the product, you do not have to deal directly with the local customers, your product appears to be locally made, and you usually do not have to invest any money in the venture. The local company receives wider local customer acceptance and often some local government support. The disadvantages are that you lose some control of the manufacturing process, the quality, and the standardization. There is also the possibility that your new partner will go into business with a variation of your product, leaving you out of the deal, or worse, becoming your competitor.

Joint Ventures

You team with a local company or companies to form a jointly-owned company that manufactures and distributes the product in the local market. The advantages are similar to a licensing arrangement, plus you have a degree of control over the manufacture, quality, and standardization of the product. The disadvantages are that you have to invest in the joint venture. There is also the possibility that your joint venture partner or partners may force you out and take over the business.

AHSI decided that the best business arrangement for their Heat-R-Tile product in a foreign market would be a distributorship in each country. Later on, if the business warranted it, they could consider a licensing arrangement in which the final assembly and possibly some of the molding could be made in-country to cut down freight costs.

First Export Decision Gate

Now that you have identified the product or products that you want to export, considered the many associated aspects of selling them internationally, and decided on the best business arrangement to set up in a foreign country, you must decide if you still want to tackle the international market. Even though you have come to the conclusion at this stage that it may be worth the effort to get into the export market, you still have to do more detailed investigation. However, if during this identification phase you came across something that would make it very difficult to export the product profitably, you may want to shelve the idea for now and save yourself some effort.

Chapter 2

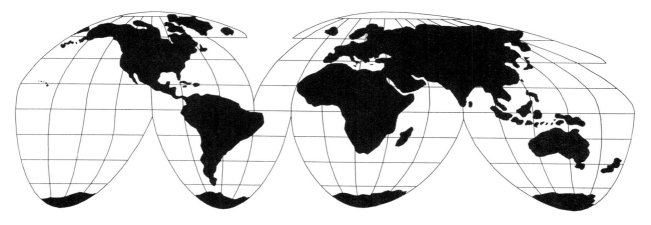

Export Costs and Considerations

Having identified and defined the product or products you plan to export, the next decision gate you must go through is to consider the various export costs. Hopefully, you will discover there are no significant cost impediments to your exporting dreams. However, there could be a significant cost or other consideration that will preclude you from exporting competitively, or there may be costs associated with certain markets that may eliminate these regions from your future plans. These issues will be dealt with in more detail in Step 3. The objective of this chapter is to introduce you to the export costs and related considerations and help you to decide if you still want to become an exporter.

Export Restrictions

Most countries including the United States control what can be imported to and exported from them. The U.S. regulations are quite complicated. The situation is made even more difficult by the fact that a number of federal departments have imposed restrictions on various exports. For example, the U.S. State Department licenses the export of defense articles and services, the Nuclear Regulatory Commission controls nuclear materials and equipment, and the U.S. Department of Commerce, Bureau of Export Administration (BXA) is the primary licensing agency for dual use exports that are commercial items with potential military applications.

The BXA is the best place to start if you have any questions about export restrictions on your products. Their Internet home page <http://www.bxa.doc.gov> begins by explaining the BXA with the following:

> The Bureau of Export Administration enhances the nation's security and its economic prosperity by controlling exports for national security, foreign policy, and short supply reasons. We administer the Export Administration Act by developing export control policies, issuing export licenses, and prosecuting violators. Additionally, BXA enforces the EAA's antiboycott provisions.

Associated with the Export Administration Act are the Export Administration Regulations (EAR). Among other things, they define the items and activities that are subject to export controls. Here is another extract from the BXA web site.

> The EAR have four principal ways of describing license requirements:
>
> i. The EAR may require a license to a country if your item is listed on the CCL and if the Country Chart in part 738 of the EAR tells that a license is required to that country. Virtually all Export Control Classification Numbers (ECCN) on the CCL are covered by the Country Chart in part 738 of the EAR. That part identifies the limited number of entries that are not included on the Chart. These ECCNs will state the specific countries that require a license or refer you to a self-contained section, i.e., Short Supply in part 754 of the EAR, or Embargoes in part 746 of the EAR. If a license is required, you should consult part 740 of the EAR which describes the License Exception that may be available for items on the CCL. Part 742 of the EAR describes the licensing policies that BXA will apply in reviewing an application you file. Note that part 754 of the EAR on short supply controls and part 746 on embargoes are self-contained parts that include the available exceptions and licensing policy.
>
> ii. A license requirement may be based on the end-use or end-user in a transaction, primarily for proliferation reasons. Part 744 of the EAR describes such requirements and relevant licensing policies and includes both restrictions on items and restrictions on the activities of U.S. persons.

iii. A license is required for virtually all exports to embargo destinations, such as Cuba. Part 746 of the EAR describes all the licensing requirements, license review policies, and License Exceptions that apply to such destinations. If your transaction involves one of these countries, you should first look at this part. This part also describes controls that may be maintained under the EAR to implement UN sanctions.

iv. In addition, under 736.2(b)(9) and (10) of the EAR, you may not engage in a transaction knowing a violation is about to occur or violate any orders, terms, and conditions under the EAR. Part 764 of the EAR describes prohibited transactions with a person denied export privileges or activity that violates the terms or conditions of a denial order.

Confused? This whole area of export restrictions is very confusing and changes frequently. Your best approach is to contact the BXA at your local U.S. Department of Commerce office to ensure you will have no legal problem in exporting your products. You will probably want to meet with them anyway for additional assistance, as described later. You do not want to be put on the *List of Denied Parties* that contains U.S. citizens and companies who are denied export privileges of various sorts.

Exporting Military Products

As mentioned earlier, the U.S. State Department licenses the export of defense articles and services. During the cold war, the NATO nations plus Japan and Australia restricted trade with the Soviet Union and its Eastern Block allies, as well as China, Vietnam, North Korea, and Mongolia. This was done through the Coordinating Committee for Multilateral Strategic Export Controls (COCOM). COCOM developed lists, such as the Industrial List, the Munitions List, and the Atomic Energy List, of products that could not be exported to the communist countries. The government strictly monitored all exports on these lists, and it was up to the exporting companies to ensure they complied with these restrictions.

Even though the old COCOM restrictions are slowly being replaced, there are additional export restrictions associated with international agreements such as the Nuclear Non-Proliferation Treaty, the Missile Technology Control Regime, and various chemical and biological weapons agreements in effect.

A new international export control mechanism, the New Forum, is currently being negotiated. The major difference in the New Forum as compared to COCOM is the countries involved. It will be open to all nations that are willing to abide by it. Another difference will be that individual member countries will not have the right to veto a transaction of another country. Each country will have a national export control program that administers the New Forum nationally.

The U.S. Department of State, Bureau of Politico-Military Affairs, International Traffic in Arms Regulations (ITAR) governs the U.S. import and export of defense articles and services. According to ITAR, "Any person who intends to export or to import temporarily a defense article must obtain the approval of the Office of Defense Trade Controls prior to the export or temporary import, unless the export or temporary import qualifies for an exemption under the provisions" of ITAR. The reason for the distinction of temporary import is that the permanent import of defense articles comes under the jurisdiction of the Treasury Department, not the Department of State which is responsible for the ITAR.

The first thing to do is to determine if your product falls within the control of the ITAR. Here is an extract of the regulations that may help you make this determination.

> The intended use of the article or service after its export (i.e. for military or civilian purpose) is not relevant in determining whether the article or service is subject to the controls. An article or service may be designated or determined in the future to be a defense article or defense service if it:
>
> (a) Is specifically designed, developed, configured, adapted or modified for a military application, and
>
> > (i) Does not have predominant civil applications, and
> >
> > (ii) Does not have performance equivalent (defined in form, fit and function) to those of an article or service used for civil applications; or
>
> (b) Is specifically designed, developed, configured, adapted, or modified for a military application, and has significant military or intelligence applicability such that control is necessary.

You must consider not only the export of the product to a particular country but also whether the product is reexported from that initial country to another country to which export restrictions apply. This restriction applies even if your product is used as part of a larger product made by your customer. For example, you may produce a component that is used in the manufacture of a defense article, and you sell it to a manufacturer in a country to which no ITAR export restrictions apply. If the manufacturer who bought your product uses it in his product that he is exporting to a third country that is under U.S. export restrictions, then your product falls under the ITAR restrictions.

So, according to the ITAR, "the country designated as the country of ultimate destination on an application for an export license ... must be the country of ultimate end use." The onus is on you to sort this out, because the ITAR states that "exporters must ascertain the specific end-user prior to submitting an application to the Officer of Defense Trade Controls or claiming an exemption."

Legal Considerations

Another legal aspect you should consider regarding export, particularly with regard to some countries, is the Foreign Business Practices Act. In the 1970s and 80s some American companies were found guilty of bribing foreign officials to get contracts in their countries.

The companies caught were in the military equipment business, where contracts are in the hundreds of millions and even billions of dollars. The payoffs were in the tens of millions. When the word got out, particularly because it was seen by the public as part of the shady world of international arms sales, it did not take the politicians long to jump on the bandwagon so as to appear to be protecting American integrity. The result was the Foreign Business Practices Act, which forbids paying off officials in another country to get business.

Unfortunately, customer payoffs happen all over the world. The practice is rampant in most developing countries and in the old Communist countries. It has been going on for centuries, and in some countries it is part of their commerce. Since the payoffs are normally done through agents' fees, these fees come under scrutiny by the enforcers of the Foreign Business Practices Act. Reasonable agent fees are accepted, but if they get too high, the law suspects that payoffs are involved. Fees or commissions up to eight or even ten percent are usually acceptable, but anything above that invites investigation by the American authorities.

Local Regulations

In the United States, federal and state regulations ensure the safety of products for consumers. For example, most electrical appliances must pass the Underwriters Laboratory and receive the UL approval. Many other countries have similar regulations and product-testing procedures. Some of them, like the Canadian Standards Association, accept the American UL approval, so no further testing is required. However, many countries require approval according to their own regulatory bodies.

Before you approach the foreign markets, find out what their regulations are regarding your product. If local testing is required, find out what is involved, how long it will take, and what it will cost. The best way to get this information is to contact the trade officials at the American embassy in these countries. You can then assess whether it is worth the effort for you to do whatever testing and certification is required.

You will also have to consider weights and measures regulations in foreign countries. The United States is the last bastion of the old Imperial system of weights and measures. Almost all the rest of the world uses the metric system. It may not be illegal in most countries to sell two-inch by four-inch lumber, but it will not be a very popular product when the rest of the construction material is in metric. As for liquid products in U.S. gallons or ounces, chances are there will be regulations against it.

Local import duties and tariffs will be dealt with later in this chapter, but there are a number of other means foreign governments use to protect their industries from competition. They may give preferential treatment to their local firms by various methods, such as not allowing government departments to buy from anyone but a local firm. Or they may exclude purchases from a particular country. Several years ago the Malaysian government was annoyed at the United Kingdom. They instituted a government policy to "Buy British Last." That is, if all aspects of competing products were equal, the Malaysian government purchasers were to select non-British products. It took a visit from the British Prime Minister to sort out the problem.

If you are marketing to foreign governments, you may also be confronted with regulations requiring local industrial benefits. That is, a percentage of the value of the contract must be reinvested in the country, usually by purchasing goods or services from local industries. The local purchases can be either directly associated with the contract or involve purchases on other projects. For example, for all contracts issued by the Kuwait government over about five million U.S. dollars, the company receiving the contract must invest 30 percent of the contract value in Kuwait businesses. Setting up and administering these industrial benefits can be very costly and should be part of your export decision.

Product Design

When you were identifying and defining the product you plan to export, you may have discovered some redesigns that would make it more appealing in a foreign market. Or you may have to redesign your product to meet local building codes or technical standards. If your product is electrical, you will have to consider redesigning to be compatible with foreign electrical supplies, not only for voltage and frequency but also for connectors. Then there is the problem of weights and measures. You may be able to get away with a soft conversion to metric, that is, to simply convert your feet, inches, and ounces documentation into meters and milliliters without changing the product. In some instances you may have to change the product itself, such as for two-by-four lumber. In the rest of the world, standard paper sizes, televisions, and VCRs, are also different from those of North America.

Now is the time to analyze the cost and effort required to implement these design changes. Some of them may be minor, so you may be able to easily include the costs in the selling price and stay competitive. But if the costs are major, you may want to seek more compatible markets or forget about exporting the product.

Labeling and Packaging

Labeling requirements, which vary from country to country, do not just involve language changes. Many countries, like the United States, require specific product information to be provided, such as ingredients, weights, and measurements. And remember that the weights and measurements will have to be in metric. These requirements can add a significant cost to the product.

The language labeling alone can be very expensive. To have a bilingual label, you will have to redesign your package to ensure all the information is presented in both languages. You may be able to do it by just placing stickers with the other language over your existing label; however, this will also be costly. A good example of the bilingual labeling requirement is in Canada where all products must be labeled in English and French. The extra cost of the French labeling can add ten to twenty-five percent to your costs.

Often overlooked aspects of labeling of international products are the customs, religions, and practices of the potential customers. Pictures of pigs should be avoided in Moslem countries, and care should be taken to avoid showing religious symbols in some countries. Revealing pictures of men or women, like those usually on underwear packages, may even be against the law in countries such as Saudi Arabia. Then there is the horror story of a company that began exporting their baby food to some African countries, with a picture of a happy, smiling baby on the package. Unfortunately, most of the customers were illiterate and purchased products based on the picture on the package, thinking there was a baby inside.

Packaging requirements of a country may also differ, so you may have to redesign your package to comply. A good example is the child-proof containers required for many products in the United States. Other countries have these requirements as well, but they can be different from those you already adhere to. However, the most usual packaging problem is associated with weights and measures. The old metric issue can jump up and bite you again.

To get information on the labeling and packaging requirements of a country, contact the nearest District Office of the U.S. Department of Commerce. If these offices cannot help you, you may have to contact the commerce officials at the U.S. embassy or consulate in the country of destination. Do not hesitate to contact these officials. It is their job to provide you with this information.

Translation

In addition to translating packaging information into the local language, you will be faced with other translation problems. Most of these, like purchase orders and contracts, will be taken care of by your agent, once you have established one in the country. However, there will be some items you may have to translate before you have an agent, such as business cards, signage for a trade booth, and brochures.

There are many translation services around that will help you, for a price, but the question is how to validate the translation, particularly if it is very technical. There is also the difference in language usage from country to country. How many Americans know what a lorry is? Yet this is the common English language term for a truck in Britain.

Spanish is also a language used in many countries, and it too has subtle differences in each country. An American company once had their brochure translated into Spanish by a professional translator from Mexico. They were very embarrassed to discover that a frequently used word in the brochure that described the coating of the product was actually the term used for condom in another Spanish-speaking country.

The safest approach you can take to the translation problem is to wait until you have established an agent in the country and then have them either do the translation or at least validate it.

Marketing

Marketing costs are probably going to be your biggest international marketing expense. These are dealt with in detail in Chapter 13, but at this stage you must consider them from a broad perspective to see if they might be too high to even consider exporting. The big costs are personnel and travel.

Assuming that you have the proper size marketing and sales force for your domestic market, you will have to hire additional staff for the international market. Depending on your product, it could take the staff a few years to obtain the first orders and generate some revenue for your effort. Can you afford to carry this additional payroll expense?

These new marketing and sales people will have to travel to the target countries, which will be a considerable up-front expense. The air fares are only a part of the travel costs. Lodging in some countries is very expensive. For example, Kuwait is a very expensive place to visit. All of the major hotels charge the same price, and it is well over $200 per night. Added to this is the extremely high cost of food, because almost everything in Kuwait is imported. A cup of coffee or tea will cost over four dollars, and a steak in a reasonable restaurant can be about $200.

So do a quick calculation of what the additional personnel and travel costs are going to be, then add these costs to your product overhead. If you still think you can be price competitive internationally, carry on. But if these costs appear to be far more than what you could recover from the foreign market, you may want to stay with your current work force and market.

Promotion

Promotional costs will be dealt with in more detail in chapters 11 and 13, but once again, have a broad look at them at this stage in your decision-making process. Make some rough estimates of what it will cost for new brochures, video tapes, trade shows, and maybe even advertisements in the new market area. These costs are usually not prohibitive, but for some markets and products they may be, so do a quick investigation of them just in case.

Agent Commissions

You will have to have an agent in each foreign market, and you definitely have to pay them. Types of agents and how they are paid are covered in chapters 20 to 23. In general, you should work with agents on a commission basis. That is, the agent does not get paid until they sell something for you. In this way you do not have any up-front or overhead costs associated with the agents, but you will have to include the agent's commission in the price of your product.

The agent commission varies from country to country and from product to product. It can be from as low as two or three percent of the sale price to as high as twenty-five or thirty percent in countries where the agent has what can euphemistically be called high out-of-pocket expenses. At this stage in your decision process, consider an agent's fee of about six or seven percent. This of course is added directly to the price of your product, but at least your competitors, unless they are indigenous companies, will have the same expense.

Cost of Getting Paid

This is not a big issue, but you should be aware of it. The usual method of international payment is by letter of credit, or LC. It starts with your customer, the purchaser, placing money for the product in their bank and asking the bank to raise an LC to be paid when certain delivery conditions have been met. The purchaser's bank then tells your bank the LC is in place and provides the delivery conditions. Your bank passes this information on to you. You ship the order in compliance with the delivery conditions, then take the delivery documentation to your bank as proof. Your bank tells the purchaser's bank that the conditions have been met and requests payment. The purchaser's bank transfers the money to your bank and you collect it.

Since this is an arrangement between banks, there is a small charge for the LC service. The charge is usually around one percent of the value of the LC and is well worth the security you get to ensure payment.

You may also get into a situation where you have to provide credit to the purchaser for a few months, usually because your competitors do. Under these circumstances you may want to get some credit insurance. There are a number of government agencies that will provide this insurance, mainly federal, but some states have them as well. The best way to find out about them is to call the nearest U.S. Department of Commerce, District Office. There is a charge for the insurance, which depends on the country you are dealing with. For some countries it is only a few percent of the value of the credit while for others it may be up to six or seven percent, depending on the country's capability and reputation for paying its bills. For some countries you may not be able to get credit insurance at all.

There is also the issue of foreign currency. Fortunately, most international transactions are quoted for and paid in U.S. dollars. However, there may be times when the customer insists on paying in his local currency. Naturally, you should strongly resist this, but if you cannot do so, be sure to add a currency risk percentage to your price to give you some protection in case the currency drops in value against the U.S. dollar. This risk percentage will also vary with the country. Your bank may be able to advise you on what it should be.

A final cost of payment consideration is countertrade or barter. This form of payment is on the increase, particularly from countries that are short of hard currency. The usual method is for you to be paid in products from the country, which can vary from local crafts to oil, beer, and wine. You then have the problem of selling these products for cash. Fortunately, there are a number of broker companies available that will do this for you, for a price of course. The price is usually quite high, depending on the product to be disposed of.

Transportation Costs

Your foreign customers will usually want prices based on delivery to their country. This can be a major cost for some products and not so for others. Perishable products will have to go by air. It may also be appropriate to ship small products such as electronics by air. Heavy, bulky products with no shelf life can easily be exported by sea, which is often the least expense mode. When doing a cost comparison between sea and air, however, take into account the many other costs associated with sea shipment.

These costs, such as rail freight to and from the sea terminal and the associated handling charges could make the cost of air shipment more feasible.

Much has been written about transportation methods and costs, but the best way to deal with them is through an experienced shipping agent, who will be able to provide you with most of the information you need. Some of the factors you must consider at this stage of your exporting decision are:

- Preparation for shipment. You may not be able to use your usual shipping containers, depending on the mode of shipping.
- Delivery to shipping agent. Most shipping agents will include the cost of picking up your shipment as part of the overall freight cost, but make sure they do so in their quote.
- Shipping costs to the foreign country. These costs will vary with the mode of transportation, whether air, rail, ship, or truck. They will vary with the type of containerization you use, standard 20-foot shipping containers, 40-foot containers, or shared container loads.
- Unloading charges. These may or may not be included in your shipping agent's quotation.
- Terminal charges. How long will your shipment wait in the foreign terminal until it is picked up and delivered to your customer?
- Longload or heavy loading charges. Is your product outside the normal shipping parameters?
- Documentation costs. You will have to pay to get the shipping documents certified, if required for an LC or other reason.
- Shipping insurance. The cost of this will vary with the mode of transportation used.
- Other insurance costs. Your shipping agent will offer additional insurance over the usual shipping insurance.

Import Costs and Regulations

The most common import costs are tariffs placed on imported products by countries, usually to protect their own industries. These are gradually being reduced through trade agreements such as the General Agreement on Tariffs and Trade (GATT), and the North American Free Trade Agreement (NAFTA). Many countries still have tariffs, however, and they could affect your competitive pricing in the country. To find out about the tariffs and other import costs in a particular country, contact the U.S. embassy in the country.

Customs charges to bring the products into the country can be an added expense that you must include in your pricing. It is not unusual to have customs duties plus handling charges leveled on a shipment by the government of the receiving country. For example, the charges in Kuwait are four percent customs duty and one percent handling charge.

Most countries have import regulations that can be costly, if only in the time and effort required to do the paperwork. Some of these requirements are:

- Certificate of origin. This can take different forms, but the purpose is to prove where the products originated. The origin may affect the tariff rate applied, or some countries will not accept products from others. For example, the United States will not allow the import of products from Cuba, and many Arab countries will not allow products from Israel.
- Import license. Some countries control imports by requiring their importers to obtain an import license for the products they are importing. To do this, the importer usually requires a pro-forma invoice detailing the products to be shipped.
- Health certificate. This usually applies to the import of animals, plants, and other agricultural products.

Finally, some countries have restrictions on what can be imported into the country. You will not be able to get around these legally. For example, Saudi Arabia and Kuwait will not allow the import of alcohol, and Singapore will not allow the import of chewing gum.

Installation, Maintenance, and Repair

If your product requires special skills for the installation, maintenance, and repair that cannot be provided by the customer, you will have to consider how you will do it in a distant country. Your options are:

- Do it with your own staff,
- Have your agent or distributor do it, or
- Sub-contract it to a local company.

Doing it yourself can be very expensive and risky. You may be able to include installation costs in your bid, but be prepared for some surprises. Your estimate of time required will probably be based on your experience in your domestic market, but things can be quite different in a foreign country. Your local supporting work force may not have the required skills or the work ethic you expect, and consequently it will take much more time than you expected to do the work.

You could also run into labor relation laws that limit the work your people can do. Then there is the problem of having staff waiting around in a country while you send them spare parts. All of this will cost you money that you may or may not have included in your price.

Having your agent, distributor, or a sub-contractor do the work can also be expensive and risky. You will have to train them, and the first question you must answer is where will the training take place. You can pay the costs of bringing the trainees to your plant, but what happens if they are not capable of absorbing the training? It is usually less risky to train people in the customer country, particularly when you are uncertain of the quality of the trainees.

Competitive Pricing

If you are in the fortunate position of having a relatively unique product with no competition, you will have to decide what price the market will bear. The income level of the country you are marketing to will be a major factor. If it is high, you can charge a high price, but if it is low, you may decide not to bother with that market. No matter how unique your product is, there will eventually be competition. Your price may have to be reduced, so do not make your revenue projections based on continued high prices.

The unique product scenario does not happen too often, and most exporters must face the competition. If you cannot beat them on price, you will have to have some pretty good other benefits to lure the customers. Price is the final frontier, however, and you must be prepared to match the competition. If all of the other expenses discussed in this chapter prohibit you from having a competitive price in a particular market, you may want to forget about that market and concentrate on one where you have an advantage.

Second Export Decision Gate

Having considered all of the export costs and other factors discussed in this chapter, you are now ready to make the next decision, whether to go on with your export plans or not. Chances are it is not yet a clear decision, although you may have been able to eliminate some market areas while others are beginning to look favorable to you. This is quite natural because there are many more issues you have to face before making your final decision.

AHSI took a look at the export costs and related considerations regarding their Heat-R-Tiles and came to the following conclusions:

- *There were no U.S. government restrictions on exporting the Heat-R-Tiles, except to countries like Cuba where the heaters would not be a big seller anyway.*
- *Except for Europe, most countries accepted the U.S. UL certification on the heaters, and AHSI had already basically decided not to bother with Europe.*

- *The only product redesign required would be the hangers they had already decided to go with.*
- *Labeling and packaging were not an issue. They would just include a translation of the one-page instruction sheet in the package, and it was mostly diagrams.*
- *Translation could be a problem, but they would rely on their distributor for help.*
- *Marketing would be through a distributor, who would also be responsible for local promotion, so this was not a problem for AHSI.*
- *Since they were going to use a distributor, there would not be any agent commission to consider.*
- *The cost of being paid would probably be low since they would only sell on the basis of an LC.*
- *Transportation costs could be significant and would vary from country to country. Also, the size of the order would determine the method of shipment. However, when they took a worst-case example of shipping small quantities by air, the end price of the heaters was still reasonable for markets that would want them.*
- *Local import costs would not be significant, and they figured the distributor would have to look after them anyway.*
- *Installation of the Heat-R-Tiles could easily be done by local tradesmen, there is no maintenance required, and repair is simply a replacement of the complete unit.*

There appeared to be no significant problem for AHSI to begin exporting the Heat-R-Tiles, except to Europe, and they decided to go on to explore the international market.

———————————————

Identify Potential International Customers

Chapter 3

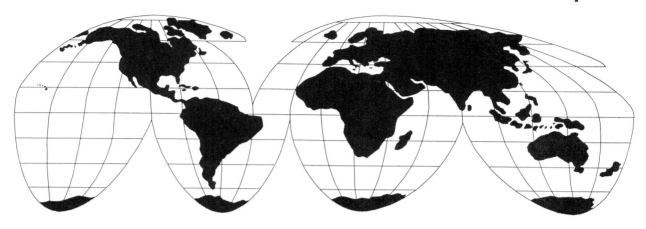

International User Benefits

User benefits are what cause a customer to buy your product and, as such, are an important part of your marketing and promotion. It is important to understand the potential benefits to be derived from your product by international customers, because this will be a major part of identifying the international markets you should be targeting.

Benefits Versus Features

There is an important difference between user benefits and features of a product. Features are part of the design that may or may not be of benefit to all customers. For example, a word processing software program may include a large selection of clip art. This is a feature, and for users who are interested only in writing text, the clip art feature is of no benefit. It may even be a detraction if it takes up too much disk space or slows down the program.

Benefits are in the eye of the customer. They are the aspects of the product that are of value or appeal to the buyer. Using the word processing example again, if the program had the capability of producing the text in columns, this feature would be of benefit to a user working on newsletters. It is the user benefits that cause a customer to buy a particular product, although these benefits are usually features of the product. In some cases, user benefits are uncovered that were never considered when the product was developed. An example of this was customers discovering that a popular bath oil also worked as an insect repellent.

If you use your list of product features as a guide to assess user benefits, be sure you are looking at it through the eyes of your potential foreign customers.

How Is the Product Beneficial to Particular Customers?

This is the question you must ask about your product with regard to the various international customers you are considering. What does it do for them that will make them want to buy it? You may want to consider the following related questions.

- Are there unique features for those particular customers that will be of benefit to them? Remember, the benefits must be from the customer's point of view, not from that of your designers.

- Does your product provide the customer with more benefits than your competitors? Again, remember that benefits differ from features. You may have a very unique feature in your product, but unless it is of benefit to the potential customers, it will not appeal to them. Saudi Arabians will not be very interested in heated seats in a car.

- Can your product solve the customer's problem better than your competition? For example, can it do it faster or with less effort?

- Is your product more cost effective? Will it cost the customer less money to obtain and use it? This is probably the most important customer benefit.

- Does your product have some novel aspect that will appeal to the customer because it offers some kind of benefit, real or perceived? For example, school bags with the latest cartoon character on them appeal to kids because it gives them the perceived benefit of having the latest thing.

The question of perceived benefits is difficult to answer, but you must consider them. Who would have guessed that the pet rock novelty product of a few years ago had any user benefits? It is very difficult, and almost impossible, to prejudge what will be a fad, particularly in the international market. In many cases what works in the United States will also work internationally, although sometimes to only a limited degree. A few years ago in Singapore, the fad was country-western bars featuring local Chinese performers emulating American country singers. Now the fad is Japanese karaoke bars.

Detracting Aspects

You should also consider any detracting aspects, or negative benefits, of your product. These may be general things which detract from the product that your marketing and sales staff have already discovered or they may be subtle issues that are detractions for only a particular international region or group. The general things are often something simple like an unappealing color, which can easily be changed. You may even be working on it already. They also can be more serious, like a feature that makes the product difficult to operate. You should be working to correct this as well. Needless to say, these general detracting aspects should be corrected for your domestic market before you hit the international market.

The detractions that affect only a particular international region or group may be difficult to identify, however, until you test that market. These detractions are usually beyond your control, such as:

- Climate. Your product may not stand up to the high temperatures, bright sun, or the high humidity of a region. For example, infra-red cameras will not work effectively in high humidity.
- Religion. There are a number of symbols that are offensive to various religions. For example, designs incorporating signs of the cross are not acceptable to most Moslems.
- Local customs. It is probably not a good idea to try to sell mini-skirts to sari-wearing women of India.

Unconventional Use Benefits

There may be uses for your product internationally that you never considered in your domestic market. These are very difficult to predict, but if you can, you may want to explore the possibilities further. For example, temporary buildings constructed from modules that can be easily transported can have many unconventional uses in a developing country, such as for schools or hospitals in remote locations.

Most unconventional uses and the associated benefits will come as a surprise to you, however. In Chile they use small, two-seater airplanes to spot schools of anchovy fish from their florescence in the sea at night and direct fishing boats to them. This use was probably not anticipated by the aircraft manufacturers. Another unconventional use of equipment in South America is the use of large watering trucks as water canons to disperse crowds. There may be potential uses of your product you never dreamed of.

Explaining Customer Benefits

The benefits of your product may be fairly obvious to your domestic customers but not necessarily to many of your potential foreign customers. In the so-called western world, people take a lot of technology for granted. People here accept the fact that technology can help them and so make the effort to learn about it. The personal computer is a prime example.

The more sophisticated your product, the more likely you will have to explain its benefits to your potential international customers. They may have a particular problem that if solved would make their lives much better, but they have never considered trying to solve the problem, or they think it is not solvable. For example, imagine the excitement of people in a remote village when you explain to them and show them how a cellular telephone can let them talk to the outside world.

In your analysis of the customer benefits of your product to international customers, include whatever is required to explain the benefits. This subject will be dealt with in more detail in Chapter 24, but you should be aware of the possible need to do this now, so you can assess the degree of effort required.

AHSI looked at the international user benefits of their Heat-R-Tiles and came to the conclusion that the major benefit was to provide occasional, augmented heat. This reconfirmed their thinking that customers in Middle East countries with cool winters could derive benefit from the heaters.

Chapter 4

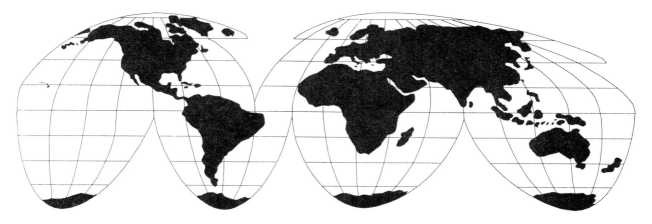

International Buyer Segmentation

A major part of identifying profitable international markets is identifying the customer groups or segments that will buy your product. Then you have to identify the countries or regions with the largest or most cost-effective segments.

What is Buyer Segmentation?

Buyer segmentation is the process of arranging the potential buyers in groups based on common aspects. The buyers in one group will have similar characteristics that will be different from buyers in another group.

There are many ways to do this segmentation, and there is a thriving industry of market researchers and research firms that will provide you with information in many forms on these various groups. Unfortunately, most of the available information is for your domestic market, and very little is available for the international market. Another problem is that you may want a different buyer segmentation for the international market than is normally used in your domestic market. How you want to segment the markets will of course depend on your product, but as a minimum for international markets, segmentation generally should be done along the lines of these factors:

- Economic
- Geographical
- Sociological
- Demographic
- Lifestyle
- Purchasing habits
- Benefits derived

The reason you want to go through the buyer segmentation activity is to narrow down the international market to the most cost-effective targets. The process will help you eliminate areas of the world that have less interest in your product than other areas, and it will highlight areas that will have more interest in the product. This will help you to begin to focus your international marketing effort.

Economic

Probably the most important way to segment international buyers is by economics. First of all, you want to be able to pick segments of the market that can afford to buy your product. It would not be a good idea to try to sell high fashion clothing to impoverished Bangladesh. If your product is more luxury than necessity, you will want to choose countries with high per-capita income.

Other economic factors of a country are also important, particularly if they relate to your product. If you provide agricultural equipment, you will want to segment the countries by their main agricultural products. Then identify the countries that produce agricultural products related to your product. You may think you already know the countries that you should be looking at, but a detailed analysis may give you some surprise new markets. For example, Saudi Arabia is a fairly large producer of grain. It is heavily subsidized by the government, but they do grow it, and they need equipment to do so.

A country's resources may also be an important way of segmenting markets, particularly if your product relates to this sector of the market, such as mining equipment or petroleum production equipment. The type of industry a country has can be of similar interest. Studying their imports and exports can provide hints regarding what they may or may not want to buy from abroad.

AHSI assumed that they would only be able to sell their Heat-R-Tiles to foreign customers who had the money to afford them. They listed countries by their per-capita income and selected only the top part of the list as possible target markets.

Geographical

Geographical data includes the physical details of a country, like terrain (coastal, desert, forest, prairie, etc.), the climate, and the population spread (urban versus rural). A good atlas will have most of the information you need, and your public library will have more. What you need will depend on your product and the type of customers you are looking for.

AHSI looked for countries with a significant urban population and a climate cold enough to require some home heating.

Sociological

Potential customer countries are segmented by social considerations such as religion, language, and ethnic background, especially for products that are consumed. A pretty obvious example is that chopsticks are a big seller in China. Chopsticks are a big export to China from some Canadian companies. If your product depends on these sociological issues, you should go through this aspect of segmentation to identify potential customers.

Demographic

Demographic data, such as age profiles, occupation, sex, and marital status, is very heavily used for market identification in developed countries. It is also important in foreign markets that have a high enough standard of living. If your product relies on this market information, you will want to segment the countries accordingly; however, it may be difficult to obtain the detailed information you require.

Lifestyle

Lifestyles of customers can be important for many products, such as processed foods, clothing, electronics, and leisure products. American food, particularly from American fast food outlets, is popular in most countries. Witness the popularity of McDonald's restaurants in Moscow and the popularity of U.S. brands of jeans in Russia.

Electronics is a product area that depends heavily on lifestyle because electronic products are most often for entertainment, despite the fact some consumers treat them as necessities. Look at all the joggers wearing portable radios and earphones. In Japan consumers treat new electronic gadgetry as status symbols. They provide a great market challenge and test facility for the Japanese electronic companies. Consumers in many other countries have similar desires to have the latest electronic entertainment. For example, in tiny Iceland, where television is limited to local broadcasts, about 80 percent of the homes have a VCR.

The fitness fad has hit many of the developing countries. Personal fitness equipment is a big seller in affluent countries of the Middle East. Golf is also catching on all over the would. Even the small island country of Singapore has dozens of golf courses.

Products relating to the American lifestyle can be very popular in other countries. However, it is very difficult to obtain detailed information on the lifestyles in foreign countries from their standard marketing information. The best way to get the information is to visit the country and talk to the potential customers. This of course is not always possible, so you will have to go with whatever information you can get.

There is, however, one important thing to keep in mind when looking for markets that depend on lifestyle. Most of the consumers of the world love to emulate the American lifestyle, even though their leaders may rant against it. Bear this thought in mind as you consider international buyer segmentation based on lifestyle.

Purchasing Habits

Much has been written about market segmentation based on purchasing habits. This book will not go into these details, but some aspects apply to the international market. Volume purchasing is a good way to segment the market for some products. The general theory in the American market is that 80 percent of the purchases are made by 20 percent of the people. This changes drastically in other countries, depending on the standard of living and the ratio of those who can afford things to those who cannot. In India, where the people range from those in abject poverty to those who can afford weddings costing tens of millions of dollars, the ratio is quite different. If you can identify the volume users of your product in a country, you will be able to gauge the size of the potential market and how to address it.

Brand loyalty is another significant purchasing habit. Beer is a good example of how customers will remain loyal to a particular brand. Toothpaste is another. You may have to overcome this brand loyalty when you enter a new market, so you should try to identify how important this issue is in the countries you are evaluating.

In the international market, country loyalty is also a factor. Consumers in a particular country will prefer to buy or not to buy products made in another country, for no apparent reason other than they always did it that way. But sometimes there are other compelling reasons for this. The most classic example is the refusal of Arab customers to buy products from Israel, although it is becoming more common to see Israeli fruits in Arab supermarkets.

There are many other purchasing habits that could affect your marketing. If you can identify them, you should try to segment the market accordingly. This will not be easy to do for most countries, but it may not be a necessary consideration for your product.

Benefits Derived

Segmenting the market according to the benefits derived by the customers could be the most important segmentation for some products. This ties in with the user benefits of computer programs discussed in the previous chapter. Here you segment potential customers according to what they get out of a product. Again, do not make the mistake of confusing user benefits with product features. They may or may not be the same.

You can start by segmenting the market into what problems the consumers have that are solved by your product. For example, if a customer has to haul small loads around and also needs basic transportation, he will derive benefit from a small truck. In this example, you would segment the market by the need to haul small loads and the need for basic transportation.

AHSI segmented the market into customers who would benefit from the heat emitted from the Heat-R-Tiles. They decided that affluent home owners, who required augmented heat in some areas of their homes, would be a major segment of the international market.

Third Export Decision Gate

Now that you have segmented the potential international buyers into market areas that apply to your product, you have to decide if the markets are large enough to go after. This is your third decision gate, where you have a third chance to decide whether to export or not. If the potential market segments appear to be large enough for you to profitably do business with, you should continue with your export plans. If the potential market is questionable, you may want to rethink the idea of becoming an exporter

If your market segmentation has shown there is enough potential to explore, it will also have identified some areas with larger potential market segments for you than others. This is another step in focusing the market you should target, because you are now in a position to discard market areas with small potential and concentrate on those with the most potential. This in itself is a major step, because you know you can safely forget about marginal markets and apply your resources to only the profitable ones. You can now also use actual market areas for your product as you work through the marketing activities described in the following chapters.

Chapter 5

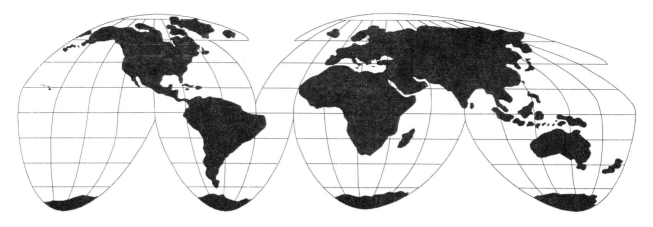

Indirect and Direct Competition

No matter how unique your product, you will always have to face competition. It will develop, perhaps not immediately but eventually. You have to assess the degree of competition you will face in each market area you are considering and select your target markets accordingly.

Indirect Competition

Direct competition is similar products made by other companies. Indirect competition is competing methods of solving the customer's requirement. Before discussing the direct competition to your product, consider the indirect competition. Some of the areas of indirect competition you may encounter are:

- Manpower. This is indirect competition to labor saving devices. It is always a consideration in developing countries where manpower is abundant and inexpensive. For example, it may be less expensive to hire people to stand hand-to-hand around the perimeter of a building to protect it from break-in than to purchase and install an elaborate alarm system.

- Technology. Customers may use a different technology and product to solve their problem. For example, fiber optic transmission cables are indirect competition to copper wire cables, and vice versa.

- Process. A different process may be used that would exclude your product. For example, you may have a software product that tracks production expenses in minute detail to detect problems and make corrections. Instead the customer wants to use a simple method of totaling up expenses by hand and does not worry about the details.

- Import restrictions. These are a form of indirect competition. The previously mentioned import restrictions of alcohol into Saudi Arabia and Kuwait and chewing gum into Singapore are examples.

- Government regulations. Regulations within a country may prevent your product from being sold. For example, Japanese labor rules require a specially trained operator to work the fish-finding sonar on large fishing boats. These people are trained only to operate Japanese sonars designed with this regulation in mind.

- Status quo. The customer may not be interested in improving what he has so does not want to change the status quo. This situation is often driven by lack of funding, but there may be other reasons people do not want to change their situation. Perhaps even you have a very comfortable chair that you have no intention of replacing no matter what new product comes along.

The indirect competition to the AHSI Heat-R-Tiles is mainly technology. There are many ways of providing supplementary heat to a room, ranging from a central furnace to a portable fan with electric element heaters. Customers can also use a different process, to simply put on more clothes or use a brazier. Or they can accept the fact that the room is cold and go somewhere else.

Identify Your Direct Competition

In any business, you must identify the products and companies in direct competition with you and get as much information as possible about them. You probably have a lot of information on your domestic competition. You will have to compete with some of them internationally; however, there will be other competitors you may never have heard of until you go into the international arena. Now is the time to look at who you will be up against and assess whether or not it is worth going into certain markets.

The easiest way to get information about the competition is by obtaining their brochures and other product literature. Several ways to do this are through:

- Trade shows. This is the best way to get info on the competition because trade shows by their very nature congregate similar product displays together in one show. You are not only able to pick up competitor's brochures but also you can often see what their product does if they have it on display. If you work it right, you may even get an enthusiastic marketer to tell you where they are selling their products and how they are doing. Remember, however, that the competition is also gathering information.

- Trade publications. This is another place that concentrates similar product information. It can be in the form of advertisements or articles on the product. Many magazines also have periodic features on products in a particular area. These are a gold mine of competitor information. When you do a search of trade publications, make sure you include those that are distributed internationally.

- Bingo cards. Many trade magazines have information request cards that allow you to circle the number given in the advertisements for more information on products; then you send the card back to the magazine. The magazine sends the request to advertisers who in turn send you a pile of information on their products.

- Conferences. Many companies like to tell the world about their products by giving papers at conferences. This can be a good source of information not only on the product but also on how it was designed and tested and even who their customers are.

- Customers. You can get information on a competitor's product by talking to customers who have purchased it or potential customers who are going around getting comparative information with the intention of buying either from you or your competition.

- Suppliers. Manufacturers' suppliers get to learn a lot about the products their components are going into, including a good idea of the volume of sales being made by the manufacturer. You may be able to tap into this information source, even though the suppliers should be discreet about what they know.

- The Internet. Many companies are jumping on this electronic bandwagon by having a home page. This resource can provide you with all kinds of information about a company and its products.

An important piece of information you want about the competition is their price. While this is not as easy to get as their product literature, you may be able to get some indications. At trade shows you can come right out and ask for the price of a product. Chances are they will tell you, but with qualifications. Internationally, a good source is an agent who represents the product in their countries, but this may have to wait until you have decided to market to a particular country and are there interviewing agents for your product.

Competitor's Strengths and Weaknesses

Once you have identified who your competitors are and obtained information on their products, you can analyze their strengths and weaknesses. You can do this under a number of headings, depending on the product. Some of the aspects you may want to investigate about their product are:

- Features
- Performance characteristics
- Style
- User benefits
- Applications
- Options
- Packaging
- Servicing
- Delivery time
- Price

You may not be able to get sufficient information from the literature to make complete comparisons to your product, but you will at least get some idea of what you are up against. If the product is not too expensive, you may want to buy one from the competition and analyze it in detail. This will give you all the information you can get on the competing product, including some of its design and manufacturing details. This is often done these days.

Information on the product is not all you need to assess the strengths and weaknesses of the competition. You also need information on the way the competitor does business and on the company itself. Annual reports are a good source of this information. You will want to assess information on several areas:

- Countries they are marketing to
- Market share
- Marketing structure
- Sales force, including agents and distributors
- Technical support provided
- Advertising and promotion methods
- Company financial situation

How the Competition Addresses the Market

This information will help you to decide on how you want to enter the market. If the competition appears to be successful in the way they are operating in a particular market, you may want to consider copying their approach. If they are not being successful or there are weaknesses in their ways of doing business, you may want to improve on their methods to your advantage.

There are several aspects you should investigate.

- What segments of the market are they concentrating on?
- Do they enter the market by initial undercut pricing, heavy advertising, or other methods?
- What are their advertising and promotion methods?
- Do they use agents or distributors, or have they set up branch offices?
- What is their distribution method?
- What is their market share?
- What is the trend in their market share? Is it increasing or decreasing and if so, why?

Competition Relative to You

Now that you have all the information you can get on the competition, you have to analyze it relative to your company and your product. The overall question you want to answer is why will a customer buy from you and not from the competition, or conversely, why will a customer buy from the competition and not from you? It is critical that you do this analysis from the customer's point of view, not from yours. This can be difficult because it is very subjective, so be as brutally honest with yourself as you can.

The best way to do this is to set up a matrix listing all of the comparison factors in the left hand column, along next to it a column for your factors, then next to that columns for the competitors. The information in each box of the competitor's columns should be a brief comment about how it relates to your product and whether it is positive, meaning stronger than yours, or negative, meaning weaker than yours. At the bottom of each of the competitor's columns, you can give a relative assessment based on the pluses and minuses in the column. This will give you an overall indication of how the products match up and who the stronger competitors are. An example matrix is shown on the next page.

Competitive Analysis Matrix

Product Aspect	Your Product	Competitor No. 1	Competitor No. 2
Features			
Performance			
Style			
Benefits			
Applications			
Options			
Packaging			
Servicing			
Delivery			
Price			
Technical support			
Advertising			
Promotion			
Market share			
Market trend			
Marketing structure			
Sales force			
Market segments			
Countries			
Enter method			
Financial			

How Will Competition React to You?

This is not an easy question to answer and is often one that is overlooked. You have to consider this issue, even if you are entering a market where there is no competition, because there soon will be if you are successful in that market. The usual situation, however, is that when you enter the market you have some form of competition, and they will react to your presence in some way. Their most likely reactions will be to:

- Do nothing. This is the usual initial response, but when they see their business waning, they usually react.

- Lower their price. This is the next most likely response, particularly if they were alone in the market until your entry.
- Change their promotion. This is another popular response to the entry of a new competitor in a market. It can sometimes get very cutthroat.
- Change the product. This happens sometimes, particularly if the existing product was alone in the market and there was no need to improve it as long as there was no competition.

The most likely response to your market entry is for the competition to lower their price, so your initial assessment of the market should not be based on the current competitor's pricing. You must be prepared for it to be lowered.

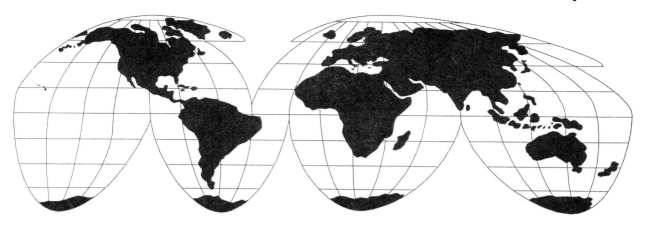

Chapter 6

Product Differentiators

Product differentiators are the unique benefits the customer can derive from using your product, compared to your competitor's product. Again, remember that it is the unique benefits as seen by the customer, not by your designers and promotion staff. Your favorable product differentiators are the reason a customer chooses your product over the other guy's.

What Are Product Differentiators?

Product differentiators are usually features or performance characteristics of a product that are of more value to a customer than those offered by the competition. Also, they can be intangible things, such as a preference to buy from your company or country as opposed to another. This latter aspect is often important in international business.

You can also have negative product differentiators, that is, why customers do not want your product. These must also be considered and your markets selected accordingly. For example, a tee shirt with an American flag on it would probably not be a big seller in Iran.

Identifying Product Differentiators

To identify the product differentiators associated with your product, you must consider what the customer is looking for in a product. What are the customers' essential requirements, and what other requirements would they like but not necessarily need? What other tangible and intangible aspects of the product are liked or disliked? Here are some of the aspects you must consider.

- What problem is the customer trying to solve, and how can your product help more than the competition can?
- How does the customer use the product, and what features of your product make it easier to use?
- What problems do the customers have to deal with when they use other products in comparison with yours?
- Does your product have economic benefits for the customer as compared to the competition, such as lower initial cost, less operating cost, or longer lasting?

Product differentiators for a particular product may differ with the customers, and you may have to identify the differentiators for each of the buyer segments you established in Chapter 4. The best way to identify them is to speak directly to potential customers, but in the international marketing arena this is not always possible, particularly at this stage. Discussing the situation with people who know the market area, such as recent emigrants, is the next best approach. A word of caution: do not rely on the opinions of people who have only visited the region for a short time. You only really get to know the people and what they prefer if you live with them.

The public library may also be able to help you with information on the consumption habits of the buyer segments you are studying. Here you may be able to get an idea about which aspects of your product will be positive or negative product differentiators. There is also the information you can obtain from your competitors. What aspects of their products are they emphasizing in particular markets? Chances are they have determined these to be favorable product differentiators for themselves, so you should have a look at these as well.

Assessing Your Product Differentiators

Once your have a good idea of what your product differentiators are, both negative and positive, you should assess them according to the importance that will be placed on them by the buyer segments you established in Chapter 4 and in comparison to your competition. The best way to do this is with a matrix of your product differentiators such as the one shown below. In each box of the segment's column make a comment and a notation whether the differentiator is positive or negative in the sector. At the bottom of each of the sector's column you can give an overall relative assessment based on the pluses and minuses in the column. This will give you an indication of the more popular buyer segments for your product.

Product Differentiator Assessment Matrix			
Product Differentiator	Buyer Segment No. 1	Buyer Segment No. 2	Buyer Segment No. 3
Feature #1			
Feature #2			
Performance			
Style			
Price			

If you have already begun to lean toward particular areas of the world or toward potential markets, you may want to extend the matrix columns to include these areas. Or you may want to develop the matrix based only on the areas you are interested in, since they were probably identified from your buyer segmentation deliberations.

Fourth Export Decision Gate

Once you have identified your product differentiators and how they compare to your competitor's products in each of the buyer segments or areas you are considering, you are ready for another decision gate regarding your entry into the international market. If your product scores high on the positive side, you are ready to challenge the international market. If your product differentiators are negative for some market segments or areas, however, you may want to disregard these and concentrate on the more advantageous buyer segments or areas.

AHSI identified their positive Heat-R-Tiles product differentiators to be:

- *Efficient heat augmentation*
- *Low operating cost*
- *More aesthetically pleasing compared to other space heaters*

They also determined they had two negative product differentiators, which were:

- *Local regulatory approval requirements, and*
- *Installation requiring an electrician.*

They were leaning heavily toward the Middle East as an initial market, since the regulatory issue had scared them away from Europe. They set up a product differentiator matrix for these two areas and decided to look at Korea as well. Here is their resulting matrix.

Product Differentiator	Middle East	Europe	Korea
Augmented heat	+	++	++
Low operating cost		+	+
Aesthetically pleasing	+	+	+
Regulatory approval		– –	
Installation requirements	– –	–	–
Overall assessment	even	+	+++

The augmented heat capability was a positive differentiator in all areas but even more so in Europe and Korea. In the wealthy Middle East market, low operating costs were not a factor, but in Europe and Korea they were. All areas would consider the aesthetically pleasing aspects of the Heat-R-Tiles about the same. As already discussed, the regulatory problems in Europe were considered very negative but not an issue in the Middle East and Korea. Installation requirements would be a problem in the Middle East but less of a problem in Europe and Korea. The overall assessment was a surprise to AHSI. They had not anticipated that their product differentiators would be so positive in Korea. This caused them to go back and take a look at other potential areas of the world.

Chapter 7

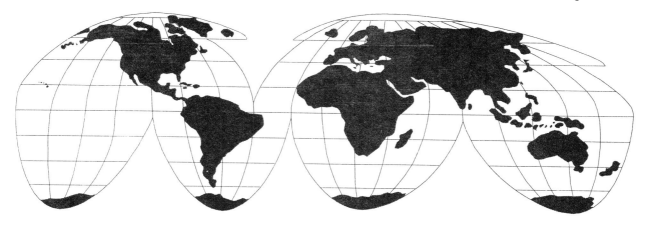

Country Segmentation

You have considered the main issues associated with marketing your product internationally in previous chapters. In this chapter you will consolidate your findings and select target countries that you will examine in further detail later in the book.

Buyer Segments in Countries

In Chapter 4 you identified buyer segments who would be interested in your product, and you probably identified areas of the world that could be potential markets for you. You have noticed that a number of the segments are common to many countries. You may also have considered countries in groups, such as Europe or South East Asia. There can be significant differences between countries usually considered in groups, however. For example, the Arab countries of the Middle East are usually grouped together, but there are significant differences between them, such as alcohol being forbidden in Saudi Arabia and Kuwait but not in the others. Now you need to zero in on specific countries to examine them in more detail, not just as parts of regions or groups.

Once again, the best way to do this is by setting up a matrix. This time list your buyer segments in a column down the left hand side and columns for each country of interest to the right. For each country, go down the column and give it a high, medium or low score for each buyer segment. At the bottom of each country column give a composite assessment of high, medium, or low for how the country rates against your buyer segments.

AHSI set up a matrix of the buyer segments they developed for their Heat-R-Tiles versus a number of countries they thought they could market to. Here is part of the matrix they developed.

Buyer Segments	Korea	Germany	Kuwait
Cold climate	M	M	L
Urbanized	M	H	M
Could afford	M	H	H
Overall	M	H	M

This process will give you a pretty good idea of what countries have the highest potential for your exports, based only on the buyer segmentation you developed. You then have to analyze each of the more promising countries from an overall marketing consideration. This is covered in the next section.

Country Assessments

Up until this point you have assessed market possibilities for your product in a general way under a number of criteria. Now you will apply those and other criteria in detail to the countries you identified by buyer segmentation as having the highest potential sales for your product. You must do this because, even though a country may appear very appealing from a buyer segmentation aspect, there could be other factors that mitigate strongly against your approaching that particular market.

To do this, you again use the matrix with the left hand column listing the marketing criteria discussed earlier, plus some new criteria. Make columns for the countries under consideration to the right of your list of marketing criteria. As a minimum, you should consider these aspects:

- Economic considerations
- Political situation
- Regulatory issues
- Cultural differences

- Ease of access
- Cost of marketing
- Competition
- Product differentiators
- Future potential

Again, score each criterion for each country high, medium, or low. However, this time your score should be based on how attractive the country is as a market for your product. For example, if it has many regulatory issues that will impede your marketing, it should score *low* for regulatory issues. If the competition is strong, it would also score a *low* for this category. If there are few regulations and no competition, both of these criteria score *high* because they are to your marketing advantage.

Economic Considerations

Some of the countries' economic considerations were dealt with when you did the buyer segmentation. Now you want to look at each country from the point of view of its overall economic state to determine if there are sufficient potential customers for your product. While the factors you will want to consider will depend on your product, they will probably include:

- Total population
- Gross national product
- Per-capita income
- Rural versus urban populations
- Income distribution

The income distribution data may be hard to obtain for some countries, but when used with the gross domestic product (GDP) and per-capita income information, it can be an important factor. For example, the average per-capita income of oil rich countries may be low, but the income distribution information will show that there is a group with very high income that could be your customers. Closer to home, the per-capita income of Mexico is considered low, yet there is a large, well-off upper class, and there is a disproportionately large number of millionaires and billionaires in the country.

Your high, medium, and low assessments for this market criteria may be difficult to make for some countries because of conflicting values. For example, tiny Singapore has the second highest standard of living in Asia, next to Japan, yet it only has a population of three million. The assessment you give each country will be very subjective and will of course depend on your product. You are looking for relative measurements, so as long as you use the same assessment criteria for each country your results should provide a useful comparison.

Political Situation

From a political view, you want to assess how stable the government is and, if it changes, how it will affect your business. It is important to assess whether the change may come about by a peaceful election or a prolonged civil war. For example, the prolonged civil war in Sri Lanka is probably not too conducive to doing business. On the other hand, if your product is for the military, maybe it is.

Political crisis in a country can cause the currency to fluctuate wildly. Look at how the Mexican peso has changed. As a result, consumers are forced to pay more for imports, and their overall standard of living drops. This will affect your sales.

If you are forced to do business in the currency of the country, the currency exchange rate can be even more of a concern to you. This is more reason for you to always try to deal in American dollars, which is usually not a problem since U.S. currency is widely used as the international standard.

Regulatory Issues

Product regulations imposed by governments are usually aimed at protecting their citizens, but these regulations can also be used to protect the country's own manufacturers against outside competition. Two examples of this are: Japan's prevention of most outside competition for commercial fishing sonar equipment on Japanese fishing boats and France's introduction of regulations requiring testing of all foreign electronic devices for electronic emissions, which poses a major bureaucratic barrier to imports.

It may not be easy to determine all of the regulatory issues applicable to your product for the countries that you are considering. There may be some that you never dreamed of, such as the example of chewing gum being a forbidden import into Singapore. Some of the issues you may want to find out about to see if they affect your product include:

- Import duties, which will vary for different countries.
- Import quotas, which will vary for different countries.
- Product testing and licensing procedures, such as the UL certification in the United States.
- Industrial benefit requirements, specifying that you put some money back into the local economy.
- Currency restrictions about taking your profits out of the country.

Cultural Differences

Cultural differences in a country can affect your business, sometimes in ways you would never have considered. The cultural differences driven by religion are fairly well documented and often must be strictly adhered to. For example, Moslems do not eat pork, and in some Moslem countries it is against the law to import pork products. In Saudi Arabia the religious issue is taken much farther. All indications of religions other than Islam are against the law. No Christmas decorations, cards, or music can be imported because they relate to Christianity. They get around the music issue to a degree by playing songs and tunes associated with Christmas, but without the Christian aspects, such as "Rudolph the Red Nosed Reindeer," "Frosty The Snowman," and "Jingle Bells." So discard any ideas of opening a Christmas store in Riyadh.

Music is the one cultural common denominator. At the height of the Gulf War, certain Iraqi singers were still very popular in Saudi Arabia, and you could hear their recordings blaring from the music stores. American country music is popular throughout the world, as are discos. It can be quite amazing to see Arabs in full traditional dress gyrating amid the flashing lights and rock music of a disco in the Sheraton hotel in Muscat, Sultanate of Oman.

Many cultural differences are often overlooked when considering foreign markets. For example, the bicycle, rather than a family car, is the main means of transportation in many countries. On the surface there may not seem to be a very big consumer market in countries like China or India for auto assessories; however, there is a growing local auto industry that may be interested in your products for possible incorporation in their products.

The overall spending habits of various cultural groups are another consideration. Studies have shown there are subtle yet important differences in how Europeans spend their money. In restaurants, the Italians spend more on food than on drinks, yet the Germans spend more on drinks than on food. The Germans also spend more on furniture than do the British.

Sorting out the cultural differences that will affect your international business is not an easy matter, and you could overlook some of the more obscure ones. You should try to get as much information as you can about these differences for the countries you are considering. For some products they will have no impact, but for others it could be extremely important. Do not make the mistake of playing down cultural differences or thinking you can get the world to change to your cultural ways. Respect these differences; some of them have been around for hundreds, even thousands, of years. If possible, turn them to your marketing advantage.

Ease of Access

How easy is it for you to get to a particular market? This question is not only associated with the cost of marketing but must be considered from other aspects as well, such as:

- The time your marketing and sales staff must spend traveling to and within the country.
- The problems you may encounter while setting up agents and distributors.
- The time it will take for your product to be accepted by the local consumers.
- The delivery and payment issues.

These issues are not easy to evaluate at this stage. The one you will find easiest to evaluate is the time your people will have to spend traveling to and within the country. You can get a relative estimate of this by just looking at a map. For example, it's a lot easier to get to Mexico than China, and getting around Mexico is a lot easier than traveling in China.

Cost of Marketing

At this stage you only want a rough, relative estimate of what it will cost you to market in each of the countries you are considering. This subject will be dealt with in Chapter 13. Your main consideration at this time will probably be the cost of transportation, and you can get a relative assessment of this by studying maps.

Competition

You should already have information on the competition from your work in Chapter 5. Use that information to do a relative assessment of the countries you are considering. You should ask yourself in which countries will your product have a relative advantage over the competition. You want to identify countries that you think will have the most interest in your product compared to that of the competition.

You will want to pay particular attention to countries with indigenous competition. For example, India is developing industries for most products, and these local products will be strong competition because of their lower labor costs. For countries like this, you may also want to take a closer look at the regulatory issues to see if they put your product at a disadvantage compared to the local products.

Product Differentiators

Having established what your advantageous differentiators are over your competition in Chapter 6, now look at countries from that point of view. Where does your product have advantages over the competition, including countries that have indigenous competitors? This marketing criteria may be the biggest reason you decide to target certain markets.

If you have a number of unique aspects to your product that relate directly to the country, give yourself a *high* score for that country. If your product differentiators are irrelevant for the country, score it *low*. And if you have only slightly advantageous differentiators, give the country a *medium*.

Future Potential

While this will be a very subjective judgment, it is also an important one. You have to look forward several years to visualize what your market could be at some future time in each country. It will depend very much on the country and the direction it is going. For example, as China rapidly opens its markets to foreign products, there could be a much bigger demand for your product in five years than there is now. The question you then have to ask is should you go there now or wait for a few more years.

Country Selections

Totaling up the assessments for each country can also be a bit subjective. In general, let the *low* scores cancel out the *high* scores. If you end up with *highs* and *mediums*, score the country according to whichever is more. You may want to put more emphasis on some criteria than others and develop a total score accordingly.

Just make sure you use the same emphasis for all of the countries so you do not fall into the trap of trying to justify a high score for a particular country because you want to go there.

The total assessment for the countries you have investigated will indicate some that are just not worth considering any further and some that have tremendous potential for your product. In all likelihood, the majority will be in a gray area in between. You will have to make a subjective decision on where you want to draw the line. It will of course depend on how many countries you are able to consider. Two or three high scoring countries are better than dozens in the *medium* to *high* range, so do not make the mistake of trying to include too many.

Later in the book, when you look at these countries in more detail, you will prioritize the countries. At this stage you simply want to select the countries that you will investigate further in the next step.

When AHSI drew up their country assessment matrix, they looked at a large number of countries and were again surprised at the ones that rated in the high category. Here is part of their matrix.

Market Criteria	Korea	Germany	Kuwait
Economic	M	H	M
Political	M	H	L
Regulatory	H	L	H
Cultural	N/A	N/A	N/A
Ease of access	L	M	L
Marketing cost	L	M	L
Competition	H	L	H
Differentiators	H	L	H
Potential	H	L	M
Overall	H	L	M

AHSI was surprised to see that Germany, that looked highly promising from a buyer segmentation aspect, was a low-potential market when other marketing criteria were considered. They were also surprised that Korea appeared to have a high market potential for Heat-R-Tiles.

Select the Best Country for Your Product

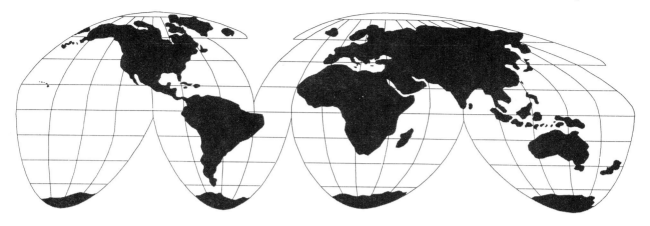

Chapter 8

Determining the Market Potential

Now that you have selected a number of countries as potential targets for your international marketing activity, you want to examine each of them further in order to prioritize your efforts. The first step is to do a relative assessment of the market potential in each country so you can compare them. You want to estimate the number or amount of your product that could be sold in each country and then do a quantitative comparison of the countries.

What is Market Potential?

For the purposes of this book, market potential is defined as the number of potential sales of your product in a particular country, if there was no competition and if everyone who wanted to buy the product did so. This is an idyllic situation, but it is a necessary first step in assessing the market and comparing countries.

Remember that you are doing a relative assessment of countries, so the numbers you arrive at for each country do not have to be precise, as long as the same criteria are used for each country.

When establishing your market potential for each country, base it not only on the current situation but also on the future market potential, even though you may have to put some conditions on it. For example, there may be a very big market potential for your product in Cuba even though American companies are not allowed to trade with them at this time. This situation could change, so be prepared. Only a few years ago Vietnam was on the same black list, yet American companies are flocking there to test the business waters now.

Country Market Information From Government Sources

Obtaining information on the market potential of a list of countries sounds like a daunting task, but it is easier than you may think. Much of the information you require can be obtained through the U.S. Department of Commerce, International Trade Administration. It is devoted to assisting U.S. companies in international trade. They have a network of approximately 2,500 trade experts in about 70 countries around the world and about 70 cities in the United States. The government commercial officers stationed around the world are there to provide you with market information on the countries they are responsible for and to help you market and export your products. The trade specialists in U.S. cities are there to provide you with the Department of Commerce international trade services. To access this information, call your nearest Department of Commerce District Office or their toll free number.

Department of Commerce trade specialists can provide a wide range of information drawn from government sources, which includes trade-related documents, product specific market research reports, and trade statistics as well as information on trade regulations, customs requirements, product standards, and tariffs. You can request information brochures that describe the services and reports available from their district offices. Here is a brief outline of some of these services, as advertised on the International Trade Administration's web site: <http://www.ita.doc.gov/>.

- Trade Opportunities Program. This program provides private and public trade leads that arrive daily from U.S. embassies abroad. These leads are printed in the *Journal of Commerce* and other private sector newspapers.
- Agent and Distributor Service. This is a customized search on behalf of U.S. companies seeking foreign representation. U.S. commercial officers abroad conduct the agent or distributor search based on requirements specified by the requesting firm. The search for agents and distributors takes 60 to 90 days and costs about $250 per market.
- Commercial Service International Contacts List. This list provides the name and contact information for over 70,000 foreign agents,

distributors, and importers who are interested in working with U.S. exporters.

- Gold Key Service. This service is custom-tailored to U.S. companies planning to visit a foreign country. The service combines orientation briefings, market research, introductions to potential partners, interpreter service for meetings, and assistance in developing a marketing strategy.

Additional Sources of Country Market Information

In addition to the government marketing information listed above, there are many more sources of information, depending on your product. This list will get you started.

- Public library. This is an often overlooked resource available free of charge. You can do the search yourself or get your staff to assist you. Librarians are usually willing to help you find information of this nature because it allows them to use their professional training.
- Trade associations. There are many local and national trade associations involved in exports, such as freight forwarders, customs brokers, and those associated with specific product manufacturing. Many of the associations provide export information for their members.
- Banks. Many banks have large international trading departments that have a wealth of information on international markets.
- Foreign embassies and consulates. These foreign representatives are more than happy to provide information about their country, but be aware that they are more interested in selling to you.

Buyer Segmentation

In Chapter 4 you used the buyer segmentation technique to narrow down the international marketplace into the most likely areas or countries for your product. You can use this same technique to gauge the potential market for your product in each country you are investigating; although, after obtaining additional information on the countries, you may want to consider different buyer segmentations for this assessment.

The information you require will depend on the product and the buyer segmentation you use, and you may not be able to get all the information you think you need. Get what you can from the sources mentioned above. You will be pleasantly surprised at what is available. It will take time to get some of the information, but doing this research is much faster and a lot less expensive than going to the countries. Anyway you are only looking for a relative assessment.

The way to achieve this relative assessment of the potential market of each country, based on buyer segmentation, is best explained by an example. Assume your product is for the petroleum business and the buyer segmentation you are looking is based on:

- Annual oil production of the country;
- Refinery capacity;
- Number of oil and gas wells;
- Miles of pipeline; and
- Petro-chemical production.

Information of this nature is readily available in annual publications associated with the petroleum industry. Here is where your local librarian can help you. You can also get information from oil and gas production trade magazines. If your product is associated with oil wells, assume that you could sell a certain number of your product to each well in the country. Knowing the number of wells, you can then get a figure for the potential market by simply multiplying the number of products per well by the number of wells in the country. This may not be a very accurate method, but it gives you a relative number with which you can compare the market potential in each country.

If your product lends itself to this type of buyer segmentation and you are able to get applicable information for each country, you will very quickly identify the more significant countries you should be targeting. You will probably find some surprises as well.

User Benefits

Once you have an estimate of the market potential for each country based on buyer segmentation, you may want to modify the numbers according to the benefits your product will offer the users in each country. The user benefit considerations will also depend on the product. Do not try to be too accurate here because you are still doing a relative assessment of each country. Using the petroleum industry example again, if your product is a modular structure that is built over manifolds and valves to provide protection from the elements, it provides no user benefits to the underwater connections of off-shore oil wells; therefore, you will have to modify you potential market numbers by removing the off-shore wells from your calculations.

Trends

Before you leave this part of the calculations, you might want to sit back and reconsider the market from the point of view of future trends. The probable market figures you have now are what the market is today, but you have to think about the future. Perhaps the standard of living in the country is growing rapidly, and in a few years more consumers will be interested in your product. On the other hand, maybe the country's inflation rate is so high that in a few years nobody will be able to afford your product.

If there are noticeable trends that affect your product, you should apply them to the market potential. For example, if your product relies on the living standard of the customers and the standard is increasing by a certain amount in the country, you may want to increase the market potential in proportion to this increase over the next few years. Similarly, if inflation is a problem, you may want to decrease your market potential.

Country Prioritization

The accuracy of the market potential you project for each country will depend on the product and the information available. What you can project may not be accurate enough to stake the future of your company on, yet it is a lot more information than you had when you started. By doing the research you will have a much better insight into your potential international market.

Assuming you used the same criteria for each country, your results should be accurate enough to do a relative assessment of the potential in each country and then to prioritize the countries in order of their market potential. You will probably find that some stand out as obvious markets to target and others as not worth your effort. You may want to discard the latter at this point and concentrate only on the others.

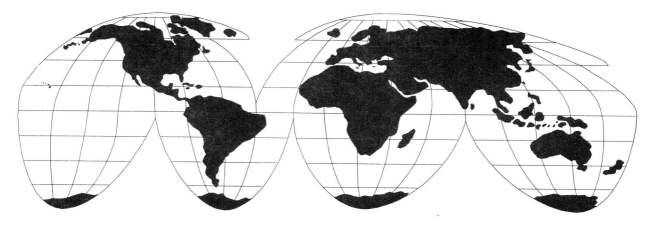

Chapter 9

Potential Market Revenue

Now that you have an estimate of the potential number of sales of products like yours that could be made in a number of countries, you want to get an estimate of the potential revenue you can realistically expect from each market. This, after all, is what you are in business for. The potential revenue is the price you get for the product multiplied by the number of sales you actually make. The sales you actually make will depend on the competition and other influences that are discussed in this chapter.

Win Probability

You may already be familiar with the concept of applying win probability figures to domestic market opportunities. This technique is often used as a tool to estimate future sales and to establish budgets based on the income from those sales. For example, you may be chasing several market opportunities or projects that you hope to win in the next year or so. Based on what you know about the buyer's desires and the competition, you assign a percentage to each opportunity that represents your estimate of the probability that you will win the business. If your chances are pretty high, you might give it a win probability of 0.8, or 80 percent. If they are low, but you do not want to entirely give up on the opportunity, you may want to give it a ten percent, or 0.1, win probability.

If you take the estimated sales value of each opportunity and multiply it by the win probability, you come up with a factored amount of the revenue you hope to get if you win it. Then if you total up the factored amounts for all the opportunities, you should get a figure that represents the total sales revenue you will win from all the business you are chasing. That's the theory, and surprisingly enough, it is usually fairly accurate if you have a number of opportunities. The trick, of course, is to develop an estimate of the value of the opportunity and of the win probability that is as accurate as possible.

You can use this same technique to gauge the potential market revenue in each of the countries you are investigating. In the last chapter you calculated the market potential for products of your kind in each of the buyer segments in each of the countries to arrive at an overall market potential for the country. You must now take another look at these buyer segments and apply a win probability to the market potential numbers. For example, if you have a number for the potential sales that could be made to the rural population of a country, estimate the win probability of these sales and multiply the potential sales number by the probability to get the factored amount of sales you can expect. When you total up the factored amounts for all the buyer segments in a country, you will have an estimate of the potential number of sales for your product in the country. That will be the amount of your product you can more realistically hope to sell in that market.

The estimate of the win probability is a very subjective figure, so you must be very honest when estimating it. It is usually based on the competition you expect to encounter, but there can be other considerations that affect it as well.

Competition

Now you must use your knowledge of direct and indirect competition, discussed in Chapter 5, to establish a win probability for the buyer segments in the countries you are considering. For example, if you know you will be up against two other competitors, an easy approach is to suppose the three of you will share the market evenly and you will win a third of the business. Thus you have a 0.33 win probability. However, maybe one of the competitors has some marketing advantages over you and the other competitor. In that case, you may want to give this competitor a 40 percent win probability, leaving only 60 percent for you and the other competitor. Your win probability is half of this remainder, or 0.3 of the potential market.

You must also factor in the indirect competition, such as what portion of the potential market will buy the product from you or anyone else. If this is only 50 percent of the potential market, you have to multiply the 0.3 by 0.5 to end up with a win probability of only 0.15. That is, you can expect to win 15 percent of the overall potential sales associated with that particular buyer segment.

Probable Market

Using the potential market numbers and the win probability method described above for each of the buyer segments in a country, you arrive at a figure that represents the probable number of sales of your product in the country. This is the probable market for you in the country. Even though the calculations you have made are based on subjective estimates, as long as the same method is used for each country, you will get a good indication of the relative opportunity in each of the countries.

Pricing

Once you have estimated the probable market in each country being considered, you must determine the price of your product in order to arrive at the potential revenue you can hope to get from each market. The price you will charge in each country may differ, and it certainly will be different from what you charge in your domestic market. In Chapter 2, a number of export costs were discussed, and Chapter 25 will address this issue in more detail. Your pricing concerns at this time are:

- Product design
- Labeling and packaging
- Translation
- Marketing
- Promotion
- Agent commissions
- Cost of getting paid
- Transportation costs
- Import costs
- Installation, maintenance, and repair

Potential Revenue

With an estimate of the probable number of unit sales of your product in each country, based on the win probabilities and the overall potential market, and with your price per unit in each market determined, you can calculate the potential revenue you can realistically expect to obtain from each market. You simply multiply your probability factor for each market by the price per unit.

Of course you will not make all of these sales and get all of the revenue at once. It will take time to set up your marketing infrastructure in the countries and for the customers to accept your product. Then, hopefully, your sales will begin to climb. When you begin to set your budgets, you will want to spread your expected potential revenue over several years. However, when determining which countries to target with your international marketing, a gross figure of the potential revenue from each country is sufficient.

Country Prioritization

The potential revenue you have just calculated for each country you are considering should be an accurate gauge of what you can expect to gain from each country. When you arrange the countries in order of the potential revenue, you may find that there is a change from the priority based on potential market alone. This is quite normal. China may have a very large potential market for a product because of the population, but only a few can afford to buy. Singapore, on the other hand, with the second highest standard of living in Asia and a fraction of the population, may have more potential customers.

The country prioritization based on potential market revenue is what you want to use to determine which countries you will target in your initial international marketing. You now have to look at each country in detail to determine your marketing approach and projected marketing costs.

Chapter 10

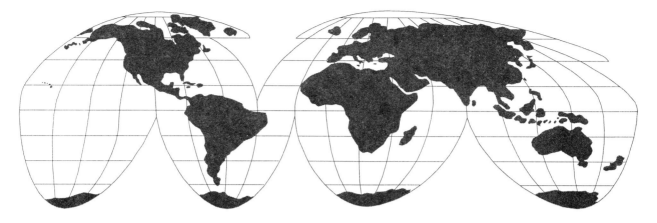

Market Entry Strategy

Now that you have selected the countries you want to market your product to, you must now devise a strategy that will get you into the market. Although you may be tempted to commit to trade shows in the countries or make trips to them immediately, do not do any of this until you have devised an entry strategy. You will accomplish much more with a well thought out game plan, and it will be much less expensive.

Foreign Marketing Cycle

Your market entry strategy and tactics should be based on the marketing cycle of the target country, which is the series of events that lead up to a sale. This cycle is particularly applicable to new technology and system products, but much of it applies to all products.

A typical foreign marketing cycle has the following stages.

- Prospecting. This is the activity required to identify new customers. There are many ways of doing this, but in foreign markets the most common is to use the services of a local agent.

71

- Create a need. For state-of-the-art products or products with new usage concepts, you may have to go through an added step in the marketing cycle if you must create a need for your product in the country. Your potential customers may have problems that can be solved by your product but be unaware that a solution exists, or they may not even know they have a problem that needs solving. This is particularly true for security equipment.
- Concept proposal. This stage is not always required, depending on the product. It happens when you find a customer who has some interest in your product but does not fully understand how it can be used. You may have to provide your customers with a short, generalized proposal showing how they can use your product to solve their problem.
- Qualification. You should qualify the opportunity as early as possible in the marketing cycle. Be sure there is a real need for your product and that the prospective customer or customers have the money to pay for it. If you do not do this early, you could spend valuable resources and time chasing somebody's dream that turns into your nightmare.
- Detailed proposal. This is a document containing technical details of what you are offering for a specific project. The accompanying price proposal is usually submitted as a separate document.
- Contracts. This is your major marketing goal.
- Delivery and installation. This part of the cycle is also important because it can lead to future business.

You are probably already familiar with most of these stages except the create a need stage, which is usually only applicable to foreign marketing. The following section explains this stage in more detail because it may need to be part of your market entry strategy.

Creating a Need

If you are marketing state-of-the-art products or products with new usage concepts, you may have to go through an added step in the marketing cycle, which is to create a need for your product in the country. Your potential customers may have problems that can be solved by your product, but they don't know it yet. They may not even know they have a problem that needs solving. This is particularly true for military and security equipment.

The usual process is to use advertising or customer meetings to explain how your product can solve their problems. Sometimes you may even have to explain the problem. Often you have to give some technical details of how your product works, but remember to keep it at the technical level of the customer. In all likelihood, you will also have to provide a written concept proposal aimed specifically at the customer's situation.

A marketer and his agent were having lunch with an admiral of a country with a relatively large coast line. The admiral was bemoaning the fact that in the clear waters off their coast they could see enemy submarines as they flew over them, but he did not know what the submarines were doing. The marketer casually suggested that they could be charting the ocean bottom so that, if they had to in the future, they could lay mines. The admiral stared at him unbelievingly and asked if submarines could lay mines. The marketer then realized that the admiral knew very little about submarines or underwater warfare.

So the marketer offered to write up a brief report on the underwater threat to the country, which he was able to do from information available in the public library. He sent the report to the admiral through the agent and never heard about it again. However, it was passed to the admiral's superiors with his name on it, and a few months later the admiral was promoted and put in charge of defending the country from underwater attack. Shortly after, they began buying the marketer's sonar product because the need was pointed out to them in the report. Having created the need, as well as a good contact in the navy, the marketer was able to do considerable business in the country.

Local Agents

In most cases, the first step in your marketing strategy is to establish yourself with a suitable local agent in the country. This is probably the most important part of a market entry strategy and is dealt with in greater detail in later chapters. This section provides the information on agents that you require at this point in your planning.

Local agents are essential to provide you with local knowledge and connections that will enable you to identify and contact potential customers, work with local laws, be aware of local customs, and navigate other confusing business practices that you will never fully understand. The main function of an agent is to market your products to the local customers; however, they can also help you in other ways, such as to:

- Validate translations of your brochures, videos, and other marketing literature.

- Advise you on local government regulations and controls, which in some countries can be very confusing.
- Arrange hotels for you that are usually much more convenient and less expensive than a travel agent can arrange.

This book uses the general definition of *agent* as "one who acts for another in business," even though there are different types of agents and various types of business relationships you can have with them, depending on your product and on the laws and customs of the country. Your market entry strategy should include a decision on the type of agent you require. The most common types of agents and business relationships are:

- Commission agents
- Retainer agents
- Commission and retainer agents
- Agents servicing other countries
- Local government-employed agents
- Distributors
- Contractors and subcontractors
- Joint venture companies
- Local branch offices
- Strategic partners

Chapters 20 through 23 provide detailed information on selecting and contracting with local agents. At this stage you may want to preview the various types of agents described in Chapter 20.

AHSI decided that their market entry strategy to each country would be to establish themselves with suitable distributor agents for their Heat-R-Tiles. They would do this by exhibiting at a trade show in the country where they could attract potential agents and, at the same time, expose the Heat-R-Tiles to potential customers.

Military Marketing

Military marketing does not just involve products that are lethal. Military forces use everything from major weapon systems, such as Trident nuclear submarines, to rolls of toilet paper, and they have to buy everything from contractors. While sales to major military systems are the domain of big companies who can afford the time and money it takes to win these contracts, there is a wide range of international military procurement open to many smaller companies.

Marketing military products is usually quite different from marketing other products to other customers, although there are similarities when you are dealing with non-military products. The approach you take to market to the military will depend on your product. You will probably also have to use an agent who specializes in dealing with the military.

It takes a few years to work through the military acquisition process in many countries and requires considerable effort from both you and your agent. When you do eventually get the contract, hopefully it is worth the effort. It can cost a lot to get to that point. If you are targeting the military of a country as your customer, be sure you have the stamina to do so.

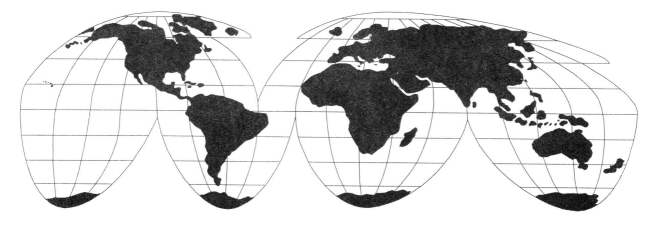

Chapter 11

Promotion Strategy

This chapter will help you develop the promotion strategy you should use in your international marketing and the promotion material you will require to reach your target audience. The strategy and material you will use for international markets will probably not be the same as what you have been using for your domestic market.

Promotion Strategy Aim

Your promotion strategy should have a defined aim and be targeted at a specific audience. The aim is usually fairly straightforward, but you should still think it through. While your aim will probably be to make potential customers aware of your product, you may also want to add some qualifiers, such as within a specific period of time.

For many consumer products, this will drive the type of advertising you need. If the period is very short, you will be forced to do a media blitz. If you want a longer period to make your audience aware of your product, you may be able to revert to slower, less expensive advertising.

AHSI decided that their promotional aim was two-fold. They first had to make suitable distributors aware of their Heat-R-Tile product, then they had to assist the selected distributors in making their customers aware of the product.

Target Audience

Identifying the target audience for your promotional material is also important. The audience may dictate the promotional approach your take and the type and content of your promotional material. In previous chapters you determined the market segments you would be targeting in each country. Now you can use these segments to determine the target audience for your promotion campaign.

A critical thing to remember about your international target audience, no matter what segment they are in, is that they are international and do not necessarily have the same customs, desires, and thought processes as your domestic customers. Do not base your promotional material on what succeeds for you at home. Try to get some idea of the kind of promotion that works in the target country. Your agent should be able to help you with this.

If your product is even slightly technical, it is important to remember that not all potential customers will understand the technical information and even fewer will be interested in it. All they want to know is what the product can do for them. Avoid deluging the potential customers with technical information. Keep this in mind as you develop your promotional material.

AHSI decided that their initial target audience in a country would have to be suitable distributors. The initial promotion material would then have to include marketing suggestions and some technical explanations of the product. Once they appointed the distributors, they would have to assist them in promoting the Heat-R-Tiles to potential customers. This would require new material that would be developed with the help of the distributor.

Brochures

You must have some kind of brochure that will tell potential customers about your product. For international marketing, your brochures should be market-oriented rather than technology-intensive. You should emphasize what the product does rather than the details about how it does it. Because your brochure may have to be translated by your local agents as they explain it to customers, do not burden them with a long technical write-up which they are liable to translate incorrectly and which will probably bore customers.

You should also consider the probability of having to translate your brochure into a foreign language. The language or languages you choose will of course depend on the countries you are targeting. Languages such as Arabic and Spanish are used in many countries; however, be aware that there are words in these languages that have different meanings in different countries. Your best approach is to have your agent do the translation or at least check it over before you print it.

Videos

Video tapes have become a very popular marketing and sales tool, but there is a major technological issue to keep in mind when using them internationally. Tapes used in North America will not work on European machines, and vice versa. In North America, the standard electronic format of the video tapes is called NTSC, while in Europe the format used is called PAL. France and Russia use an even different system. You can run across any of these three formats throughout the world. In general, the NTSC is used in the western hemisphere, and the PAL format is used everywhere else.

Do not think you can overcome this video tape incompatibility problem by taking your own TV monitor, because your TV may not work on the electrical supply of the country you are visiting. North American TVs are designed to operate on the standard 120 volt, 60 cycles or hertz electrical power used in North America. In Europe and much of the rest of the world, the electricity is 240 volt and 50 cycles per second, so your TV will not work there. The answer is to have your videos in both NTSC and PAL format.

An important rule to remember about the content of the video tapes is that people who watch them in a foreign country will be limited in their ability to understand English. Even those with good English capabilities will not understand many of the American idiomatic expressions. Keep the wording simple, and above all, do not use colloquialisms like "The net of all this is a highly inflated bottom line." The listener will spend the rest of the tape trying to figure out why you are talking about nets and how you inflate a net.

Advertising

Without consulting with your agent, you should not consider local media advertising in a foreign country as your means of market entry. This type of advertising is fraught with problems such as whether you should use billboards, newspapers, radio, or TV; who will pay for it, you or your local agent; and how you will ensure the ads are correct in the foreign language and culture. This form of advertising is best left to the discretion of your agent once you are better established in the market area.

You may, however, want to consider magazine advertising, particularly in magazines that target your audience, are in English, and have wide international distribution. There are many of these, such as *Jane's Defense Weekly* that is read by military people around the world. You may even want to try some magazines in the appropriate foreign language, such as Spanish or Arabic. If you use magazines that have a card for readers to fill out for more information, you will be pleasantly surprised at the response. As a market entry tool, these ads and responses will give you an estimate of the interest in your product and will also flush out potential agents.

Trade Shows

Trade shows are an excellent market entry vehicle to promote your products, to test the response to your product in a new market, and to identify potential agents. However, trade shows have become a product in themselves, and as such there are too many for potential customers to attend them all. Before you decide on a trade show, check it out carefully to make sure the customer audience you want to target will be in attendance in numbers that will make your efforts worthwhile.

You may not have to go far to have an international audience visit your booth at a trade show because many shows in the United States attract attendees from around the world. Foreign visitors are usually agents looking for products to sponsor in their homeland, so here you may be able to find someone who can get you started in his or her country. Similarly, multinational trade shows are held throughout Europe and are gaining popularity in the Middle East and Asia.

Once you have decided to use a trade show for your market entry, there are a number of issues that you must resolve in order to ensure a successful show. These issues will depend on your promotion strategy and your target audience. Chapter 24 covers most of these considerations.

AHSI decided that their best mode of entry into a new market was by way of a trade show aimed at local householders. They assumed that local contractors, distributors, and potential agents would also attend the show. Here they could get an idea of the local acceptance of the Heat-R-Tile product and identify potential distributors or agents at the same time.

They would have some of the trade booth artwork in the local language and would translate and print one of their standard brochures as well. They would provide press kits for the local media and make up special information kits for potential distributors and agents.

Other Promotional Methods

There are a number of other promotional methods you may be able to use in your foreign market entry, but these will depend on your product. Direct mail is one of them. It is not as difficult as it sounds in some countries. For example, if your product is for the construction industry, you should be able to get a list of architects in a particular country from their local architectural society. You can send each of them a package of information. Before you do this, however, you should have established a local agent for them to contact and for the follow-up.

Articles about your product published in relevant international magazines are another excellent market-entry technique. Quite often, if you provide the magazine editor with a written article and suitable artwork, they will publish the article. They will probably want you to buy some advertising space, which may be a good idea as a complement to your article. This can be a very cost-effective way of advertising.

If your product is fairly technical, you may want to present a paper on it at a suitable conference. This will expose it to people directly involved in the subject. The paper will be published in the conference proceedings, and your information will reach others who read it. You can also use copies of the paper in the future as a handout.

A growing trend in some countries is to hold seminars on products. These can be a useful marketing tool, provided the product lends itself to this type of promotion. The seminar can be as short as a few hours or can last a few days.

Follow-up

Every marketing and sales course stresses the need for follow-up. This is even more important in international marketing where the phrase "out of sight, out of mind" is brutally true. Your promotion strategy should include plans for frequent follow-up.

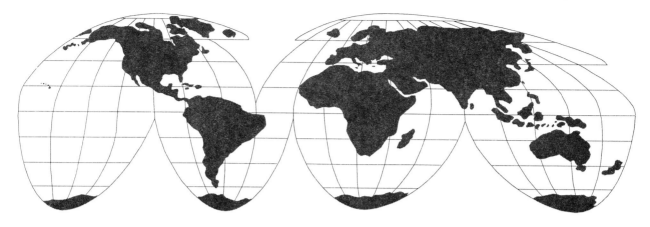

Chapter 12

Marketing Plan and Schedule

Having established your market entry and promotion strategy, you can now set up a marketing plan and schedule. For each target country, identify the required activities and attach reasonable completion dates to them. Then integrate the plans and schedules of each country into an overall plan and schedule, consolidating activities as appropriate.

Agent Selection

As discussed in Chapter 10, your market entry strategy will begin with the selection of a suitable agent for each country. You may want to break this down into sub-activities such as to identify potential agents, interview potential agents, select an agent, and negotiate the agent agreement. These important international marketing activities are explained in chapters 20 through 23. However you do it, you must allow a suitable amount of time to go through the agent selection and contracting process.

If your potential agent identification process involves getting suitable names from the government and other sources and then contacting them, it will take several months. You may be able to obtain enough information to make a selection without visiting and interviewing them. However, be very cautious if you go this route, particularly when you negotiate the agent agreement. Make sure you have an easy out if your selection proves to be wrong.

No matter how you do your agent selection, you must allow time for it in your marketing plan. The following are some suggested times.

Agent Selection Timetable

Potential agent identification	4 months
Agent interviews and selection	1 month
Agent agreement negotiation	1 month

Promotion Activities

Planning and scheduling your promotion activities may not be easy, because you seldom have control of the dates of key events. If you decide to use a suitable conference or trade show, you will have to tie your schedule to the date of these events. Similarly, if you want to use government incoming or outgoing missions, you are at the mercy of their scheduling. The only promotion activity you have control over is the visit to the country you have organized. But it may not be as effective as a visit in conjunction with a trade show.

Selecting an appropriate trade show also takes time. The best way is to peruse appropriate trade magazines. They often provide lists of upcoming trade shows around the world. The trade shows themselves frequently advertise in these magazines as well. Once you have made contact with a few of the show organizers, you will be on their mailing lists and forever inundated with information on future shows.

You will have to select a show at least four or five months in the future, in order to make the booking deadline for the booth and to allow you time to prepare for it. The show organizers will require you to book at least four months in advance and make a payment on the booth a few months before the show. You will need much of this time to prepare your artwork and promotion material. The suggested times to allow for preparation are as follows.

Promotion Timetable

Select and book trade show	4 months prior to show
Design show booth	3 months prior to show
Prepare artwork and material	2 months prior to show
Ship trade show booth	2 weeks prior to show

Promotion Material

You have, no doubt, already experienced the hassle of getting promotional material prepared, particularly if you have had deadlines to meet. International marketing requires the same kind of material, with the added complication of foreign translation. Your first marketing sortie into a country, usually a trade show, will probably involve at least a brochure or fact sheet translated into the language of the country. You may also want to get some business cards translated and printed with English on one side and the local language on the other.

Assuming you are having just one of your existing brochures redone in the local language, here are the suggested times you should allow for this activity.

Brochure Timetable

Translation	2 weeks
Validation of the translation	1 month
Brochure layout and artwork	2 weeks
Printing	2 weeks

As mentioned in Chapter 11, you should not rely only on commercial translators for the correct translation, particularly for languages that are used in several countries. To be safe, have the translation validated by somebody from the specific country to ensue there are no embarrassing words or phrases used. This goes for business cards as well as brochures. Sometimes the translator will try to do a literal translation of your company name or title and get it wrong. For example, Truck Bodies Incorporated could end up as Automobile Drivers Company.

Passports, Visas, and Carnets

Make sure you have all the required travel documents long before you leave on a marketing trip. A valid passport is an obvious requirement, but make sure it is not expired or about to do so. Many a business trip has been delayed waiting for a passport renewal.

Many countries require some form of entry visa, and some also require you to have an exit visa. Find out the country requirements long before your trip because obtaining a visa can sometimes take considerable time. For example, to get a visa to visit Saudi Arabia you must have a letter of invitation from a Saudi citizen or company that is certified by the Saudi Arabia Chamber of Commerce, stating they will be responsible for you when you are in the kingdom. You also need a letter from your company, certified by your local Chamber of Commerce, stating that the company will pay for your way out of Saudi Arabia. These letters, a completed visa application form that also asks for your religion, a fee, and your passport are submitted to the nearest Saudi consulate. Then you wait for them to call and tell you the visa is ready for pickup. This can take a few days or a few weeks. In the meantime you are without a passport and unable to travel anywhere outside your own country.

International Certificates of Vaccination should be considered if you are traveling to a country with a questionable medical situation. The document itself is a small booklet about the size of a passport that lists the dates of vaccinations for yellow fever, cholera, diphtheria, polio, and other diseases. It can be obtained from your doctor when you get the vaccinations. The purpose of the document is not necessarily to let you travel to the country with the health problem but to allow you to enter another country after your visit, including your return home.

If you plan to carry demonstration items with you, you should have an international carnet (pronounced car-nay). This document allows you to temporarily import the items into a country and also to bring them back home, without paying duty on them. The carnet is obtained from your local Chamber of Commerce and, before you can use it, it must be validated by a customs official of your own country. This involves taking the equipment down to the customs office and having them check to ensure that the equipment listed exists, that the serial numbers listed are correct, and so on. Sometimes this procedure can be done on your first trip out of the country with the carnet if you are hand carrying the equipment, but then you must ensure you have all of the equipment that is listed on the carnet.

Carnets are not used by every country in the world. Countries that do not adhere to the carnet system have some other local method of controlling temporary import and export of goods. The usual approach is to have the importing company post a customs bond. The amount of the bond is returnable when the goods have been reexported out of the country. For example, Kuwait requires a customs bond for all temporary imports in the amount of eight percent of CIF (cost including freight) of the goods. The money is eventually returned after the goods have been reexported. In practice, these customs bonds are handled by the shipping companies, although you must pay the money up-front.

Country Plan and Schedule

Now you can put together the marketing plan and schedule for each country you have decided to target, based on the four considerations discussed.

- Agent selection activities
- Promotion activities

- Promotional material acquisition
- Travel documentation

Lay this out in a composite plan that lists the required activity and the date by which it must be completed. The best way to explain this is by the following example.

For their market entry into Korea, AHSI decided that they would exhibit at a suitable trade show aimed at local householders. This would expose their Heat-R-Tiles product to customers and would also enable them to meet with potential agents. They planned to have identified a number of potential agents prior to the trade show and interview them after the show.

In the January edition of an international heating and air conditioning business magazine, they saw an ad for a heating and air conditioning trade show in Seoul, Korea, in October. They decided to use this as their market-entry vehicle. They developed the following marketing plan and schedule for Korea.

Activity	Complete By
1. Register for trade show	End June
2. Design show booth	End July
3. Translate brochures and cards	End July
4. Validate brochures and cards	Mid August
5. Prepare brochure layout and artwork	End August
6. Print brochures and cards	Mid September
7. Complete artwork and ship booth	Mid September
8. Obtain visas	End September
9. Obtain carnet	End September
10. Identify and contact agents	End September
11. Make travel arrangements	End September
12. Attend trade show	Mid October
13. Interview agents	End October
14. Select agent	End November
15. Prepare agent agreement	End December

Integrated Plan and Schedule

Once you have drafted your marketing plan and schedule for each of the countries you are planning to target, you should integrate the plans into one. This will give you a chance to sort out conflicting travel dates and other commitments and alter some of the individual country plans, if necessary. This will also enable you to amalgamate certain activities to reduce the marketing costs. The marketing costs, discussed in the next chapter, may cause you to alter your integrated plan or the individual country plans. With a well thought-out marketing plan and schedule, you will be able to effectively budget your time and resources.

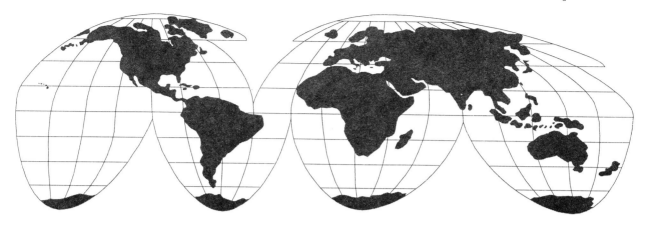

Chapter 13

Marketing Costs

Your marketing plan will have costs associated with it. Before you put your plan into action, you should establish at least a rough estimate of these costs. In so doing, you may discover that your plan is beyond your budget and will have to be reduced in scope or altered in some way. It is better to realize this and adjust accordingly before you begin your international marketing activity, rather than have to make the adjustments later when you have already made commitments.

Demonstration Equipment Costs

Some products can be effectively marketed without a demonstration, but usually the customers want to see what the product will do. Some form of demonstration is normally required, and it usually involves equipment, for either the product itself or to show it off. The costs associated with this demonstration equipment are often underestimated, and they can be significant.

If the demonstration is to be done with the product itself, allowance must be made for the marketing staff to have the required equipment to demonstrate. Companies will sometimes relegate old models or faulty units to the marketing department to keep the costs down. This can be worse than having no demo at all. You cannot impress customers with non-working or old products, no matter how well you explain to them the improvements of your latest version.

Another thing to consider is that your product may have to be altered for the international market. This is particularly true for electronic products. As mentioned earlier, the electricity supplies and connections in most of the world are different from those of the United States, so your demonstration units will have to be altered to accept the local voltage. Sometimes it is simply a matter of getting an adapter to match the local electrical outlets. If your product involves TV displays, however, you could be in for some expensive changes to accommodate international electrical voltage and frequency.

If your product involves the printed word, it of course will have to be tailored to the local language. If it involves dates, you may have to change it to comply with local calendars. For example, some of the Muslim countries use the Hijrah calendar that starts in the year 622 and is based on lunar months. Even colors may have to be changed to comply or appeal locally. If you suspect any of this applies to your product, check with the Department of Commerce officials or the trade officials at the U.S. embassy in the country you are considering.

All of these changes, including those to the basic demonstration equipment, cost money. You will have to factor this into your marketing costs. In some cases it may be a determent, but in others it may be insignificant.

Travel Costs

These are the costs most novice international marketers think of first. Air fare is the most obvious and is usually the largest portion of the travel costs. Do not budget based on specially-priced fares because you will probably not be able to meet the restrictions associated with these fares. Consider regular-priced tickets that give you the flexibility to alter your plans because it is very likely you will have to do so.

Local travel within the country can be quite expensive. Just look at a map of Chile and think about how much the air fare will be to get around that country. Other public transportation can also be expensive. Have you traveled on British Rail lately?

The form of local travel you probably will use most, taxis, in some cities such as Paris will cost about 50 dollars for a 15-minute trip. In many cities it is impossible to simply telephone for a taxi to take you back from a meeting, because the taxi service is not organized for this and often there are no street addresses to direct the taxi to. In such cases, you will be forced to hire the taxi by the hour and have it wait for you to take you back from your meeting. You must therefore be sure you budget adequately for local travel within a country.

Hotels, at least the kind you would want to stay in, are also expensive. You usually have to stay in business-class hotels that can cost around $300 a day, but you usually get your money's worth because the hotels are very elegant, except in Paris and London. In those cities you still have to pay the $300 or more, but for that you get only a tiny room barely large enough for the bed.

Meals can be another significant expense because, in many countries, you will want to eat only in safe restaurants such as those associated with the major hotels. Needless to say, the hotels know they have a captive clientele and charge accordingly. In many European countries, breakfast will cost about $25 and lunch about $40. If you want a steak for dinner, be prepared to pay $60 or more. Even a cup of coffee is around $5.

Often forgotten travel costs are telephone calls and faxes back home. Hotels can add a surcharge up to 200 percent on calls, so you are much better off to use a telephone charge card. In many countries, such as in the Middle East, however, the American telephone charge cards are not accepted. A five-minute call home can cost you $40 or $50. Your best tactic is to call your office and quickly tell them to call you back so that the charges are based on your regular U.S. rates.

You will be forced to entertain customers on your travels, and this can be very expensive. Lunch and dinner are the usual forms, and you will want to take them to fairly respectable restaurants. The food will be expensive and the liquor even more so. In many countries it is the expected thing to do, so you had better budget for it.

Promotion Activity Costs

Your major promotional activity associated with your market entry strategy will probably be exhibiting at trade shows. This can be a costly business because your expenses are not just the rental of the booth space. Some of the costs you should budget for are:

- Booth space rental. Booth sizes are usually multiples of a standard nine-square-meter booth, which is 10 feet by 10 feet. Depending on the country and the trade show, the standard booth can cost anywhere from $1,200 to $4,000.
- Booth services. You will have to pay extra for electrical power, furniture, and cleaning. This can cost another $500 to $2,000.

- Booth artwork. You will have to design your booth and produce the artwork for it. These costs could be a few thousand dollars, depending on how elaborate you want it to be.
- Demonstration equipment. These costs were described previously in this chapter.
- Shipping. This cost will depend on how large your demonstration equipment is, the booth artwork, and where the trade show is. Your local shipping agent can give you an estimate for budgetary purposes.

Another cost that you should consider is your staff time required to prepare the demonstration equipment and operate it at the trade show. This can run into several thousand dollars, depending on the equipment involved. Their travel and foreign living expenses must also be considered.

Promotion Material Costs

Chapters 11 and 12 described the promotion material you should consider for your market entry. It is difficult to provide accurate examples of these costs because they will vary with the complexity of the material and way you choose to have it produced. Here are some rough guidelines.

- Translation. A two page information sheet, fairly technical, could cost up to $1,000.
- Brochure layout and artwork. A relatively simple, two-page information sheet in black and white with pictures will cost about $500 to $1,000. If you use color pictures, it could be $2,000 or more.
- Printing. A two-page, black-and-white information sheet will be inexpensive to print, only a few hundred dollars, depending on the numbers. Color will cost over $1,000, depending on the number printed.

In this day of sophisticated computer graphics programs and color printers, you may want to produce the brochures yourself; however, you still have to budget for the time of your staff. Remember that the output of colored printers can also be expensive, particularly when you are printing large numbers of copies.

Overall Costs

For each of your target countries, you should now put your estimated costs together with your market entry plan. This process is best explained by the following example.

For their marketing plan to enter the Korea market, AHSI estimated these costs.

Activity	Costs
Trade show booth space rent	$ 1,500
Show booth design	1,000
Artwork production	1,200
Brochure and card translation	1,000
Brochure layout and artwork	500
Brochure and card printing	800
Ship booth	2,400
Air fare for 2 people	9,600
Hotel and meals, 2 people 8 days	4,000
Local travel and entertainment	1,000
Total	$23,000

After you have done a cost estimate for each target country, put them together and see if there are any costs that can be shared. For example, a trip to Korea may be combined with a trip to China, at considerable cost savings. You should also look at the timing of the expenses because they may stretch across two of your budget years. The whole question of budget will be addressed in the next chapter.

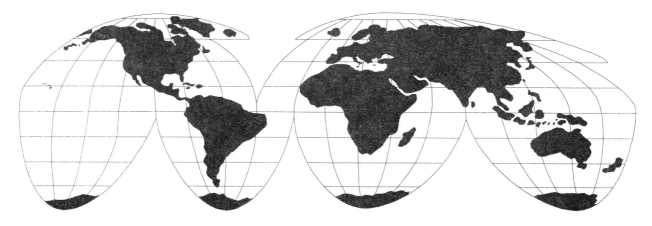

Chapter 14

Overall Market Entry Decision

You have now selected a number of countries you want to export your products to, and you have estimated the cost of entering each of these markets. Your next move is to make the hard decision as to whether or not the costs are worth your potential profits and if you can afford them.

Marketing Budget Constraints

No company is without budget constraints, and the marketing budget is often the most vulnerable. You must now take a good look at what your international market entry plan is going to cost to see if it will fit within your budget. If you're lucky, your plan will span two financial years, so you'll be able to spread the costs farther. No matter how you do it, you will still have to put out a lot of money to enter the international market.

If your estimated costs are over your budget, do not make the mistake of hoping that your estimates are too high. Chances are they will be too low. You could get yourself in real trouble, so accept the numbers and look for ways of cutting the costs. The best way is to base your cuts on the cost effectiveness of each market entry and each activity within that market entry plan. Your comparisons should be based on your anticipated revenues and profits from the market

Potential Revenue

The potential revenue and the associated profit you expect to get from each market area or country you have selected should be used to decide where to cut your market entry costs to meet your budget. In Chapter 9 you addressed the issue of the potential market revenue from each country. Based on this, you made your country prioritization. Review those calculations to see if there were any large discrepancies between the countries you have decided to market to. Perhaps the last one or two on your priority list were considerably lower in potential revenue than the others. If this is the case, consider dropping the lower revenue countries to get within the budget.

Another important way to cull out a not very cost-effective market is to look at the time it will take you to get the projected revenue. In some markets you may be able to get orders fairly quickly, but others may take a while to develop their revenue potential. You obviously want to go after the quicker paying markets and leave the slower ones till later, when you can afford to exploit them.

Profit-to-cost Assessment

In the calculations that developed your revenue estimates, you would have assumed certain profit margins for each market. Take another look at these figures and compare the expected profit to the estimated marketing costs. You will of course want to go after the countries with the highest profit-to-cost ratios. Your decision will be easy if there is a wide disparity between the ratios. If there is little difference between them, do not make a hasty decision. Remember that these figures are based on estimates only and, in reality, some markets could be better than they look.

Reduce Marketing Activity

There are two ways you can reduce your marketing activity to fall within your budget. You can reduce the activity in each or some of the targeted countries or drop some of the countries from your plan. First look at the revenue, profit, and cost considerations discussed in the last sections to see if a particular country market is a candidate for disregarding or delaying market entry. If so, see if the marketing cost savings from dropping this country will bring you within your budget. If it does, your problem is solved. However, your decision will probably not be this easy.

In all likelihood, all of your chosen target markets will still look pretty good, and you will want to go after them all. If so, your market cost reductions will have to come from somewhere else. The only other way is to reduce the marketing activity within the markets. Do this by looking at each activity within the market entry plan for each country to see if it can be reduced or dropped. Here are some things to consider.

- Demonstration equipment. Do you have to take demonstration equipment on your initial trip? Perhaps you can delay taking it until you have established an agent and customers who definitely want to see the equipment, rather than take it with you on speculation.

- Number of travelers. Is it necessary to send as many people to the target countries as you initially estimated? Perhaps the initial trip can be handled by fewer people.

- Select an agent without visiting the country. This is not recommended, but it could be a major cost saver; however, you may not be able to select the best agent for your business.

- Promotion material. Maybe you can go with your current promotional material and not have to translate and produce brochures in the language of the particular country.

In making these cost reduction decisions, you may want to apply the three cardinal risk management rules.

- If the uncertainties are high, keep the amounts at stake low.
- As the uncertainties decrease, the amounts at stake can be increased.
- Continuously reevaluate the situation, making timely go and no-go decisions.

Revised Market Entry Plan

After you have made your marketing cost cuts, have another look at the individual country market entry plans to see if they are still effective. You may want to readjust your cuts to emphasize one country or another; or you may want to drop one or more countries and use the money you save to improve your marketing in the more promising countries.

No matter how you do it, you should end up within budget with your final plan to enter the international market. Make sure you are happy with the plan because you are going to have to live with it for quite a while. More importantly, your company's international success and, possibly, its future will depend on the viability of this market entry plan.

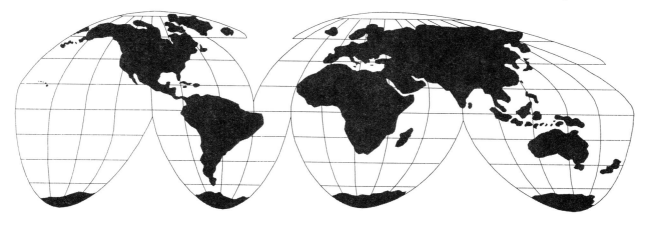

Chapter 15

Commitment and the Withdrawal Decision

You have done your homework, and you have determined there are profitable markets for your products in some identified countries. You must do two more things before you start your marketing plan: be sure your company will commit to the plan, and establish some criteria to withdraw from the marketing activity in a country if it is prudent to do so.

Senior Management Commitment

No matter how promising the international market is and how effective a marketing plan you have, it will all be in vain if you do not have the serious commitment of your senior company management. This statement is true in larger companies where the marketing department reports upwards and in small companies where the owner or CEO has decided on the international arena but staff members have to be convinced. However, the usual problem is associated with senior company officials to whom the marketing staff report.

It is critical that the company's top management agrees to the international marketing plan and are prepared for the long-term commitment associated with it. They are the ones who must provide the resources necessary for the marketing activity, and they must be prepared to do so over the period it takes to get those first critical orders. Too often senior management is under the delusion that as soon as you visit a foreign market the orders begin to flow. You know this is not the case, and you must ensure that your senior management knows it as well, otherwise you could be fighting a stiff battle for marketing resources in the not-too-distant future.

Your marketing plan should be presented to the senior management with the following three questions clearly explained.

- What is in it for the company? This information will come from the market potential evaluation and the potential market revenue calculations you made in chapters 8 and 9.
- How much will it cost? This is the marketing cost data you developed in Chapter 13. You should also present the profit and cost figures you used to zero in on particular markets.
- How long will it take? This is a critical issue that you must get across and that the senior management must accept. Try to have some method, such as milestones, that you can use to reply to them in the future when they begin to question why the marketing is taking so long and costing so much.

Empowerment by Senior Management

Senior management must not only agree to the marketing plan but also fully empower the marketing team to carry it out. Budgets must not only be allocated for the marketing but management must also avoid micromanaging them. For example, if a particular trade show is in the plan and has been estimated for in the approved budget, senior management should not question why you are spending money on it. Similarly, marketing should be given free rein in obtaining the marketing materials, within the budget.

Senior management should be involved with the final legal arrangements with agents, but they should empower the marketing staff to select the agents without interference. It is not uncommon for an agent to approach a senior company official and to convince him or her they should do business together. The company official then foists the agent onto the marketing team, much to their annoyance. You should alert senior management about this possibility in advance so they can refer all agent approaches to the marketing team.

Empowerment is a two-way street. Even though you may have been empowered to do what you want to within the marketing plan and budget, you must make sure that you stay with the plan. There will be many temptations to stray from it, such as an opportunity to exhibit very inexpensively at a trade show in a country outside the plan. Forget it. You must stick with your plan in spite of how appealing the opportunity is. Chances are that you previously rejected that country as a potential market, so why should you change your mind now? Also, straying from the plan will seriously jeopardize your credibility with senior management at a time you really need it.

Withdrawal Decision

Throughout this book decision gates in the selection of suitable markets for your products have been discussed. You must also continuously evaluate your situation in each market area and, if required, be prepared to make the hard decision to bail out and cut your losses. This is a lot more difficult than it sounds because you will be encouraged to stay in the market by your agent, who will be painting an optimistic picture no matter what is happening. The decision will be yours alone, and you must develop some guidelines to work from.

You can set some time guidelines in association with your marketing strategy and marketing plan, but these are difficult to do accurately when you are first entering the market. Nevertheless, you should set up some point at which time you will quit the area if you have not made sufficient progress. You will probably have to do this in some form for budgetary estimates anyway.

Once you begin the marketing process in an area, you will get better indications on how to make your withdrawal decision. You should start looking for these criteria as soon as possible so you can make the decision as soon as possible. When you withdraw from a non-performing market, you can devote more effort and resources to a more promising one.

There are a number of criteria you can use for your withdrawal decision, but they are all usually based on the simple fact of not finding enough customers who will buy your products. Do not mistake this with not finding enough interest. You may discover a lot of interest for your products at a trade show in a country but after a while learn that they cannot afford to buy or there are other circumstances that will prevent them from buying.

The best way to sort out the real market from what the agent tells you is for you to visit the potential customers themselves. When you talk to the customers and ask them when they will buy, you should be able to get an indication of how real the opportunities are. If you judge them to be questionable, dig deeper. Don't just rely on your agent's word. If you decide to stay with the opportunity, your probing should spur the agent on to work harder to get the business.

After all is said and done, do not be afraid to cut and run from a non-performing market area, no matter how much effort you have devoted to it. If the business is not there, get out. There are plenty more opportunities that you can concentrate on and get better results. After all, there is a big international market out there, and somebody is bound to want your products.

Prepare to Visit Your Target Country

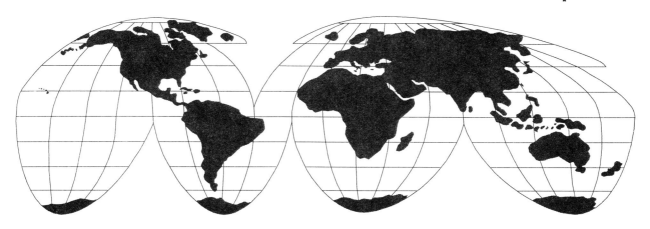

Learning About the Country

In international marketing, you must be prepared to travel to many countries. Do not make the mistake of thinking that things will be the same as what you are used to in the United States, because you will probably be dealing with a different climate, culture, and way of doing business. The old adage that preparation is half the battle is very true when visiting foreign countries.

Language, History, Religion, and Culture

Many people think that the main thing they have to do before visiting a foreign country is to learn the language. This is definitely not true in international marketing. For one reason, if you are dealing with many countries, you would have to learn several languages and probably not be very proficient in any of them.

Fortunately, throughout the world most of the business people you will deal with know English, or they will have somebody with them who does. However, learning a few basic words like *thank you* and *hello* will be very much appreciated by the local people.

It is much more important to learn about the country you are visiting. Some basic things you should find out about are its history, the form of government, the predominant religions, and the culture. Appendix B contains much of this information, and more can be obtained from your public library and the Internet. You can also buy an appropriate travel book. Your family probably will want you to do this so you will know where to buy gifts for them.

The history of a country can explain a lot about it. The classic example of this is Saudi Arabia. In the 18th century, the Saud family aligned itself with the Wahabi religious movement and began to conquer and unite portions of the Arabian Peninsula. Over the years the descendants of the original Saud family and Wahabi rulers gained control of the area and formed the Kingdom of Saudi Arabia in 1932. The linkage with the religious movement accounts for the highly religious character of the country even to this day.

A country's form of government will sometimes dictate the way it does business. Using the Saudi example again, it is a kingdom in which the royal family has the final say in all major government activities. Thus, to win government business, you must be sure your agent is somehow associated with someone from the royal family. Another example is Thailand, which on the surface is a kingdom with a ruling elected parliament; however, the military has considerable influence in all government activity. This is something to keep in mind when seeking government business.

A knowledge of the country's religious and cultural makeup will help you avoid making embarrassing and sometimes costly faux pas. Many countries are highly religious, and their religious objects and activities must be respected. In Moslem countries you should know about the limitations on using the left hand, and if you are female, you should learn about the severe dress codes in many of these countries. Customs such as bowing in Japan should be understood and, when appropriate, followed. In Thailand, rather than a handshake you may want to use the *wai* gesture of bringing both hands together in the prayer position. These simple considerations may not seem important to you, but they could be very important to your customers.

Communications

Foreign business people rely on modern communications just as much as U.S. businesses do, and perhaps even more. It is quite common to see a group of businessmen sit down at a restaurant table in a Middle East country, in full Arab dress, and pull cellular phones out of their pockets and place them on the table. These same businessmen probably also have pagers in their pockets.

Fax machines are widely used throughout the world. These are particularly useful in overcoming the time zone problem. For example, when Californians are going to work, Europeans have just completed their day at the office. The fax then becomes an excellent way to communicate. A question sent during the day from California can be answered over night, during the working day in Europe, and the reply can be waiting the next morning in California.

In many countries, however, telephone and fax lines are not always a secure way of communicating. The lines may be tapped by the government, and your competitors may also have access to your transmissions. If you doubt this, see how easy it is to buy a fax interception machine in the U.S., then imagine what is going on in less regulated societies.

Computers are also widely used by business throughout the world. The major word-processing programs common in the English speaking world have also been designed for many other languages. Many hotels provide computers to the guests for a small charge. It is quite common to travel with a portable computer, so customs agents in most countries will not question you about it. Some of the things you may find useful to have in the computer or on a travel disk are:

- Company letterhead
- Company standard fax form
- A standard letter of intent
- A standard agency agreement
- A draft proposal

With the proper attachments to the computer, you can use it as a fax machine right from your hotel room, and you can collect your electronic mail from back in your office. The computer is also very useful to keep a day-to-day log of your activities that you can later use to write up your trip report and action items, on the computer, of course. For those so inclined, a few computer games may help to while away the lonely hours in hotel rooms when you can't understand the local television.

Local Climatic Conditions and Food

Before you take off on a business trip to a strange land, check out what the climate and weather conditions will be. You may think you know what to expect, but it can be much different than you anticipated. Then there is also the season change. For example, if you travel to Chile in July, take an overcoat. It's winter down there then.

Your biggest problem will be underestimating the heat and humidity. Singapore and Thailand are famous for their high temperatures coupled with high humidity, both well over 90. You will find that you are frequently changing your shirt during the day, so make sure you have plenty. You might expect the Middle East to be extremely hot, as well. It is in some places and at certain times. While it can get over 50 degrees Celsius, that's over 125 degrees Fahrenheit, humidity is seldom a factor. Also, there can be uncomfortably cool evenings in December, so take a light jacket or sweater with you. Appendix B will give you an idea of the climatic conditions in most of the countries you will be traveling to. It also provides suggestions about what to wear.

Food can be a major problem when you travel, and Chapter 19 discusses some of the hazards and how to avoid them. In general, when you eat in the major hotels you will have no problem finding the types of food you are accustomed to. Eating in local restaurants is a different situation, and you must be very careful. In some countries there are local food rituals you may get involved with while entertaining customers. Quaffing vodka in Russia is a well-known example, but the snake restaurants of Taiwan are something else. The brave pick out their own poisonous snake and are treated to a drink concocted of the reptile's venom and blood.

A more common problem concerning food is that it may not always be available when you want it. This often happens when you arrive late at your hotel and all the restaurants are closed. A solution to this problem is to carry a few of the diet bars available in drugstores. Each bar has the nutrition equivalent to a full meal, and they are easy to pack. You will also find them useful for breakfast, which often is a colossal waste of time in a hotel restaurant.

Political Situations

You should also do a quick study of the latest political situation of the countries you are going to visit or pass through. It could be on the brink of civil war or under threat of a country-wide strike, and you don't want to be caught in those circumstances. France is prone to strikes, and it is very difficult getting around when none of the public transportation is operating and the country is a huge traffic jam.

The political situation may also affect your business. Many countries have periodic disagreements with the United States that can result in additional travel visa requirements or trade boycotts. Iran still treats the United States as the great Satan. The U.S. government also imposes restrictions on its people traveling to and doing business with certain countries. Cuba is a close example.

Chapter 17

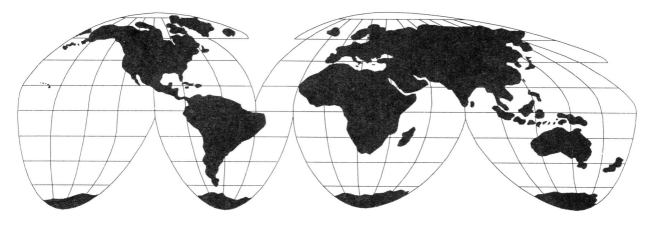

Local Business Practices

Business practices vary throughout the world. This chapter discusses some of the main issues in this regard. You should prepare yourself for them, and have the patience to accept them. Patience plays a big role in international marketing.

Weekends, Holidays, and Office Hours

When you are planing your trip, check out the local business hours and holidays. You don't want to arrive at the start of a national or religious holiday and have to wait until it is over before getting on with your business. Similarly, you don't want to start your visit on the first day of a weekend. The local office hours can also be a surprise. Appendix B provides information to help you with these local situations. The following paragraphs will explain why they are important.

Weekends are not the same the world over. This can be very confusing. In most Arab countries you will find it difficult having Thursday and Friday off, then starting the work week on Saturday. Thursday is like Saturday in North America, although many offices work only until noon.

The rest of the day is spent with family. Friday is the religious day of rest, with Friday prayers equivalent to the Christian Sunday church services. Then it's back to work Saturday. Some of the western embassies and compounds even celebrate the end of the week with TAIW parties — Thank Allah it's Wednesday.

In Israel the Sabbath is Saturday, so their weekend is Friday and Saturday. This is the case in a number of other countries as well. Then there are countries that cannot officially decide whether the weekend is Thursday, Friday, Saturday, or Sunday. The result is the confusion of some offices being closed on some days and others on other days. Pakistan is one of these mixed situations where they designate the weekend as being Friday and Sunday. You can imagine how much work is done on Saturday.

Religious observances and holidays must also be considered. The most serious of these in the month of Ramadan in the Muslim world. Ramadan is the last month of the Islamic Hijrah calendar, which is based on the phases of the moon. In 1998 Ramadan is approximately the month of January. During the month, between sunrise and sunset Muslims are not allowed to eat, drink, smoke, or have sex. This is strictly adhered to in countries such as Saudi Arabia and Kuwait where anyone, including non-Muslims, caught breaking the fast is thrown in jail. So the working day shifts to the working night, and people sleep during the day.

The Christmas period in European countries is a time when little is accomplished. Closer to home this period lasts about a month. In Mexico nothing is done in government circles, so the government offices simply close. The same can be said about Washington D.C., but the offices maintain the facade of being open. National holidays can also last for a few days and can be very trying on your business patience. Holidays such as the beginning of the new year are particularly disruptive, and they do not always occur on the dates of your new year. For example, in Asia during Tet, for which the dates vary, little gets done because many businessmen have hangovers from the ongoing celebrations.

Once you get around the problems of weekends and holidays, your next test is to sort out the office hours. These vary from country to country and also within the country. For example, in many hot countries government office hours are from early morning, sometimes around seven, to early afternoon. Then they are closed the rest of the day. Other businesses in the same country may begin work around nine in the morning, close around one in the afternoon, reopen around five, and finish the working day around eight in the evening. Many business meetings are held even later at night, sometimes around midnight. This is easy for your hosts because they spend the afternoon sleeping, so you might consider doing likewise.

Appointments

Appointments in foreign countries are not always easily arranged prior to your arrival there. Even once you have established an agent, you will find they are still reluctant to schedule customer appointments for you until after you arrive. The reason for this is that travel plans are not always adhered to. Just think of how many times have you had to cancel or change a business trip at the last minute.

Your local agent does not want to prejudice their relationships with their customers by scheduling and then canceling meetings. Instead, they wait until you are in the country before setting up the meetings. Consequently, you may have to wait a few days until you make your first customer contacts. You can use this time to get acclimatized and to discuss other business with your agent before you get involved with the customers.

Punctuality is not a universally-accepted practice, sometimes with good reason. For example, it is almost impossible to judge how long it will take you to go anywhere in Bangkok because of the legendary traffic jams that seem to happen instantly. Appointment times are thus assumed to be approximate, and you may have to wait for hours to meet with senior officials. This lack of devotion to time is encountered throughout the world, but you should not let this become your habit. Do not schedule appointments too close together. Arrange for only one meeting in the morning and another in the afternoon or evening. Besides allowing for the lack of punctuality, this will give you time to do other business.

Appointments in foreign countries are often inexplicably changed at the last moment. This is often caused by somebody with higher influence convincing the person you are to meet with to meet with them instead. This is understandable because you will sometimes get your agent to pull stings to enable you to have a meeting, and chances are that you will bump somebody else from their meeting. Sometimes your meeting time is changed to have you meet with a more senior official who has taken an interest in your product, so be prepared to be flexible about arranged meetings in foreign countries.

Local Customs and Dress

Local customs and dress can be very important to your customers in some countries. Appendix B mentions the major local customs to be aware of. You will want to check your tourist travel book for others. For example, in Muslim countries, never eat pork or drink alcohol in front of a Muslim. Also, never pass anything to them, particularly food, with your left hand. In Thailand, never sit with one leg crossed over the other, with the bottom of your foot pointed in the direction of a person. This is an insulting gesture to the person.

As discussed in the previous chapter, find out what the recommended dress for Westerners is before you start your trip, and pack accordingly. Business suits are usually acceptable anywhere in the world, but you may want to take additional light shirts for hot climates. Do not try to emulate the dress of the local population. Picture the sight of a Chinese businessman rushing through a hotel lobby in Riyadh, wearing the common Saudi Arabian floor-length white shirt and red checkered headdress, looking absolutely ridiculous as he tries to keep the headdress from falling off. Then imagine how his Saudi customers react to this display.

Local Travel

Local travel is usually provided or arranged for you by your local agent. This is one of the many reasons to have an agent in the country, as will be discussed later. The agent knows the local traffic laws, the city, and particularly the location of your customers. They will also follow the local driving habits, which can be pretty scary.

The author was once being driven by his agent in a very large Mercedes to a meeting in Jeddah. They were late, and the agent, in full Arab dress, was frantically punching numbers into his cell phone as he drove. He was trying to call the man they were meeting to tell him we were late, but he kept getting a busy signal. The air was blue with Arabic curses as he repeated the dialing. His passenger sat frozen in the passenger seat, trying to look brave, as they sped down one of the major, six-lane streets of the city, dodging traffic at 180 kilometers an hour, which is about 110 miles per hour.

Rental cars are available in most countries. All you need to rent them is an international driver's license. This license is easily obtained from the American Automobile Association by just presenting your regular driver's license and paying a fee. However, getting a rental car and driving yourself is not a smart move in many countries. Do you think you can drive on the left hand side of the road in the narrow streets of London? As a foreigner in some countries, if you have an accident, all the blame will be placed on you. It may take weeks or months to sort things out, possibly while you are in jail.

Another problem you will have with a rental car is figuring out how to get to where you want to go. Addresses as you know them do not exist in many countries. Streets may not have names, or even if they do, the locals may not use them. How do you stop and ask for directions when you don't know the language? Even if you know enough to ask the question, chances are you will not understand the answer.

It is usually best to rely on your agent or on taxis. The safest taxis and the easiest to obtain are those connected with the hotel you are in, and they usually have air conditioning that works. You can have the hotel concierge phone the office you are going to visit to get the directions then explain them to the taxi driver in his language. Make sure you have the taxi wait for you, so you have a ride back to your hotel. It is often wise to hire them by the hour, so they won't mind waiting for you while you have your business meeting.

On a trip to Peru the author did not follow the advice to keep the hotel taxi to take him back, which resulted in an interesting adventure. At the end of a business meeting with a company, one of their staff went out into the middle of a busy street to flag down a taxi. It turned out to be an old Volkswagen Beetle with a very large driver who overflowed into the passenger seat. On the way to the hotel they got caught in a traffic jam. The driver was convinced that he could speed things up by hanging part of his huge body out of the window to more effectively shake his fist and yell at the other motorists. This left him with only one hand for driving, and it was fully engaged blowing the horn. In a fit of frustration he motioned to his passenger to shift the gears for him, which the passenger did out of curiosity to find out what would happen next. Much later, they managed to arrive safely at the hotel.

Local Meetings

Do not be annoyed if you experience many interruptions during your meeting with a local businessperson at their facilities. These interruptions are common practice in many countries and are not an indication of lack of interest in you. It is just the way they operate. The reason for the interruptions can even give you an idea of how important the person is and what the company is all about. Just be patient while your host sorts out other business. In a few minutes they will return to you to pick up where they left off.

Another potentially uncomfortable situation you will experience is sitting through long meetings in which you cannot understand a word that is being said. Your agent will be speaking on your behalf. Occasionally they will ask you something in English then continue the discussion with the customer in their language. Do not get annoyed during this kind of meeting because it is quite normal. Just remember that your local agent is your spokesperson not only when you are there but also when you are not. You have to trust your agent.

Always try to find out as much as you can about the position and authority of the customer you will be meeting with. Your agent should be able to tell you this, but make sure they are not inflating the importance of the customer merely because this was the best appointment they could set up. Sometimes the person you are meeting with will have no authority whatsoever and the company sent them just to appease you, or the person may have considerably more authority than their position indicates. You may also end up in a meeting with a high-ranking official who misunderstood the reason for your visit. This can be very intimidating and ego shattering.

In Kuala Lumpur, while evaluating potential agents, the author visited a large agency headed by a Tengku, which is a Malayan prince. The embassy had set up the meeting. The author was pleasantly surprised when he was escorted into a large, expensively decorated office that could only be that of the Tengku. After a suitable waiting period during which the company escort and the author stood and did not speak, the tapestry on one of the walls parted and a distinguished Malayan gentleman entered and took his seat at an ornate desk.

"Present yourself to the Tengku," the escort whispered. The author walked across the office to the desk and offered his business card. It was not taken by the gentleman.

"What is your product?" He asked in perfect English.

The author gave a quick overview of the product and handed him some brochures that he slowly scanned. He then silently rose and, without saying another word, left through the tapestry.

The escort led the author out of the office and commented, "The Tengku is not interested in your business."

Be prepared to meet with customers in a variety of places and don't be surprised when your agent takes you to a very unlikely location for a meeting. Even though it may seem odd to you, it may be very natural to them. Your product will be a determining factor. For example, if your product is for the fishing industry, you may have to meet on one of the customer's company boats. The venue may be necessary so they can more fully explain what your product must do for them.

Reluctance to Give Bad News

You will run across situations in which your customer or even your agent is reluctant to give you bad news. You will find this is a general tendency around the world. Often they will go to extremes to avoid having to tell you, like making excuses for not being able to meet with you or not answering your faxes and telephone calls. Sometimes it is so obvious that you quickly get the message. This problem can be critical in your early market entry days when the local people are reluctant to tell you there is no market for your product or when the agent you chose is unable to sell your product.

Always be aware of this reluctance to give bad news or to say no. If you suspect it is happening, try to come up with a way to find out the truth, but do it in such a way that your customer or agent does not lose face. For example, if you think an expected contract is taking far too long and may not happen, you might ask your agent about what would happen if you lose the contract. You could also ask about how you should go after other contracts since this one is taking too long to come in. With this approach to the situation, it is easier for the agent to let you know that you lost the contract.

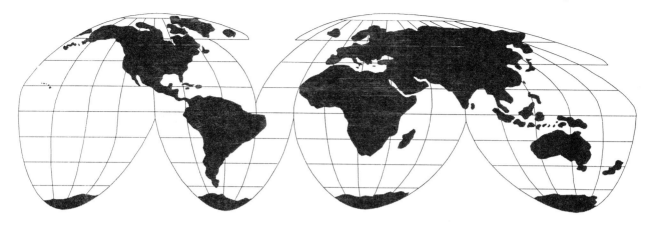

Chapter 18

Travel Considerations

International business travel requires more consideration than a holiday trip outside the country. On a holiday you usually do not have to meet with others or stick to a schedule. On business trips you must do both, and sometimes the future of your company may depend on the success of the trip. This chapter provides some travel information for your first international marketing trip.

Travel Arrangements

When you plan your trip, try to allow as much time as possible in each country. A good rule of thumb is to allow at least three days per stop, preferably more, and no more than three countries in two weeks. Above all, do not plan to travel at night and do business during the day with very little sleep. Allow time for acclimatization and overcoming jet lag. For example, try not to schedule any meeting on the day of your arrival. When traveling across several time zones, such as to Asia or the Middle East, you may want to spend a day along the way in a place like London or Paris to overcome some of the jet lag.

Arrange your flights carefully, and do not assume you can easily change your arrangements once you arrive at your destination. In many countries, the travel agents are not like those in the United States. They often work with only one airline, making it very difficult to arrange a trip to places where that airline does not fly. Another problem can arise with in-country travel changes. There may not be suitable flights available when you need them. Also be sure you are booked on a reasonably good airline because airline safety and schedule considerations are not the same all over the world.

Once on a flight from Madrid to Rome the author noticed his tickets indicated the airline was IA. Because he was in Spain, he assumed it was Iberia Airlines, the national carrier of Spain. He was wrong. It was Iraq Airlines. His luggage was searched at the aircraft before loading it, and he was given a personal search on entering the aircraft.

The flight itself was very pleasant, but on arrival in Rome, the aircraft was ordered to a remote part of the airfield where the Italian Army surrounded it. The passengers deplaned under the watchful eye of armed soldiers, then military busses took them into the terminal. As the author stood in line at passport control, thinking the ordeal was over, an elderly man in front of him collapsed on the floor. The author looked around in panic to see who shot the man, but the man had actually suffered a heart attack.

Make sure you have appropriate hotel reservations before you arrive because there may not be any suitable rooms available without a reservation. You could arrive in a place like Kuala Lumpur without hotel reservations only to discover all the good hotels are booked due to a major Asian conference in progress. Then all you can find is some sleazy old hotel used mainly by the local sex trade, where the check-in clerk is very surprised to hear you do not want the room by the hour.

Travel Documents

Make sure you have all the required travel documents long before you leave on the trip. A valid passport is an obvious requirement. Make sure it is not expired or about to expire so that your business trip is not delayed waiting for a passport renewal.

Many countries require some form of entry visa, and some also require you to have an exit visa. Find out the country requirements long before your trip because, as mentioned in Chapter 12, obtaining a visa can sometimes take considerable time. Another thing to be aware of is the type of visa you obtain. Some South American countries issue a business visa on short notice; however, with this visa you may not be able to leave the country unless you pay income tax for the time you are there.

If you are traveling to a country with a questionable medical situation, you should get an International Certificate of Vaccination and any recommended vaccinations. They may be required for you to enter another country or to reenter the United States.

If you plan to carry demonstration items with you, you also should have an international carnet. This document allows you to temporarily import the items into a country and to bring them back home without paying duty on them. The carnet document and procedures are more fully explained in Chapter 24.

Local Documentation

You must ensure correct handling of local documentation, which can be confusing at times. For example, on entry into Kuwait you pick up your visa at the airport, provided somebody has arranged for it for you. The procedure is to wait in a line until your name is called. You are then given a completed application form in Arabic and directed to an immigration officer. He collects four Kuwaiti dinars, about 15 dollars, from you, sticks some stamps in your passport, stamps them, and hands all the paperwork back to you. Do not discard the visa application, thinking you no longer need it. It is also part of your exit visa from the country.

An even more confusing situation involves a form you must fill out when entering China. On it you must list the valuables you are carrying, including personal jewelry. When you leave, the local officials will ask for your copy of the form. They will not allow you out of the country until the form is returned.

Travel Tips

Because many publications provide travel tips, this book will only give you some suggestions to make your marketing travel a little easier. As mentioned earlier, always allow time for acclimatization and overcoming jet lag before you begin doing business. When traveling to Europe, you normally fly overnight from North America and arrive about 7 A.M. It is difficult to check into a hotel early in the morning, so try to prearrange to be able to do so. Then go to bed for only three or four hours, force yourself to get up, and treat the rest of the day as if it was a regular day in the new time zone. This routine can often ease the jet lag, but there are many other suggested methods as well.

Some airlines provide additional benefits to their traveling clientele, so find out about these. For example, British Airlines has a special transient lounge at Heathrow Airport for people stopping over between flights. The lounge offers private showers, which are much appreciated when you have just arrived from an overnight flight from Asia or the Middle East and are about to get back on another airplane to North America.

Now a word about what to pack. The governing rule is that the hotels you will be staying in will have laundry and dry cleaning facilities, so take only enough shirts and underwear to last you until you can make use of the laundry services. Similarly, take only a couple of suits, preferably wearing one on the flight. Select suits that are compatible with the same accessories, such as ties and shoes. The last thing you want to do is travel with both black and brown shoes.

Finally, consider what to do with all those heavy company and product brochures. Rather than pack all that you think you will need on the trip, take only enough for your first few stops. Send the rest ahead by courier to your agent or your hotel. You can also do the reverse and send the material you collect back to your office by courier or ordinary mail.

Visit Preparations

Appendix A contains a checklist you can use to prepare for an international business trip, and Chapter 19 provides some hints about how to prepare yourself to avoid local hazards. Here are some tips on money that will help you along.

Do not bother to get travelers' checks in the currency of the country you are visiting. Take travelers' checks in U.S. dollars, because it is the standard hard currency around the world. You can cash them at standard rates, and often you can pay for your purchases directly in American dollars.

Almost all international airports have currency exchanges where you can obtain the local currency; however, they are not always open when you arrive. It is wise to take a few dollars worth of the local currency with you to pay for your visa, if necessary, and for a taxi to your hotel. You can get the currency for most countries at the foreign exchange section of major banks.

Major credit cards are accepted throughout the world, and you should always take a variety of these. Using credit cards also limits the amount of travelers' checks or cash you will need.

Chapter 19

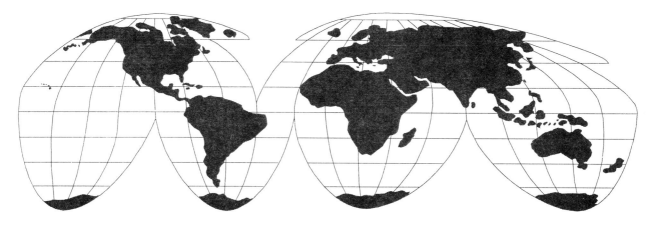

Avoiding Local Hazards

In addition to the unexpected business problems you will run into in international marketing, there are many personal hazards that you must avoid in other countries. You've heard the warning jokes about not drinking the water, and most of them are true. Now, however, there are more severe threats to one's personal safety in many countries. They range from simple theft to serious illness, terrorists, and being caught in a civil war. This chapter discusses these hazards and offers suggestions to avoid them.

Illness

Illness in a foreign country is the most common hazard you will face, and diarrhea is probably the most frequent illness that hits the international traveler. It can be caused by many things including viruses, bacteria, toxins, or just excessive indulgence in alcohol and foods that are irritating to the stomach. Most of these problems can be found in any country, but in many developing countries they are rampant.

A common source of diarrhea is the water. Many hotels provide bottles of mineral water or other pure water in the rooms. If these bottles are in your room, you should not use the tap water for drinking or cleaning your teeth. Also, if some form of pure water is not supplied in your room and you suspect the tap water, do not use it, even if you have to brush your teeth with gin. Another common source of diarrhea for the traveler is uncooked foods such as salads and fruits. As a rule, avoid raw vegetables and fruits that do not have a natural protective skin such as oranges and bananas.

There is medication available to counter the symptoms of diarrhea. Do not leave home without it. If you don't have any with you when you need it, drug stores in most countries carry some form of diarrhea relief. It is a big seller around the world.

A young woman on holiday in a Latin American country, in spite of her companion's warnings, tried some local food from a food cart on the street. Within hours she was in an emergency ward in the local hospital and a few days later was evacuated by air to a hospital near her home. She had contracted a form of internal parasite that will stay in her body for the rest of her life. You know the moral of this story.

You must also make sure you have adequate travel medical insurance. It can be obtained for each trip, but the most convenient way is to have your company take out an annual policy that covers you whenever and wherever you travel. Even with the insurance, it can sometimes be a major problem finding a competent doctor. Your agent or the hotel should be able to help you.

Diseases

The dreaded diseases such as cholera and polio that you no longer worry about in the United States are still a part of life and death in many parts of the world. For example, vaccinations against cholera are recommended for a number of countries. Inoculations are also recommended for diphtheria, tetanus, polio, and typhoid. Even if you do not contract any of these diseases, on your return from an infected area you may be required to provide proof of inoculations before you are allowed entry to a country. The proof is usually an International Certificate of Vaccination that is described in Chapter 12. Since the health situation in each country changes regularly, the best thing you can do to make sure you have adequate immunization is to contact your local medical authorities for up-to-date information.

When going to many tropical climates, it is recommended that you also take medication to prevent malaria. This disease is still prevalent in much of the world. New strains have evolved that are immune to the usual quinine-based medication, so for some locations you will have to get more specialized drugs. The medication is usually in the form of pills that you take for a few weeks before your trip, during the trip, and a few weeks after the trip. Make sure you get the pills early.

The most common disease threats are those of a social nature. In some countries the business of prostitution is well controlled, but stay away from it. It can be tempting in countries such as Thailand, where they have elevated the sex business to a national institution. The Pat Pong district of Bangkok is a complete community devoted to the pleasures of the night. It has clearly defined borders inside of which one can find regular grocery stores, clothing stores, and even an American Pizza Hut. However, the main business enterprises provide sex for all tastes. Though tempting, it is extremely dangerous, particularly with the AIDS virus running rampant around the world.

Theft

Your credit cards, passport, airline tickets, and money are all very attractive to thieves around the world. Within minutes of being stolen, your passport and airline tickets will be sold by the thief. There is a very high demand for these items. You should always carry a list of your credit card numbers in a separate location from the cards, so if they are lost or stolen, you can easily provide the numbers to have them canceled. A simple way of doing this is to make photocopies of all your cards as well as the front pages of your passport. Carry the photocopies in your suitcase and your briefcase for easy reference when needed. Leave a photocopy at home and with your secretary as well.

Another good precaution is to carry some suitable identification in addition to your passport. If your passport is lost or stolen, you can more readily get assistance from the local embassy staff. This is important because there will be many instances when you have to surrender your passport to local authorities as you enter government buildings or for other reasons that are often inexplicable. You will feel very vulnerable in a strange country without a passport, but if you have some other form of official identification, you know you can still get help from your embassy.

The author had a frightening theft experience in the airport in Lima, Peru, a major South American hub. The height of activity takes place around two in the morning. This allows aircraft to depart and arrive on the Eastern Seaboard of the United States during the working day. He was returning home from a trip to Chile and Peru. As he stepped up to the check-in counter he heard a voice behind him.

"Señor, come with me."

He turned and saw what appeared to be a police officer. Then he looked questioningly back at the airline clerk.

"You have to go with him," she said in a quiet voice, "and take your luggage with you."

He was led into a small room where there were two more officers. One had his gun out and was pretending to be polishing it. The other took the suitcase and began going through it.

"Take your clothes off, Señor," the first officer ordered.

The author was pretty scared and in no mood to argue with them. They went slowly through the pockets of his clothes but took nothing. His luggage was a different story. They made sure he saw them take an electric travel alarm and some souvenirs. Then they told him he could get dressed and leave.

When he got back to the check-in counter, he was shaking like a leaf. As he waited to board the aircraft, he saw the police do the same thing to two other single travelers. The first was a middle-aged, well-dressed man who also emerged from the inspection room in a shaky state. The next was a sloppily dressed young man who looked as though he should be inspected. However, in a few minutes he walked out as casually as if nothing had happened, tucking his wallet back in his pocket. Then the author realized what was happening. The police were trying to get people to bribe them to avoid the inspection. The young person obviously did.

Personal Safety

The threat of being accosted on the street exists throughout the world. Since you can be punched out by a local derelict at five o'clock on a Friday afternoon on Fisherman's Wharf in San Francisco in the middle of a crowd, imagine what can happen in less developed countries. In Russia in 1995, there were more than 31,000 murders, a per-capita rate of about three times that of the United States. An increasing number of these murder victims are foreign businesspeople.

The best thing to do to enhance your personal safety when in potentially dangerous locations is to use common sense and not take chances. Make sure someone who knows you is aware of your itinerary and where you will be staying. It is also advisable to check in with the U.S. embassy or consulate, if possible.

Kidnapping

Kidnapping for ransom money is a popular crime in several countries, most notably Russia and Columbia. For an idea of how bad the Colombian situation is, consider the fact that recently the mayor of Madellin proudly announced that they were getting it under control. He said the rate was down from over 50 a month to less than 30. Most of those kidnapped are wealthy locals and, in some cases, foreign executives of local companies. Nevertheless, make sure this is not a problem in the country you are visiting. If it is, take the precaution of never traveling alone or into risky situations.

Terrorists

The threat of terrorism has eased somewhat in recent years, but it is still a fact of life in many parts of the world. Americans are often the chosen targets of these killers. The most sinister recent development is terrorists targeting tourists in some parts of the world. Incidents in Egypt and Algeria have received considerable press, but attacks against tourist have also happened in Spain, Columbia, Panama, Peru, and other countries.

To help avoid terrorist attack, make sure you are aware of the political situation in the country you plan to visit. Find out if there is a terrorist threat. If the threat exists, try to avoid the country. If you can't, then as a rule try to keep a low-key appearance. Also, avoid outward indications of your company and products, particularly if you are in any way involved with the military. Above all, do not emblazon your brief case and luggage with stickers depicting military products or affiliations.

Civil War

Varying degrees of civil war are happening in many countries every day. Most of the time, travelers into the country are not affected, but there is always the possibility that you could become caught in a flare-up. In some countries, low-level civil war activity has gone on for so long that the people consider it only a minor inconvenience. An example is Peru where the Sendero Luminoso, or Shining Path guerrillas, have been blowing up things for years, and now other groups are joining in this activity. Before you travel to a country, check out the political situation.

A friend of the author was on a marketing and equipment delivery trip to Sri Lanka when their civil war exploded into pitched gun battles. He was overseeing the delivery and installation of some of his company's medical equipment in a hospital in Jaffna, in the northern part of the country, where most of the ethnic problems are centered. The sounds of gunfire drove most of the people from the hospital, but he and some of the staff could not hear anything where they were located. When he and a doctor attempted to leave by the main door, they realized they would be caught between two warring factions shooting it out on the street.

The doctor led him out a side door and into a nearby store where the owner was frantically trying to close the front shutters before the battle reached him. A few minutes later a truck was stopped by armed men right in front of the store. They ordered the driver out and shot him, then drove away in the truck. Through the shuttered windows the visitor watched this activity in horror, then turned to discover that the doctor and the storekeeper had fled without him.

The street fighting was still a few blocks away, but he had to get out of there and out of the city. He had with him a copy of a city map that fortunately showed the hospital and the airport. He spent several terrifying hours hurrying through deserted streets heading in the direction of the airport. Just before dark he arrived at the airport, which was teaming with government soldiers who paid no attention to him. The airport of course was closed to civilian traffic as military aircraft ferried troops into the city from other parts of the country.

It took several hours to locate an official who was willing to listen to his problem. To this day he does not really understand what happened, but apparently his passport and the fact that he was bringing them hospital equipment helped. The next thing he knew he was on an Air Force airplane flying back to Colombo, the capital city. With Air Force help, he was able to get a commercial flight out of the country.

Select a Marketing Agent

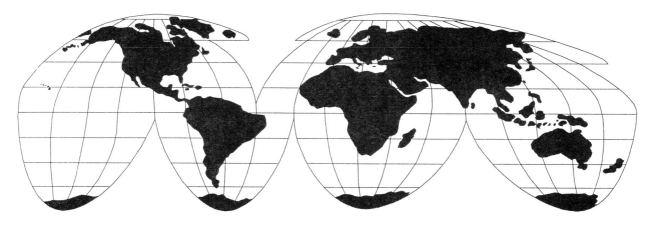

Chapter 20

Local Marketing Agents

Some kind of business arrangement with a local representative or agent is necessary to successfully market your product in almost any country in the world. The agent will help you work in what is often a very different business environment than you are accustomed to. There are many reasons for using agents, and there are many different kinds of business relationships with agents. No matter how large a company is, few are immune to this basic requirement of international marketing. This chapter introduces you to the concept of agents.

Agents, Representatives, Consultants, and Advisors

There are a number of different terms used throughout the world to describe a company's local representative in a foreign country. Sometimes these titles have different meanings, and sometimes they are just semantics to get around a local law. Even though there are various forms of agents, as will be explained in this chapter, this book uses the term *agent* to mean the person or company that represents your company for marketing purposes.

Another term for agent is *representative*, a term often preferred by U.S. lawyers drawing up contracts for use by a company to employ an agent. Some countries resent this term, however, preferring to use *agent* instead. Kuwait is such a country. It requires the agency agreement to be registered with the government, but the term used must be *agent* not *representative*. Perhaps it has something to do with the translation of the agreement into Arabic. Usually this is not a big issue, and your agent can advise you of the correct terms for their country.

Consultants are often different from agents, in that they may work for you in addition to, and with, your agent. This arrangement is becoming popular in many countries. The reason is that your agent may not have the right connections with some of your potential customers and needs help in covering this part of your business. For example, you may have a good agent marketing your product to the construction companies in a country, but they do not have the required connections to get you into the oil industry. They then find some other agency that can address this market, and they make a deal. Your original agent remains your registered agent in the country, while the other agency acts as a consultant and assists them in getting the other business.

Normally your agent will pay for the services of this other agency out of the commission you pay them, but sometimes the consultant will want a separate agreement with you. The consultant may also want you to pay their commission directly. Under these circumstances you will have to reassess the value of this arrangement, as well as the worth of your existing agent. A good compromise is to pay the consultant's fee, but deduct it from your registered agent's fee.

In some countries, like Bahrain, it is against the law to use agents when dealing with the government or military. The reasoning is that use of an agent adds to the price and opens the door to bribery and corruption. You will find, however, you still need somebody in the country to help you with your marketing. A common term for that person or company is *advisor*. The agreement and remuneration arrangement you make with the advisor will vary, but you must be very careful not to break the laws of the country, so their first bit of advising should be how to make your relationship legal. Before you sign with the advisor, speak to commercial officials in the embassy, or other companies doing business in the country, and satisfy yourself that you are making the right decision.

Why Do You Need An Agent?

It is amazing how many business people are still of the impression that business throughout the world is carried out the same way it is at home and that they do not need some foreigner to help them sell their product.

They soon learn they need the local knowledge and connections of an agent to identify and contact potential customers and to work with local laws, customs, and other confusing local business practices that they will never understand.

The main function of an agent is, of course, to find local customers for your products. The local users of the product may be quite different from those in the United States. It will be up to your agent to identify the real customers. For example, you may be considering selling communication equipment to the police of a country that has a large coast line. But your agent may point out that the real customer is the navy because they are responsible for all police activity ten kilometers inland from the shore.

The agent's connections are the most important reason for using them. These connections are discussed in detail in the next chapter because they are an important element of agent selection. The right connections can get you into the local market very quickly. The lack of these connections can waste a lot of time. An agent who sells household products can easily get you in to see the buyers from large supermarket chains in the country. However, this same agent may have no connections with the military, so you have to use a different agent to sell these same products to the army.

In addition to helping you market your product to the more obvious customers, a good agent can uncover other opportunities for you. Once they understand your product, they may be able to identify other types of customers who could use it if it was slightly modified. For example, the Mexican agent of a company that manufactures walk-through metal detectors used by airport security also found a bank customer who wanted to use the detectors at the entrance to the bank to detect hidden weapons on potential robbers.

Agents can help you validate translations of your brochures, videos, and other marketing literature. You might also use an agent to verify that the name you are giving to a product is not offensive to the local people. There are many international marketing horror stories about this typical faux pas. If you have any doubt about a product name in a country, check with your agent or the U.S. embassy.

Local government regulations and controls in some countries can be very confusing. It is part of an agent's job to know these regulations and controls and how to work within them or, in some cases, around them. For example, in some countries such as Australia, products must go through lengthy testing before they are approved for sale. This is much like the testing done by the Underwriters Laboratory in the United States. An agent can monitor and assist in this process and, as is often required, take steps to expedite it.

Legal Requirement for an Agent

In some countries the law requires you to have a local agent represent you. This provides the local government with some control over what is being marketed into the country, which in some societies is very important. The law will probably require the agent to be a citizen of the country. So make sure your prospective agent meets this requirement before you get too involved with them. Your legal agreement with the agent will probably also have to be in accordance with the laws of the country.

Some local agent laws can sometimes have a significant effect on your business in the country, particularly if the law binds the agent to you for life. Even if they do nothing for you and you switch to another agent, you may still have to pay commissions to the first agent. The concept is something like divorce and alimony. You should therefore include in your market research activities an investigation into the marketing agent laws of the country. This data is usually available from the trade officials at the U.S. embassy in the importing country.

Types of Agents

As stated earlier in this chapter, this book uses the general definition of *agent* as one who acts for another in business. However, there are different types of agents and business relationships you can have with them. The following sections describe the most common types of agents and agent business relationships. You may actually need more than one agent in a country if you have different products or different customer profiles. For some of your products you may want to set up a distributorship, while for others you may want a commissioned agent. There is no legal problem in doing this as long as the products and the customers that each agent is to handle are properly stated in the agent agreements.

Commission Agents

The commission agent is the most common agent arrangement. It is also the simplest because the agent gets paid a percentage of the sale only when they make the sale. The main advantage in this arrangement is that the agent has a very big incentive to sell as much as possible for you. The more they sell, the more they make. The disadvantage is that if they find your products are harder to sell than some of their other lines, they may not bother with them.

The commission rates vary from country to country, depending on how much effort the agent must make and on how much overhead they have. Commissions can be as low as two percent and as high as 25 percent. The commissions can also vary according to the sales volume. For example, the agent may get ten percent for sales up to $100,000, eight percent for $100,000 to $1,000,000, and six percent for everything over $1,000,000.

Most exporters would love to have the problem of paying commission agents a lot of money, because this equates to a lot of completed sales. For this reason, the commission agent is the most popular method of doing international business and is highly recommended, provided of course you choose the right agent.

Retainer Agents

Retainer agents are paid a fixed amount to work for your company for a defined period of time. They normally do not get any commission, and in fact are really only paid salespersons. They are usually contracted on a yearly renewable basis to work a stated number of days per month on your behalf for a fixed amount of money.

There are two major disadvantages to this business relationship. The first is that the agents know they will get paid whether they do anything for you or not, so why spend the contracted time on your behalf. It is very difficult for you to check on whether or not they are doing the work for you because you are not always in frequent communication with them. Resulting sales can be an indication of their effectiveness, but perhaps they could be doing even more. This is the second disadvantage because there is no incentive for them to get additional business by expending just a little more effort. They will be paid the same amount no matter how much business they generate for you.

These disadvantages do not necessarily mean that you should never use a retainer agent. In some countries, this is the only type of agent available. Most agents will not take advantage of this situation because they want their contract renewed the next year.

Commission and Retainer Agents

There is a growing trend for agents to work on a combination of fixed payments and commission. This is particularly true with regard to government and military marketing because of the length of time and the effort it takes to make a sale to these customers. Another reason is that often the agent's marketing expenses are too high for the allowed commission to cover; therefore, a retainer can augment the commission so that the two sources of income cover the agent's overhead.

This is the best of both worlds for agents. They get paid regularly whether they do anything or not, and then when they do make the sale, they get a commission as well. There are ways of leveling this playing field, which will be discussed in the next chapter.

Agents Servicing Other Countries

In some countries, you will find agents who also sell in several other countries. This is particularly true in Singapore where agents will sell to Malaysia, Indonesia, Sri Lanka, and other neighboring countries. This is not usually a problem and can even be to your advantage because you will have to deal with only one contact in the region. However, be aware of political, religious, or ethnic frictions between the countries that could limit an agent's effectiveness.

There are some multinational companies that act as local agents for several manufacturers throughout the world. They usually specialize in marketing a particular product line, such as security equipment or medical supplies. Although the commissions or discounts required by these companies may seem high, it can be very cost effective for you as an international marketing division. If you can locate a suitable company like this that is willing to take on your products, you will not have to read the rest of this book.

Another type of out-of-country agent is based in the United States but sells to other countries. These are usually nationals of the foreign country who were educated in the United States and who have set up a U.S. company to sell U.S. products to their home country. To help them in their operation, they associate themselves with other agents in their home country. This can be a good arrangement for you because it cuts down on the communication problems. Your legal concerns are also considerably eased because you will be able to set up an agreement with the agent according to the laws of your country, rather than those of the foreign country.

There is a growing trend for U.S. citizens to set up agent businesses in the United States that deal with a foreign country through local contacts in that country. This type of agent can ease your communications and legal concerns. However, you should make certain that their in-country associates are the proper people for your products and customer base. You must ask yourself if it may not be more advantageous to deal directly with their in-country associates or with some other in-country agent.

Local Government-owned Agencies

In some countries, the local governments have set up companies to act as agents for foreign companies that want to do business with the government. This is done for a variety of reasons. They operate as do other agents except they have the distinct advantage of selling to their employer. It may also be an unwritten government policy to deal only with government-owned agencies. If you are targeting the local government as a customer, you should check out this possible agent arrangement with the U.S. embassy.

Distributors

Another common international business relationship is that of the distributor who purchases products from you and resells them. The distributor is usually granted exclusive rights to sell the designated products in a designated territory for a designated time period. Distributors vary from little more than a commission agent to those who stock products and parts as well as provide complete installation and repair service.

Some distributors will purchase the products from you at a wholesale price and mark them up as they wish. Others will sell the products at your recommended selling price, and you give them a discount depending on the sales volume. This latter arrangement is advantageous to you if you want to have standard prices throughout the world.

A distributor can make or break your company reputation in the country. If the distributor stocks sufficient spare parts and provides good repair service to the customers, they can greatly enhance the reputation of your product. On the other hand, if the distributor cannot support your product adequately, your business will suffer. It is therefore very important to check out the technical capabilities of a potential distributor if you want them to provide installation and repair service for your products. You will have to train their staff and maybe even provide them with special tooling. You will want to make sure they will be around for a while, so you should check out their financial situation as part of your selection process.

Contractor and Subcontractor Relationships

For some products, you may want to set up a contractor and subcontractor team relationship with an in-country company. This is particularly true if your product is fairly sophisticated equipment that is part of an overall system. An example of this is an automatic car washer that requires a specially designed building, an aspect you may not want to become involved with. Customers in most countries will want to buy the complete system, that is, the building and the car washing equipment.

Your best approach will be to find a suitable in-country company that will handle the building requirements and be the prime contractor for the project. You will be a subcontractor to them, providing the car washing equipment. Your subcontract may also include services to help the contractor design the building and possibly to provide project management. The in-country contractor is thus responsible for a complete system that can be more easily marketed, and then they will look after future maintenance and repairs.

The type of company you select to work with will depend on the product and, to some degree, the sophistication of the country. Your selected team partner does not have to be someone who completely understands your equipment because you can provide overall design and management service. However, some additional factors you should consider when selecting a suitable in-country partner are:

- Does the company have at least some technical capability?
- Does the company have the financial resources to take on the project?
- Does the company have the personnel resources to perform their part of the work?

Another big advantage of the contractor and subcontractor business relationship is that the in-country contractor has all of the responsibility of dealing with the customers, including acting as your agent. There is also an advantage for the in-country prime contractor in that they are free to charge whatever they like for the overall project.

Joint Venture Companies

A joint venture company (JV) is a form of business organization set up by two or more companies to carry out a business venture in which each of the founding companies has an interest. The founding companies jointly own the JV company and share in its profits and losses. The JV company usually subcontracts back to the founding companies for goods and services associated with the business venture.

An example of a joint venture is when a U.S. electrical generation equipment manufacturer and a U.S. electrical transmission equipment manufacturer want to do an electrical project in a foreign country, but they need a local labor supply and a local business presence. They find a suitable in-country company to supply the labor, and the three companies form a JV company in the country. The JV has a local business presence and labor source, and it buys the equipment from the founding U.S. companies. This type of business arrangement is becoming popular in developing countries because it employs local labor and enhances the country's industrial development.

A major advantage of this arrangement is that the JV company is looked upon as a local company in the country. As such it will be favored for future contracts, particularly government contracts. Compared to other foreign companies, the founding U.S. companies have an advantage when selling their products into the country. The disadvantage is that the JV company is subject to the laws of the country, which can be a problem particularly if the in-country JV partner becomes overbearing. This is a frequent problem in Russia. The selection of joint venture partners must be very carefully made.

Local Branch Office

A branch office in a foreign country is part of your company and is usually set up to be the local distributor of your products. It functions like most other branch offices, but to be effective it must employ locals who know the local situation and customers. The advantage of this business arrangement is that your company has complete control over pricing, product quality, and other business concerns.

The main disadvantage is that the branch office is subject to the laws of the country, which can be a problem particularly in the area of employee relations. So before considering setting up the branch office, ensure that all legal implications are thoroughly checked out.

A point to remember about a branch office is that it will always be considered a foreign company by the locals, whereas a distributor is considered a local company even though they deal with foreign products. You will want to assess this image consideration before setting up a branch office in a foreign country.

Strategic Partnering

As the world trade shifts into large trading blocks like the North American Free Trade Agreement and the European Economic Community, it is becoming advantageous to set up strategic partners within these trading blocks. For example, a U.S. company may set up a strategic business relationship with a company in Germany. This gives the U.S. company access to the European market through its German partner, and the German company has access to the North American market.

Increasingly, strategic partnering is becoming a requirement in order to penetrate another trading block, so selection of a suitable partner is a very important activity. There is always the question of who is helping who the most. There is also the danger that your foreign partner may become your competitor in your own country. Nevertheless, this is an important business trend that must be considered.

Selecting the Most Suitable Type of Agent

The type of agent or business relationship you select will depend on your products, the country you are marketing to, and the way you want to do business. These are several factors that will affect your selection process.

- Market considerations. What is the best way to penetrate the target market? Will your customers expect after-sales service? Is there potential subsequent business with customers? Is it advantageous to be a foreign supplier?

- Marketing costs. What business relationship will provide the most cost-effective marketing? A commissioned agent is probably the least expensive, but is it effective for your product? If you need a distributor arrangement, would it be appropriate to open a branch office?

- Proposal considerations. Will detailed proposals be required in the local language, and if so, who will do the translation? Can you propose a complete solution to the customer's requirements, or will you have to involve other companies? How many proposals will be required, and how much will they cost?

- Technical knowledge. Does the local representative require a high level of technical knowledge to handle your product? Is long-term training required? Do they have the staff to undertake the training?

- Installation and support. Who will do the installation? Who will handle the follow-up support? What are the costs associated with these?

- Legal considerations. What kind of business relationships do the local laws allow? What other legal obligations are associated with each business relationship?

- Business relationship considerations. How can you measure agent effectiveness? Can you easily switch to another agent if your first one does not work out? What are the costs of changing agents? What is the initial and on-going cost of an agent?

As stated earlier, before you begin your search for an agent you must decide what you want them to do and what kind of business relationship you want to set up with them. If you are dealing with different products or different customer profiles, you may want to set up more than one agent. The above factors should be considered from this aspect as well.

Chapter 21

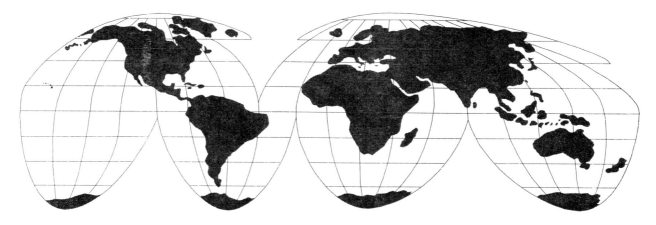

Identifying Potential Agents

Once you have decided on the type of agent you want for each country, the next step is to develop a list of suitable contenders for the job. There are several ways to go about getting the names of potential agents. Sometimes agents will come to you, but usually you have to find them. This chapter outlines some of the methods to use and the assistance available to you to identify potential agents.

Agents Approach You

Don't be surprised if agents approach you to be your representative in their country. In some ways, the fact that they have approached you is a sign of their aggressiveness. They will have heard of you from any of several sources, some quite surprising. For example, an agent may approach you because a customer in the country had suggested he do so. This situation is definitely worth following up because of the potential customer interest. Make sure the interest is real, however, and not just a ploy to get you signed up.

An agent telephoned a company with an interesting pitch. The military of his country was impressed with one of their products and wanted to buy some. The company checked out the agency and found that it was a one-man operation but also that the man was the son of a senior general in the military. They signed up the agent and made the sale.

The usual way agents find out about you and subsequently contact you is by reading your magazine ads or by obtaining your brochures from trade shows. These situations are discussed in the next sections. No matter how an agent hears about you, if the contact sounds plausible, ask for details on their company and business. A viable operation will reply with the information you ask for, and you can begin assessing the potential agent. If they are nonviable, chances are they will not even bother to reply to your information request. Here are some of the basic questions you should ask in your letter.

- What is the size of the agency, in personnel and gross sales?
- What products do they specialize in?
- Who do they sell to?
- What are some of their recent achievements?

A point to remember in drafting your letter is that it may be translated into the local language by someone in the agency and then passed on to a senior manager. The translator's English may not be very good, so avoid idiomatic expressions. Use simple English and avoid jargon phrases like "give me the book on your product line."

International Advertising

If you advertise in magazines that have international distribution, you will be inundated by mail from agents all over the world. Some of these can be quite legitimate, but mainly they are small operations probably writing to you and every other advertiser in the magazine. Some of these can be quite humorous both in their approach and due to their use of the English language. Don't judge them by their English, however, just remind yourself of how well you would write in their language. As stated in the previous section, if the agent sounds plausible, reply with some qualifying questions.

Trade Shows

In addition to exhibiting your products to prospective customers, trade shows are an excellent method of identifying potential agents. Major trade shows in the United States are attended by potential buyers and agents from around the world, so you may not have to go far to contact agents. Similarly, agents from several countries will attend a trade show in a near-by country, so if you exhibit in a suitable country, you can often get responses from several neighboring countries. The subject of trade shows is more fully covered in Chapter 24.

Government Assistance

The U.S. Department of Commerce Trade Opportunity Program (TOP) provides considerable assistance to American companies seeking foreign marketing agents. They can be reached at the Export Assistance Center nearest you, or you can call them or check out their web site.

TOP Export Assistance Center
(800) STAT-USA or (202) 482-1986
http://www.ita.doc.gov/uscs/uscstop.html

Some of the other agent services provided by the Department of Commercial are:

- Agent and Distributor Service. This provides you with information on qualified agents to represent you and your products in a particular country. The list of potential agents they develop for you is based on the product literature you provide to them.
- Commercial Service International Contacts. This provides contact and product information on thousands of foreign companies interested in U.S. products.
- Gold Key Service. Experienced trade professionals in your target country will arrange appointments for you with prescreened contacts whose interests and objectives match your own. There is a charge for this service ranging from $150 to $600.

To make use of these services, contact the nearest U.S. Department of Commerce District Office. These offices are located throughout the United States, including Alaska and Hawaii. You can also contact the Department of Commerce commercial counselors in the country you are considering. They are located in cities throughout the world.

Foreign Organizations

Many countries, particularly in Europe, have local organizations that promote their member agents. The International Union of Commercial Agents and Brokers based in Amsterdam is an umbrella organization for agency organizations in European countries. They can provide you with an up-to-date listing of their member organizations, which in turn can provide you with a list of their agent members.

International Union of Commercial Agents and Brokers
020-4700177
FAX 020-6710947

There are additional in-country institutional sources of information on local agents that you may also want to refer to. The main ones are boards of trade, industrial and trade associations, and banks. Many countries have a local trade association of sorts, such as the Board of Trade of Thailand. Their main purpose is to stimulate exports from the country, but their members are often both exporters and importers. They publish documents outlining the business of their members, which are usually available at their embassy.

There are many industrial or trade organizations in the United States that have export interests. While they may not be able to provide a list of agents, they may be able to put you in contact with someone in their counterpart association in your country of interest. The regularly published newsletters of these organizations sometimes list foreign companies looking for business connections, which may also be of interest to you.

Other Agent Identification Assistance

Foreign embassies and consulates can provide you with lists of potential agents and business partners in their home country. However, the main objectives of these embassies are to promote their own exports, to attract investment, and obtain technology that will generate jobs. If you can tie in your business approach with any of these objectives, they will be happy to help you. If your product can eventually be produced in whole or in part in their country under some business arrangement with you, they will be particularly interested in working with you.

The author once met the ambassador from Swaziland at a cocktail party and casually mentioned that he represented a company that produced prefabricated buildings made of plastic panels. She became very interested when he explained that the buildings could be easily assembled using unskilled labor and that the panels themselves could eventually be made in her country.

A few days later, he got a call from the embassy to come in and see her. She gave him information on a suitable team partner in Swaziland, wrote to them about the product, and also got local government authorities' cooperation.

Most major U.S. banks have foreign service departments that have access to many international business contacts. Foreign banks operating in the United States have even better contacts in their home market. The banks are usually quite happy to assist you in locating agents in particular countries on the assumption they will get some business from you when you start exporting to that country.

You can get information on potential agents from other companies that are actively marketing in the country. Do not hesitate to contact your friends in other companies and ask them about the agents they have in the countries in which you are interested. This is just another form of what is now referred to as networking. Even your competition can sometimes help you select a suitable agent, although the ethics of this approach may be questionable. When you identify whom your successful competition is working with, you could try to have that agent take on your company instead, perhaps by offering a better remuneration package.

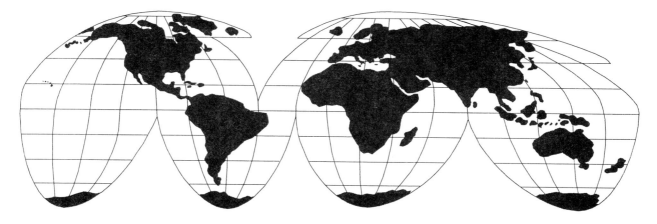

Chapter 22

Selecting Marketing Agents

As explained in Chapter 20, the local agent is not only your business contact in the country but an extension of your company. The amount of business you have in a country is a direct function of the agent you select. Many companies make the mistake of using the first agent that contacts them, much to their chagrin later on. Be prepared to spend considerable time making the agent selection, both during your visit to the country and on your return to your office.

Visit Agent Facilities

You should always try to visit the prospective agents in their country. If possible, do not just interview agents in your hotel but visit the facilities of the agents you are assessing. This will give you a much better idea of their size, specialty, and overall way of doing business. When you visit them, it is also easier to meet with the more senior managers of the company. Bear in mind, however, that appearances can be deceiving, and a very humble operation may have very good contacts for your particular business.

The author once came close to making a very bad agent selection because he did not visit their facilities. The product was a complex system that required construction-type installation with many components purchased within the country. The marketing and business approach was to try to team with a local construction company as the prime contractor. The author's client would be a subcontractor to the local company, providing the product and consulting services to do the project.

The author's client company had been in touch with a company in Saudi Arabia that appeared to fit our requirement. The company's promotional literature listed whole cities that they had constructed, as well as many large government buildings. The owner appeared to have excellent connections and was active in many relevant associations. So the author and his client began to negotiate a team agreement with them via telephone and fax, but after several months and considerable legal fees, they still had no agreement.

The author had the opportunity to go to Saudi Arabia on other business, so he arranged to visit the would-be agent. It turned out they were no more than a shell, with only a few employees. All the experience they advertised came from another agency, in which this company's owner had been a major partner. However, he was kicked out of the partnership a few years earlier and was trying to set up his own business using the false credentials.

On the other side of the coin, the author was very pleasantly surprised in a visit to an agency in Chile. He had inherited this agent from a bankrupt company whose product line his client had bought. The agent appeared reluctant to stock spare parts, only ordering them as they were needed, so the author doubted his size and capability and was considering dropping him. A visit to the agent facilities changed his mind.

On a marketing swing through South America, he stopped at the agency in Santiago. Their office had only about ten people in it; there were no spare parts or technicians in sight. They told him that all of that activity took place in the coastal towns where they had branch offices, which made the author even more skeptical. A few days later, he visited one of these branch offices and was astounded to see the huge warehouse they had. This indicated they were a very viable agency. He later learned the reason they did not want to stock spares was that they were planning to drop the product because of the treatment they had been receiving from the bankrupt predecessor.

Gather Agent Documentation

Gather as much documentation as possible on the agents you are evaluating. You should already have some information that you used to put the agent on your list of potentials. During the agent interview or facility visit, you want to collect as much more as possible. The documentation obtained from these companies is usually their marketing literature, which can be misleading. You should try to get information from other sources as well, such as from customers.

You may be able to obtain significant financial and capability information on companies using the Dun & Bradstreet service, depending on the country you are dealing with. For a fee, Dun & Bradstreet will provide such data on companies as ownership, activity, and financial status. This data can be very useful in assessing the viability of the company. Unfortunately, companies that you are interested in may not always be in the Dun & Bradstreet data bank. This does not necessarily mean that they are not legitimate companies.

Interview Questionnaire

Always interview agents using an itemized questionnaire. This can be done openly in front of the interviewee without any embarrassment. Doing it this way adds to your credibility because it shows them that you are serious about setting up a business relationship with an appropriate company.

The questionnaire will ensure you cover all the main issues you need to know about the company. Sometimes even a vague answer to a specific question can provide enough information for you to make a judgment. When you do the final assessment, the questionnaire also ensures that you will be comparing the same categories of information on all of the agents you interviewed. Questionnaires will vary depending on the type of agent or team partner you are seeking. Some of the basic elements your questionnaire should cover are:

- Company name or division
- Personnel contacted
- Specialization
- Size
- Ownership
- Recent achievements
- Other representation
- Customer contacts
- Aggressiveness
- Type of business arrangement

Company Name or Division

This is not as straightforward as it may seem. In some countries, companies are interwoven for a variety of reasons. Also, some smaller companies may be a division of a much larger company, giving the smaller company considerably more depth than appears to be available.

A company was looking for a Korean company to team with on a large electric project. After meeting with several would-be agents, as opposed to potential teaming partners, the company official was becoming despondent. Fortunately, the situation changed dramatically when he was interviewing the president of what appeared to be yet another two or three-person marketing agency.

The company's name was KEE International, which he had initially assumed was named after a founder. However, the casual question of what KEE stood for changed the situation considerably. It came from the parent company, Korean Electrical Engineering, which had hundreds of employees supplying electric maintenance and repair service throughout the country. This was exactly the kind of company he was looking for.

Personnel Contacted

At the beginning of an interview, try to identify what positions the people have in the company and to whom they report. This will set the tone of the interview. The marketing or salespersons will be judging your product on how easily they can sell it. A marketing manager will look at a wider picture but still from a sales point of view. Senior company people, like presidents or managing directors, will tend to consider your business from a more strategic aspect.

Try to speak to the senior company officials, but at the same time, do not talk down to the marketing people who will be your soldiers in the field. You should also be on the alert for inter-company connections that can benefit you.

One evening in Riyadh, the author had a meeting with a very pleasant sheik and his technical advisor. They wanted to manufacture the product in a factory they had in the country, but the author was not interested in this. A few days later, he was visiting another company in Jeddah that seemed like the kind of company he wanted. As he thumbed through their literature, there was a picture of the sheik from Riyadh. He was actually their managing director for special projects but during the meeting had stressed only his latest project that was the manufacturing factory. This combination now made an appealing business relationship.

Another interesting thing about the people you initially contact in a company is that they may not be natives of the country. Quite often you will meet with Americans, Britons, or other foreigners working for the company. This is not unusual in many countries because they hire these people as a technical bridge between their suppliers and their customers. Try to identify who they work for and what their role is because these people may have considerable influence in the company and with customers.

Specialization

Make sure the agent you select specializes in your type of products or deals with your potential customers. One of the first things you want to find out about a company is what they specialize in. If you sell car radios, it is probable you will not get much business through an agent who sells to the fishing industry.

Their response to inquiries on this subject can sometimes be very misleading. They may try to look as if they specialize in your product so they can get your business and start a new business area of their own. For example, after the Gulf War almost every agency company in the Middle East was setting up a security equipment department.

Size

The size of an agency company is not always significant. It depends very much on the products you are trying to sell and, more importantly, the customer market you are trying to reach. To move most consumer products in a country, you will want an agency that has many contacts. This usually means a large company with branches throughout the country. The same can be said for office products for which you probably want a distributor with outlets in all the major towns and cities.

For highly specialized products aimed at a very focused customer group, you may want to deal with a very specialized small company. This is particularly true for military products to developing countries, where a one-person agency might do the job, providing the agent has access to the senior officers of the military. A successful agent company can be large or small, depending on many factors. You will have to be the judge, but remember that big is not always best or right for you and your product.

Ownership

While ownership of an agent company may not seem important, in some countries it can have a great impact on your business. For example, in Indonesia many of the transportation-related companies are owned by the military, as are many of the agent companies. A military-owned agency will probably bring you more transportation-related business than one not associated with the military.

In Malaysia there is an ownership situation of a different dimension. The indigenous population of the country, called Bumi Putras, make up only a fraction of the population. The other major ethnic groups are Chinese and Indian, who are the businesspeople of Malaysia. The government has passed laws supporting the Bumi Putras, and one is very important to your selection of an agent. That law requires all the government departments, including the military, to make purchases from or through a Bumi Putra-owned company. If your customers in Malaysia are government or military, make sure the agent you select meets this requirement.

In most of the Arab countries of the Middle East, the ruling families have considerable influence over what is purchased and sold in the country. As a result, many agencies are owned by members of the ruling families. There are, however, many of these companies in each country. The trick is to identify the right one.

It can sometimes be difficult to identify the ownership of an agency, but in some countries it can be very important. Before you begin your agent selection in any country, find out if ownership is an issue. The U.S. embassy people can help you in this regard.

Recent Achievements

The recent achievements of an agent are a good indication of how effective they are. They can give you an idea of the type of customers dealt with, the products handled, and the size of the projects completed. Make sure, however, the advertised achievements are valid and not just marketing hype. For example, they may tell you they have represented an American supplier who just got a large vehicle order in the country. When you check with the American company, you may learn that the agent in question had just recently been signed up to market maintenance contracts only and that the vehicle sale was accomplished by another agent.

Find out as many relevant achievements as possible from the agent to help you qualify him. During the interview, ask for more details about the achievements, and then try to verify they are valid examples. Indicate you will verify his sale with the company he represented, and see if they modify their story.

Other Representation

The list of companies and products the agent represents is also an indication of how effective they will be for you. You may not want someone who already represents companies with products similar to yours, but you want to make sure they handle products of interest to your potential customers. If you are looking for someone to sell construction material, an agency representing companies that sell only food may not be the agent for you. If you want them to sell air conditioners, however, they may have the right kind of customer contacts. Another thing to watch for is conflict of interest. If the agent already represents a list of companies in your field, make sure that their products are not in direct competition to your products. If they are, the agent will have loyalty problems, and your trade secrets could get passed to your competition.

The quality of the companies the agent represents is also an indication of how good the agent is. There is quite a difference between an agent who represents a large list of small companies with obscure products and one with a small list of very well-known companies and products. The reason for representing only obscure products is very likely because the agent is not qualified to work for the well-known companies.

Customer Contacts

In many countries and for many products, an agent's contacts are far more important that anything else. For example, in Saudi Arabia the trick is to get together with an agency associated with a member of the royal family. For large government purchases, this association will give you access to the senior person who makes the purchase decision. For commodity sales, the association will ensure your products are handled by the right wholesalers and carried in the right shops. There are many other countries where things work similarly, where you want agents with contacts who are senior government officials or influential politicians. In countries run by the military, the sought-after contacts are senior military officers.

Do not make any harsh judgments about this way of doing business. It has been going on since the dawn of civilization and no amount of moral persuasion will change it. If you want any more proof of how entrenched it is, just look at the lobbyist system that affects many of the decisions made by Congress, including those involving large government purchases.

Aggressiveness

Aggressiveness in an agent is a major factor. There is no use having an agent if they are not going to get out there and sell for you. Not only do they have to have the right contacts but they also have to be willing and able to work them. The problem is how to determine how aggressive an agent will be on your behalf before you make a commitment to them. You can get some indication from the quality of the other suppliers they represent and from their recent achievements. You can also get information from others who know the agent, particularly customers.

Type of Business Arrangement

There are many types of business arrangements with agents, distributors, and team partners in foreign countries, as discussed in Chapter 20. The type of arrangement you need will depend on both your product and the market you are dealing with.

The type of business arrangement you want must also be a consideration in agent selection. Discuss this openly with the potential agent during your initial interview. If the agent is vague about what they want, try to pin them down. The business arrangement will form the basis of your contract with the agent and of your future together.

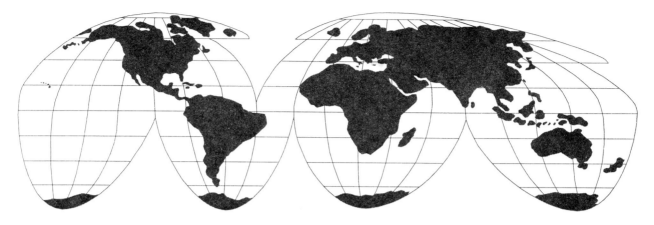

Chapter 23

Contracting and Paying Agents

Once you have selected a suitable agent, it is very important to be sure your business relationship is fully documented in a contract, including how the agent will be compensated. This chapter presents the main issues that should be covered in agent contracts, including various options for paying agents. The information given here should not be considered a substitute for legal advice. It is strongly recommended that any contracts you make be done with the advice of your lawyer.

Why Do You Need a Contract with an Agent?

Many agents will insist on a contract before they do anything on your behalf, which is usually a reasonable position. Some will get very pushy and demand you sign a contract before they will even discuss marketing your product with you. Do not waste any time with these agents. On the other hand, some agents may not want a contract until they identify some business for you. This is the situation you should aim for. It gives you a chance to assess the agent's capability before you commit to them. The agent in turn can test the viability of your product in their market area. You can give them a letter of intent stating that you will negotiate a representative contract when they identify a suitable business opportunity. If they do find some business for you, however, you will eventually have to have a contract.

The main reason for a contract is to ensure that both you and the agent understand the kind of relationship you have and each other's responsibilities within the relationship. You may want to limit the agent's activities to certain products, customers, or territory. The agent in turn will want to try to get exclusive representation of all your products, to all customers, and to several countries. Then there is the all-important question of how the agent is paid. These issues, and often many others, are the reason you both want a contract.

In a contractor and subcontractor relationship, the agent or prime contractor may want to wait until they obtain some business and then rely on the terms of the purchase order they give you. This sounds simple, but it has its pitfalls. Well into the project you may discover your prime contractor was expecting things from you that you did not consider in your pricing. Before you get caught in a bind like this, at least draw up a memorandum of understanding that identifies how the work and responsibilities will be split when your prime contractor agent does get some business for you.

You must also consider the possibility that the agent will not honor the contract. This is a common occurrence is some countries, and there is very little you can do about it. As they say, it comes with the territory. The territories where this is bound to occur are usually known to the embassy trade officials in the country, so if you are worried about the possibility of this happening, check with these officials.

Basic Contract Considerations

Agent contracts vary according to the type of agent relationship, the product, and the territory. Some basic issues that must be covered in a contract include:

- Contract date
- Parties in the contract
- Purpose of the agreement
- Products involved
- Territory involved
- Responsibilities of the agent
- Responsibilities of your company
- Agent compensation
- Duration of the contract
- Termination of the contract
- Law governing the contract

Each of these issues is briefly discussed in the following paragraphs using extracts from actual contracts where applicable. Remember that this information is not a substitute for the legal advice you should obtain to draw up a standard agent contract for your company.

Identification of the Contract Date and the Parties

This is the opening part of the contract. It establishes the contract date and identifies who the contracting parties are and where they are located. Here is a typical example.

Sample Contract

IDENTIFICATION AND DATE

THIS AGREEMENT made this _____ day of _____, 19__ between ABC Manufacturing Inc., 1234 Main Street, Town, Florida, USA, (hereinafter referred to as "ABC"), and Super Agent Limited, 25 Chula Soi, Surawongse Road, Bangkok, Thailand, (hereinafter referred to as "AGENT").

The establishment of the date is important, because it will determine the exact date on which the contract terminates or is to be renewed. Also, if you were doing business in the territory before the contract, you have a definite date prior to which the new agent will not be compensated for any business obtained.

The beginning of the contract also names the contracting parties and states their addresses for additional identification. An exact street address may not be given, because in some countries it may not exist.

Purpose of the Agreement

This is the meat of the agreement where it details the type of agent relationship. It identifies the products involved and the territory in which the agent can work on your behalf. This is a typical example.

Sample Contract

PURPOSE

1. APPOINTMENT

ABC appoints AGENT as its exclusive sales representative to promote the sale of the products set forth in Appendix A (hereinafter referred to as "the Products"), within the territory described in Appendix B (hereinafter referred to as "the Territory").

The question of exclusive and non-exclusive agency is usually a thorny issue with an agent. The agent will, of course, want an exclusive representation.

In some circumstances, however, you may not want to use the agent exclusively because other agents may also be able to serve you in the same territory. Sometimes an agreeable compromise is to give them exclusive rights for one territory and non-exclusive rights for another.

Products

The products that the agent will try to sell for you are usually listed in an appendix to the agreement so they can be easily changed in the future. While many agents will want to handle all of your products, quite often an agent is good with one product or customer base and not with others. You could very easily have more than one agent representing different products in the same territory. Here is a typical product appendix.

Sample Contract

PRODUCT DEFINITION

APPENDIX A

to

ABC and AGENT agreement of the _____ day of _____, 19___.

THE PRODUCTS

    The ABC Products to be promoted by AGENT in the Territory are as follows:

    1. Bathtubs, including fixtures

    2. Sinks, including fixtures

    3. Toilets

    4. Urinals

Territory

The agent will want to have as much territory as possible, including neighboring countries. Agents will use such arguments as, "Our business covers all of the Asian countries, and we must have exclusive representation in the complete area." If possible, you should resist these initial demands and define a small territory so they can prove themselves. You can also give them non-exclusive rights to some other territory and see how they do. If they turn out to be worthy of additional territory, you can amend the applicable appendix in the contract accordingly. A typical territory appendix is shown here.

Sample Contract

TERRITORY DEFINITION

APPENDIX B

to

ABC and AGENT agreement of the _____ day of _____, 19___.

THE TERRITORY

The Territory in which AGENT has exclusive rights to promote ABC Products is as follows:

1. The Eastern Province of the Kingdom of Saudi Arabia

2. The Sultanate of Oman

Services and Responsibilities of the Agent

You will want to detail the main services you expect from agents and stipulate the terms and conditions under which they should work. Many of the services are basic to most businesses, but some companies will have additional services that an agent must perform. Here are examples of the basic services required of an agent to be included in an agreement.

Sample Contract

SERVICES DEFINITION

2. SERVICES AND RESPONSIBILITIES OF AGENT

The services to be provided by AGENT to ABC shall include, but are not limited to, the following:

a. Analyzing the market and developing marketing plans;

b. Promoting ABC products within the Territory;

c. Identifying, contacting, meeting with and briefing potential customers, and further qualifying their requirements;

d. Assisting in preparing and delivering bids and proposals;

e. Communicating with customers for follow-up business;

f. Assisting in collecting payment for sales made;

g. Assisting ABC personnel visiting the Territory; and

h. Carrying out other related activities as agreed upon by both parties.

The last item ensures that other services are covered when they arise. For example, at some time in the future you may want the agent to translate a brochure for you.

Responsibilities of Your Company

Your company will have to provide support to the agent. Examples of typical support responsibilities follow.

Sample Contract

COMPANY RESPONSIBILITIES

3. RESPONSIBILITIES OF ABC

ABC shall be responsible to the AGENT for the following:

a. Providing suitable product information and promotional literature;

b. Responding as soon as possible to inquiries and request for bids or proposals received from AGENT; and

c. Assisting AGENT in promoting the Products in the Territory.

The last item should be kept as vague as possible, because you do not always know in advance how you will promote your products in the territory. You may use advertising in international trade journals or local media advertising, or you may do nothing. Be very careful about committing to definite promotional activities until you have a better understanding of the territory.

Agent Compensation

There are various methods of agent compensation which depend mainly on the type of agent relationship. Most agent relationships are based on a straight commission in which the agent gets an agreed percentage commission based on the value of the sales transactions generated. This is the best arrangement for you because you have to pay them only after they make a sale and you collect for it. This arrangement also puts pressure on the agent to sell on your behalf because without a sale, they have no income from you.

The commission percentage varies with the product and other circumstances. For high value transactions it may be down around two to four percent, and for some activities it may be 15 percent or even more. Some agent commissions are as high as 25 percent, but these are usually in countries where the agent has the added expenses associated with paying others to help get the sale.

If the agent compensation is straightforward, such as a fixed percentage of all sales made by the agent, this can be simply written in as one of the main clauses of the contract, as shown here:

Sample Contract

COMPENSATION CLAUSE

4. AGENT COMPENSATION

AGENT will receive from ABC a commission amounting to five percent (5%) of the dollar value of any sales made by ABC to buyers in the Territory introduced by AGENT. The commission will be paid to AGENT by ABC each time payment in whole or in part is received by ABC.

Compensation by Retainer

Chapter 20 described retainer agents and the disadvantage of this arrangement to you. The main reason agents want to be compensated by a monthly retainer is to generate some income while they develop sales that will take a long time to happen. For example, it can take years to develop a sale to the military, and an agent must have some continuing compensation to keep them going.

Retainer compensation is usually a monthly fee paid directly to the agent. In return, you are provided with a monthly report of activities and progress. The fee can be as low as a few hundred dollars a month to several thousand a month, depending on the market and the product. Some contracts will stipulate that, for the retainer, the agent must work a specific number of days for the company each month.

The agent's time can be monitored to some degree by requiring a monthly report. Although it is in the contract as a requirement, however, it is seldom specified in detail. In practice, a typical report is a one or two-page letter in which the agent explains what is happening with regard to your business. In practice, the report is often overlooked by the agent who, like most salespeople, hates paperwork.

Combination Retainer and Commission Fee

Some agents will insist on a commission plus a minimum monthly retainer or a consulting fee. In addition to the basic reasons for a retainer fee, there is sometimes another reason for this arrangement. The commission allowed in the country or by the U.S. Foreign Business Practices Act may not be enough to cover all of the agent's expenses. The retainer can be considered a consulting fee for other services so the expenses can be met.

This arrangement is not as good for you because agents know they will get some compensation even if they do nothing for you. One way to get around this problem is to have the retainer or consulting fee as an advance against future commissions. The following extract from a contract illustrates this method of compensation.

Sample Contract

COMPENSATION CLAUSE

5. AGENT COMPENSATION

For its marketing service to ABC, AGENT will be compensated with a combination of commission and hourly consulting rates as follows:

a. AGENT will receive from ABC a commission amounting to six percent (6%) of the dollar value of any sales made by ABC to buyers introduced through AGENT. The commission will be paid to AGENT by ABC each time payment in whole or in part is received by ABC, and will be paid on any sale or exchange from any source whatsoever effected by ABC to the buyer introduced through AGENT. The amount of the commission payments will be reduced by the amount of hourly rate payments made in accordance with sub-paragraph 5.b below.

b. AGENT will be compensated for the marketing activities on an hourly rate basis at rates stated in Schedule A of this agreement, and ABC will pay AGENT for all expenses associated with these activities. The compensation will be paid to AGENT by ABC at the end of each month that the activities took place, unless otherwise agreed to by both parties, and the sales commission payments referred to in sub-paragraph 5.a above will be reduced by the amount of the hourly rate payments paid to AGENT by ABC.

Distributor Compensation

In a distributor agent arrangement, the agent is compensated with a fee, either through a profit arrangement or through discount payments. In the fee or profit scenario, you sell your products to agents at a wholesale price and they mark them up and sell them. The markup is their income for the activity. This is a very clean arrangement for you because once the product has been purchased from you, your responsibility ends, except for warranty and similar considerations. The disadvantage to you is that you have no control over the prices that will be charged.

If you want to control retail prices, you can have a discount arrangement with the agent. Agents agree to sell your product at a price set by you, and you pay them an agreed upon discount fee, usually a percentage of the sale.

Your business arrangement can be such that either the end customer pays you directly and you pay the agent the discount fee or the customer pays the agent who, in turn, pays you the final purchase price, less the discount.

Duration of the Contract

The duration of the contract must be clearly stated. This also will vary with the type of agent relationship as well as the product. If you are engaging an agent to sell a common item such as bathtubs, you may want to try out the person for a year to see how he or she does. However, if you are selling large systems or products that take considerable time to develop a market and make a sale, you will have to give the agent reasonable time to get the contracts. To avoid unnecessary paperwork, you may also want to have the contract renew automatically, if agreeable to both parties. A typical example is shown here.

Sample Contract

DURATION CLAUSE

6. DURATION OF AGREEMENT

This agreement will be in effect for a period of two years from the date first above written, and will automatically renew annually thereafter on the anniversary of the date first above written, unless terminated by either party.

Termination of the Contract

The agreement should allow for termination of the contract by either side before the expiration date. You may want to terminate the agreement because the agent is not doing the job, and the agent may want to terminate because they have found a better supplier. The usual approach is to allow termination by either party after a defined number of days after informing the other party in writing of the desire to terminate. Here is a typical example.

Sample Contract

TERMINATION CLAUSE

7. TERMINATION

This agreement may be terminated by either party at any time by informing the other party in writing at least 90 days prior to the termination date.

Law Governing the Contract

The agreement should state under what law it is to be interpreted and the method of settling any dispute. Try to have it under the state law of your own company, but this may not always be possible. Some countries demand that agency agreements come under the law of the country in which the sales are being made, which gives you little choice. This is a typical example.

Sample Contract

GOVERNING LAW CLAUSE

8. GOVERNING LAW

This agreement shall be interpreted in accordance with the laws of the State of _____, and all disputes arising from this agreement shall be settled under the same laws.

Other Contract Considerations

There are many more issues that may be covered in the agreement, depending on the agent relationship, the products, and other factors. This is why you should obtain legal advice when drawing up an agent contract. Some of the other items you may want to consider are:

- Advertising costs in the territory
- Trade show costs and attendance
- Sub-agents working for the agent
- Amount of stock the agent or distributor must carry
- Shipping arrangements
- Shipping insurance
- In-country training
- In-country maintenance

Team Agreement Considerations

If your agent relationship is contractor, subcontractor, or some similar joint venture, you should have a much more detailed contract that specifies who is responsible for each aspect of the joint activity. It is wise to sort out these details at an early stage before you have a contract from a customer. This can be done with a memorandum of understanding that specifies the responsibilities that will be assigned to each of you when you get a contract from the customer.

The responsibilities that must be covered will, of course, vary from project to project. Here are some of the most common considerations associated with a large or complex project.

- Who will be the prime contractor with overall responsibility and direct communication with the customer?
- Who will be the program manager, or which company will provide the program manager? What are their duties and who will they report to? What authority will they have?
- Who is responsible for the overall project design, and who is responsible for the various subsystems of the design?
- Who is responsible for supplying each of the components of the project or for acquiring components from other sources?
- Who will be responsible for installing the overall project, and who is responsible for installing the various components?
- Who will train the operators and maintainers?
- Who will supply future support to the customer for modifications and other needs?

Contract Certification

In some countries, your agent contract must be certified by officials of the country in order for the agent to be considered to be your legal representative. This can be a problem unless you can easily visit the embassy or consulate of the country for the certification.

Mexico, for example, requires that the agent contract be certified if the agent is going to be involved with selling your products to the Mexican government. The procedure is to have your own lawyer or a notary public produce a letter saying that you have appointed the agent. You then take the letter and a copy of the contract to the Mexican embassy and ask to have it certified. There is the standard bureaucratic waiting period, after which they will ask you to pick up the document. You will be amused by the elaborate application of sealing wax and long official ribbons. You will be less amused by the fact they charge you for this service.

Determine Your Promotion and Pricing

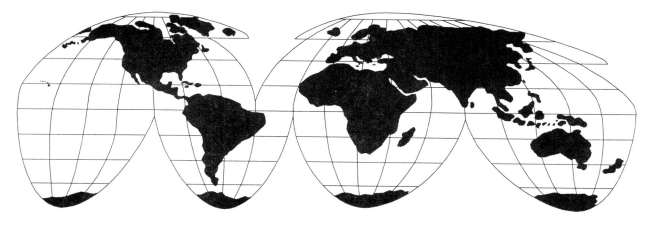

Chapter 24

Promoting Your Product

Much has been written about how to promote your product, so this chapter will address only some practical considerations associated with promoting your product in the international market. In some ways it is similar to marketing in the United States, but in many ways it is not.

Brochures

As everyone knows, you must have some kind of brochure to tell customers about your product. For international marketing, your brochures should be market-oriented rather than technology-intensive. You should emphasize what the product does rather than go into long detail about how it does it. Remember that your brochure will probably have to be translated by your local agent as they explain it to their customers. Do not burden them with a long, technical write-up that is liable to be translated incorrectly and that will probably bore the customers.

You should eventually consider translating your brochure into the foreign language. The language or languages you choose will, of course, depend on the countries you are targeting. Languages such as Arabic and

Spanish are used in many countries, but remember that there are words in these languages that have different meanings in different countries, such as the example of the choice of a word for covering translated in Spanish to a word which is slang for condom in at least one Spanish-speaking country. Your best approach is to have your agent do the translation or at least check it over before you go to press.

When you are producing a new brochure, even if you are not yet prepared to have it translated into a foreign language, you may want to allow for the future translation. The most expensive part of printing a brochure is the colored pictures and artwork. In the production process, the colored work is usually printed first, and the words, usually in black, are then printed onto the colored work.

When you print the brochures, have extra copies made with just the colored work printed on them. Then when you decide on another language you want the brochure to be in, you just have to print the translated words onto the colored work. With today's computers and desk top publishing software, you can do this in-house very inexpensively, particularly if your agent can do the translation.

Other Marketing Material

In addition to brochures and video tapes, there are several other forms of marketing material available. Gifts with company logos are a useful addition to marketing in many countries. As you know, there are many such items available now, ranging from cheap and useless to unique and expensive. Try to select something uniquely tied to your product. Also bear in mind the status of the customer who will receive the gift. An Arab sheik will not be impressed with a plastic key chain.

As mentioned in a previous section, you may have to provide customers with a concept proposal to help them understand your product and to convince them that they need it. Using the car washing equipment as an example again, the customer may think they should get into the car washing business, but they really do not know what it is all about. You do not know enough about the territory to give them a detailed proposal, yet your agent needs something more than just brochures to increase the customer interest. So with the agent's help, you give the customer a concept or preliminary proposal that explains how they might set up a car washing business with your equipment. Because you do not know all the requirements and expectations of the customer at this time, you should keep it fairly vague and not commit to anything. In particular, do not quote exact prices. They will insist on a price, but limit it to a very high quotation, given orally by the agent with many caveats. Even then, many customers will hold you to that price, so make sure it is higher than the formal quote you and your agent will give them later with a more detailed proposal.

In many cases, you will have to provide the customer with a detailed proposal, including final prices, that they will turn into a contract. The proposal will probably have to be translated into the local language, and here is where the agent is very important. Your agent will do the translation and put the proposal in the form that is usually used in the country. You will have to provide your English version of the proposal and the accompanying art work. Remember that the translated version will also require the art work, so you must provide the agent with as many copies of it as needed. You will marvel at how elaborate some of these final proposals are and the justifiable pride that the agent takes in them.

Advertising

International and in-country advertising as discussed in Chapter 11, is very much dependent on the product and the target audience. If you decide to do local, in-country advertising, you should work closely with your agent to ensure the best results. If you decide on international advertising, for example in a specific magazine, make sure the magazine readership includes your target audience.

However, you may want to consider magazine advertising, particularly in focused magazines that are in English and have a wide international distribution. For example, *Jane's Defense Weekly* is read by military people around the world, even though it is in English. There are other specialist magazines that also have a large international distribution. Most of these are in English, but they are also in other languages. If you can identify a suitable international magazine that is read by your potential customers, it may be worth considering running some ads in it.

You will find that replies to international advertising are in an interesting pattern. The initial responses are from customers you are targeting. These are usually serious, and you should follow them up immediately. At this time you will also begin to get responses from would-be agents, and this will continue for a while. Finally, and particularly if your product involves new technology, as the magazine is read in institutional libraries around the world, you will get requests for information from academics. These people probably have no intention of buying your product. Nevertheless, you should respond to all of the queries.

Trade Shows

Trade shows are an excellent way of promoting your products, testing the response to your product in a new market, and identifying potential agents. However, trade shows have also become a product in themselves, and as such there are too many for the potential customers to attend. So, before you choose a trade show, check it out carefully. Make sure that the customer audience you want to target will be in attendance in numbers that will make your efforts worthwhile.

You may not have to go far to have an international audience visit your booth at a trade show because many shows in the United States attract attendees from around the world. The foreign visitors are usually agents looking for products to sponsor in their homeland, but they may be able to get you started in their country. Similarly, multinational trade shows are held throughout Europe, and they are gaining popularity in the Middle East and Asia as well.

Once you have decided to use a trade show to promote your product, there are a number of issues that you must resolve in order to ensure a successful show. These will vary with the product, but the main ones are:

- Booth size and type. Booth sizes are usually multiples of a standard nine-square-meter booth which is 10 feet by 10 feet. You then have to choose the type of booth, whether a corner, an island, outside for products like vehicles and aircraft, or a chalet that is a popular exhibit space at air shows. Booth space is usually allocated on a first-come, first-choice basis, and often the companies that have been exhibiting at the show the longest have the opportunity to keep their usual space or to upgrade.

- What to exhibit. You must decide not only what product to exhibit but also how to exhibit it. Will you use the product itself as the main part of your booth? Will you use a mock-up? Will you use a crowd grabber? The idea of having a belly dancer or similar attraction perform at your booth is very passé because it only attracts people, not necessarily customers.

- Artwork. No matter what you exhibit, you will need some artwork in the booth to illustrate your product or, at least, your name. Do not forget that the artwork takes time to produce, and the bigger the booth, the more artwork you will need. Also remember that at least some of the artwork should be in the language of the host country.

- Literature. While you will certainly need brochures to hand out, you should also consider having more detailed information packages available to give to visitors who appear to be seriously interested in your product, such as the concept proposals mentioned previously. Here too, at least some of the literature should be in the language of the host country.

- Press kits. Prepare a number of press kits to give out to press people when they come around looking for material to write about. Even if they do not come around, go and find them and give them a kit. The kit should have a brief, magazine-style article about your product. You should also include eight-by-ten glossy photos of your product that they can publish with your article. You can include your brochures, but the press people will be more interested in the article and the pictures.

Make sure your local agent is deeply involved with your booth at a trade show. The show gives them a chance to show off your products to their customers, and if they are assertive, they will contact potential customers and have them visit the booth. You can do the pitch to the customers, using the agent as an interpreter. This can be a major part of your marketing activity in the country.

There are three types of trade show visitors, and your agent should help you sort them out. The first, and least important, is the person who goes along just picking up brochures without even looking at the products on display. While they may contact you at some time in the future, the chances of a sale are slim. The next type is the one who takes up a lot of your time with questions about your product but who has no intention of buying it. You can often nail them down by asking what they intend to use the product for, and if they waffle, you can disregard them, politely, of course.

The third and best type of trade show visitor is the one who returns to your booth later. At first visit they will briefly study the product on display, maybe ask a few questions, then pick up your brochures and leave. When they return, you know they are serious because in the meantime they've had a chance to read the brochures and think about the product. They may even have discussed it with colleagues. The fact that they have returned to your booth is an indication that you are on their short list and they want to talk business.

While at your booth, be sure to get all the information you can about a serious visitor. Their business card is a good start, but also find out their interest in the show and how it relates to your product. Do not be afraid to take notes in front of them. This shows you are very interested in what they are saying, and of course the notes will be very useful for following up. And follow up you must.

Temporary Importing and Exporting of Goods

To take demonstration equipment into a foreign country for trade shows, demonstrations to prospective customers, or for prospective customers to try out for a short period of time, you must become involved with temporary importing and exporting. In effect, the equipment is exported from your country, imported into the foreign country, then exported from the foreign country, and imported back into your country. This activity could incur import duties in both the foreign country and your own. Most countries recognize this problem and have taken steps to avoid these duty costs.

The most common way of temporarily moving equipment across international borders is by an internationally recognized document called a carnet. It was developed by the International Bureau of Chambers of Commerce, and it allows you to export goods temporarily into another country and reexport them back to your own country, without going through extensive customs procedures or paying duties.

The carnet is obtained from your local Chamber of Commerce, and before use, it must be validated by a customs official of your own country. This involves taking the equipment down to the customs office and having them check to ensure that the equipment listed exists and that the serial numbers listed are correct. Sometimes this procedure can be done on your first trip out of the country with the carnet if you are hand-carrying the equipment, but you must be sure you have all of the equipment that is listed on the carnet.

The most important practical consideration about a carnet is to ensure that all of the equipment you will ever be taking temporarily out of the country is listed. If you have several different demonstration units, even though you do not always take them all, list them all on the carnet. If you do not take some of them on a particular trip, you note the exceptions on the four vouchers and counterfoils that you will use on the trip. One voucher is used to export from your country, one to import into the foreign country, one to export from the country, and the fourth to import back into your country. Similarly, make sure that all support equipment such as power supplies and demonstration stands are also listed on the main carnet. If you don't take them, they can also be shown as exceptions for that particular trip.

Make sure that the names of all the people who may ever have to transport the equipment are listed on the carnet. Do not limit it to people in your own company, but consider agents or people in associated companies who may be involved in the future. However, if in the future a new person becomes involved, their name can be added to the carnet by a letter to the issuing office. Listing the correct names on the carnet is important because the customs officials will not allow the equipment to cross the border if someone using the document is not on the list.

If you are hand-carrying equipment on a carnet, you should plan your trip with the customs office in mind. Remember, you have to start the process by going through your own customs when you leave the country. Thus, you have to make sure that they will be open when you arrive at the airport for your flight. This sounds obvious, yet there are many early-morning flights out of the United States that leave from locations where the customs office does not open until much later. You must also consider the customs office hours in the foreign country because you must check in there when you both enter and leave the country with the equipment.

When shipping goods on a carnet, try to limit the number of containers involved. It is very easy for one or more to get temporarily lost in transit. Customs officials in the receiving country may not clear your shipment until the missing containers arrive and the list of equipment on the carnet is complete. Many people exhibiting at trade shows have had to carry on without their main demonstration as the result of these circumstances.

Carnets are not used by every country in the world. Those that do acknowledge the carnet process are shown in the table below. Countries that do not adhere to the carnet system usually have some local method of controlling the temporary import and export of goods. The usual approach is to have you as the importer or exporter post a customs bond that is returnable when the goods have been reexported out of the country. For example, Kuwait requires a customs bond for all temporary imports in the amount of eight percent of CIF (cost including freight) of the goods. The money is eventually returned after the goods have been reexported.

Carnet Countries

Australia	Hungary	Poland
Austria	Iceland	Portugal
Belgium	India	Romania
Bulgaria	Ireland	Senegal
Canada	Israel	Singapore
Cote D'Ivoire	Italy	South Africa
Cyprus	Japan	Spain
Czechoslovakia	Korea	Sri Lanka
Denmark	Luxembourg	Sweden
Finland	Malaysia	Switzerland
France	Malta	Turkey
Germany	Mauritius	United Kingdom
Gibraltar	Netherlands	United States
Greece	New Zealand	Yugoslavia
Hong Kong	Norway	

These customs bonds are usually handled by the shipping companies, so the exporter turns the money over to the local shipping company that will ship the goods from the United States. The local company works closely with a receiving company in the country where the goods are going. Between the two companies, the money and the paperwork get handled correctly, hopefully. When the goods are shipped out of the country, the local foreign shipping company does the paperwork to get the bond money back. It eventually flows back to the shipping and receiving company you started out with. You then get your money back from your shipping company.

Needless to say, if you are involved with non-carnet temporary import and export, it is essential to use a reliable, competent, and experienced shipping company. The shipping company, with the help of their counterparts in the foreign country, can advise you of the requirements associated with temporary importing into the foreign country.

Local Briefings and Seminars

On each of your visits to the country, have your agent arrange for you to brief potential customers, either as an introduction to your product or to reinforce previous exposure. These briefings are also important to the agent, not only from the customer aspect but for their own knowledge of your product. Each time they hear your pitch, they will become more familiar with the product. The customer's questions and your answers will also be an important learning process for them.

Quite often, the customers you are briefing will want the briefing done in their language, and your agent will have to act as an interpreter. Bear in mind, however, that they will probably understand some English even though they will not always understand what you are saying. It's amazing how quickly they learn English when you take them to lunch.

When your agent is setting up appointments for you to brief customers, make sure they also arrange the support equipment you will need. Do not totally depend on briefing equipment you take for granted at home, and do not assume that the agent has made the required arrangements. Be prepared to improvise. Remember that the form of electricity varies around the world, and you can never be sure that the briefing room will have an electrical outlet. Do not bother with 35 mm slides, but rely mainly on overhead projector viewgraphs that are used throughout the world. Have hard copy of the briefing to leave with the customer. The hard copy is also very useful as a briefing aid if there is no projector available, which is often the situation.

Seminars on your product are also a very useful marketing tool, provided of course that the product lends itself to this type of promotion. The seminar can be as short as a few hours or last a few days. The usual procedure is for your agent to send out invitations by fax to potential customers they have selected to attend the seminar at an announced time and place. Keep in touch with your agent when they are making these arrangements to make sure all the facts are right, including the dates when you can be there. You will then give a detailed briefing on the product to the assembled customers. The briefings can be as elaborate as you want to make them. The main thing to remember is that the people attending are probably genuinely interested in a product of your type. In many countries you should be prepared to do the briefing through an interpreter, usually your agent.

Customer Visits to Supplier

In some situations, you may be required to have the customer visit your facilities. This is particularly true with government and military business, in which the individual, and sometimes his family as well, are fully compensated for their travel. If this can be arranged and you look after them well at your end, it can be a major factor in closing the deal.

The author once had to host some foreign customers who were visiting a security company he represented. The plan was that they would all meet for dinner the first night and go on from there. When the author and his client's representative arrived at the visitor's hotel, only the elder leader of the delegation was there.

They waited in the bar for the two younger members of the delegation for over an hour, then the leader casually suggested they go to dinner. They did not see the other two until late the next morning, after they had missed some of the briefings. The author later found out that they had spent the evening in a local brothel, probably with the blessing of the elder and envious leader.

The visit must have been a success, because shortly afterward the company got an order from them.

Follow-up

Every marketing and sales course stresses the need for follow-up. This is even more important in international marketing, where the phrase out of sight, out of mind is particularly true. The best follow-up is to keep in regular touch with your agent. Sending new brochures or new product information is not enough.

Telephone or fax your agent every week or so, either for an update on a hot customer they are working or just to talk. You can tell them about contracts you have won in other countries, for example. This is the kind of information they can use in their own marketing efforts. You may want to get their input on new brochures or new company gifts you are planning. All of this makes them feel part of your company, which can be a significant motivator.

Personal Relationships

You will find that, as your international business grows, you will make many personal relationships with customers and agents in various countries. In many countries, good personal relationships are very important for good business relationships. These personal relationships in foreign countries are important because they help you to learn their customs, and it helps you realize that people are much the same the world over.

The author became very close to his agent and his family in Thailand. One evening in a fancy restaurant in Bangkok, the agent's wife carved the Peking duck herself, then took most of it home in a doggy bag. Throughout the evening, the teenage daughter was embarrassed and complained about having to be out with her parents instead of with her friends, and the eight-year-old refused to eat anything. Does this set a familiar scene?

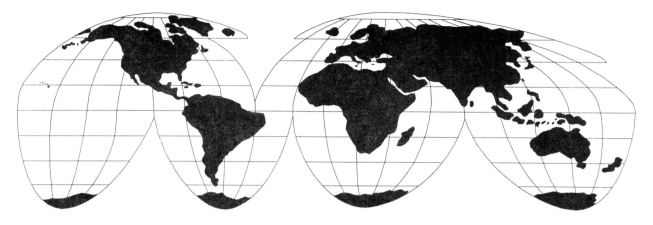

Chapter 25

Pricing and Payoffs

The pricing aspects of international marketing can be a challenge. As part of your marketing effort, you will have to deal with the price questions, which may include various methods of payment, industrial benefits, countertrade, and other aspects. There is also the question of commissions to be paid to agents and representatives. In addition, in many countries you must face the inevitable under-the-table payment issue. These aspects are addressed in this chapter.

Pricing for International Sales

There are several pricing methods for international sales that can be used, depending on the product and the market you are considering. Three of the most popular methods are:

- Domestic costs plus. This is the easiest pricing method. You simply take your domestic price and add on your export costs. You may want to refine it a bit by subtracting your domestic marketing costs from the domestic price before you add on the international marketing costs.

- Full cost calculation. You review all of your costs associated with the product, including those associated with your domestic product as well as the new costs introduced by the international market.

- Marginal costing. You identify the fixed costs currently being covered by your domestic sales that will not increase with increased sales, and you exclude them from the costs of the products going into new markets. You do, of course, add up all other costs. This gives you a more competitive price because of the lower base cost. In some situations it could even be lower than your domestic price.

You will probably arrive at different prices for each country, depending on the costs associated with the country. For strategic purposes, however, in some situations you may want to consider deviating from the price you arrived at through normal calculations. For example, you may want to do market-penetration pricing to quickly establish yourself in a particular market. To do this, you initially sell your product at a lower price than the competition, then as your product becomes known, you gradually increase the price.

If there is no initial competition for your product, you may want to sell at a price as high as the market will bear. When competition surfaces, you can lower your price to meet it. Because of the higher profits you made in the beginning, you can afford to sell even lower and possibly drive out the competition.

Pricing your product for international sales involves several additional costs that must be considered in your final price to the customer. Many of these costs may also apply to your competition, but some may not. As you go through the international pricing activity, bear in mind how your competitors will be doing their pricing. It's a very competitive world, so you have to be competitive to survive in it.

The first thing to do is review your basic costs for items that could change in the international market. For example, if your product involves installation and setup (set to work) as part of the price, the cost could be substantially higher in the international market. If you are using your own personnel, you must allow for their travel and living costs in the new market. If you are relying on local labor to do the work, you must be sure they are as available, qualified, and productive as you are accustomed to. To be on the safe side, you may want to add an additional percentage to these costs for risk management. You never know what will happen in a foreign country, but you can be sure you will have little control over it.

A good example of unexpected extra installation costs was experienced by the author in a Latin American country. He had sold some equipment to the country's navy, which they were going to install in their vessels under the supervision of the company technician. The technician frantically called after he had been in the country about five days. It had taken them three days to make the first boat available for the installation, and that was just the start of the problems. The shipyard that was to do the work was not very well organized. Nobody seemed to know anything about the project. To top it off, the technician was being escorted wherever he went by an armed guard. He was a nervous wreck, thinking they had him under some kind of arrest.

The author called the agent in the country to get him to sort things out. The agent explained that the armed guard was to protect the technician because that part of the country was notorious for bandits and kidnappers. How do you explain this to a scared technician? The agent said he would talk to his naval contacts.

A few days later, a calmer technician called to say that things had changed remarkably. The head of the shipyard had been fired. The remaining workers were being extremely cooperative in getting the work done, and it was soon to be completed. However, the company had to absorb the unexpected costs associated with the technician's extended stay and the bonus holidays he received to get over his experience.

Another point you must consider is that you and your foreign customers may have very different expectations with regard to what they are buying. This can result in additional warranty costs, extensive delays in receiving your payment, or even total rejection of the product after it is delivered. Again, you should add some risk management costs to your basic pricing to cover this situation.

If you must alter your product, your production equipment, or the labeling, the costs must also be accounted for. Here you must decide the number of sales over which you will amortize your costs. Your agent should be able to provide you with information to aid in this decision, but be conservative and expect the worst.

A company was asked to bid on a chemical product for the Vietnam war. They really did not want the business, so in their bid they amortized all of their equipment and set up costs over only a six-month production period. They won the contract and began several years of production which, after the first six months, provided embarrassingly high profits. The product was Agent Orange.

Export Costs

Your foreign customers will usually want prices based on delivery to their country, including all insurance and customs costs. Much has been written about these usually encountered export costs, but the best way to deal with them is through an experienced shipping agent who will be able to provide you with most of the information you need. Make sure you have this information before you make your bid so you can include these costs. Here are some of the items you must consider.

- Preparation for shipment. You may not be able to use your usual shipping containers, depending on the mode of shipping.
- Delivery to shipping agent. Most shipping agents will include the cost of picking up your shipment as part of the overall freight cost. Make sure it is in their quotation.
- Shipping costs to the foreign country. These costs will vary with the mode of transportation and the type of containerization you use.
- Unloading charges. These may or may not be included in your shipping agent's quotation.
- Terminal charges. How long will your shipment wait in the foreign terminal until it is picked up and delivered to your customer?
- Longload or heavy-loading charges. Is your product outside the normal shipping parameters?
- Documentation costs. You will have to pay to get the shipping documents certified, if required.
- Shipping insurance. The cost of insurance will vary with the mode of transportation used.
- Customs duties. Customs charges to bring the products into the country can be a surprise additional expense if you do not include them in your bid. Find out about them before you bid, and make sure you include all of these costs. It is not unusual to have customs duties plus handling charges leveled on the shipment by the government of the receiving country at, for example, four percent for customs duty and one percent for handling charge.
- Other insurance costs. Your shipping agent may offer additional insurance over the usual shipping insurance.

Additional Pricing Considerations

Once you have established your costs for the export product, you must consider usual overhead costs that will increase. Your marketing costs have certainly increased and so have your communication costs, so it is probable your overhead will also increase. You should therefore consider increasing your gross profit to cover these costs. Also, you may want to add some overall risk management costs.

Another consideration is to build into your bid an additional percentage for negotiating allowance because your initial bid price may not be accepted by the foreign customer. You will be surprised at how happy a customer is when, after considerable debate, you are able to drop the price by five percent. If this cushion was built into the bid, you can also be happy. You will be even happier if your built-in negotiating allowance was ten percent.

You should always quote in U.S. dollars and try to get the ensuing contract in U.S. dollars. This is a currency metric used throughout the world and also in quotations by companies outside the United States. With inflation running at hundreds and sometimes thousands of percent per year in some countries, if you quote in their currency, by the time you get their money it may be worthless. Insist on being paid in American dollars. If, however, for some reason you must quote in the local currency, be sure you include in your pricing a risk factor for currency fluctuations. Your banker may be able to help you with this.

Agent Commission Pricing

Only when you have established your overall cost and the price you want to get for the product do you apply the agent's fee. Do not simply add the fee to your price because the agent is expecting a percentage of the final price paid by the customer, not a percentage of the price you will get. What you will receive is the final customer price less the agent's fee. This is a surprisingly common mistake made in bids, which can be costly. For example, assume that you have established the price you want to receive for the sale at $1,000,000. If you simply add a ten percent ($100,000) agent fee to this figure for a bid price of $1,100,000, you have just lost several thousand dollars. The agent fee is ten percent of the sale price. If your bid price is $1,100,000, the agent would get ten percent of it, or $110,000, which is $10,000 more than you allowed for. The net price to you would be only $990,000.

To work out the final price including the agent's fee, you must divide your price by one, minus the agent's fee. In this example you divide the $1,000,000 you expect to get as net payment by (1 – 0.10 = 0.90), with the resulting figure of $1,111,111 as your bid price. The agent gets ten percent of this, or $111,111, and you end up with your $1,000,000.

Another thing to consider is how you make the commission payments to the agent. In most instances, the agent payment procedure is very straightforward. When you receive payment, you simply send the agent a check for his commission or discount. However, some agents will want to establish special arrangements to collect their money. They will want this for several reasons, but usually it is to counter inflation or minimize taxes. A typical request is for the agent's money to be deposited in U.S. dollars in a U.S. bank. The agent can then use credit cards through the U.S. bank to pay for expenses in U.S. dollars. This way the agent's income is not eroded by inflation at home, and sometimes an agent can make money on the exchange rate fluctuations.

The most unusual agent payment procedure the author was involved with was for an agent from Iceland. As the agent explained it, commission payments made directly to him in Iceland would be taxed immediately by the government at over 50 percent, regardless of the expenses associated with earning the money.

He set up a company in North America into which we made his payments. The author was the local director of the company, and the official company head office address was the author's home. The agent's commission payments were made to the North American company and deposited in a North American bank from which he paid his expenses.

Countertrade

The practice of countertrade in international business is rapidly increasing. Countertrade is often very complex, because it can involve a number of parties quite divorced from the initial agreement to buy and sell a product. The problem is not as daunting as it may sound, because there is a growing number of brokers who will handle the situation for you. For example, a government may want to pay you in coffee beans. A broker may be available who will take the coffee beans and issue an LC for the payment. But to do this, they will charge a percentage, typically six percent, of the total value plus expenses. These added costs must be applied to the purchase price you quote to your customer.

The above example is the simplest form of countertrade, known as barter, where goods are traded for goods. When dealing with foreign governments, you may run into a form of countertrade known as counterpurchase. Here the foreign government agrees to buy your goods, and over a period of time you have to buy a variety of goods from them, usually at a ratio different from a straight one-to-one exchange. Your problem is to dispose of the goods to get your money. Be very wary of this arrangement, unless you know the quality of the foreign goods and are positive you can sell them.

Industrial Benefits

More and more governments are demanding industrial benefits when they make major purchases from other countries. One form of industrial benefit is the requirement that part of the project work be done in the receiving country. This gives them a chance to employ some of their locals and may provide these employees with experience in technology they would not normally be able to get.

During the Gulf War, Saudi Arabia discovered that most of their imported technical labor deserted them, and they were left with only a few of their own people capable of filling the gap. After the war, they set up a program to prevent this in the future and to update their own people on technology. This involved setting up a company that now employs Saudi citizens to manufacture components for and handle maintenance on military equipment purchased by the kingdom. Foreign suppliers of military equipment are asked to put some of the work into this Saudi company as an industrial benefit.

Another commonly required industrial benefit is to have part of the order built in the exporting country and the remaining part built in the importing country. This is particularly applicable to vessels, vehicles, and some forms of electronics. For example, the first three fast patrol boats of an order of six are built by your company, then the rest of the order are built under license in the country purchasing them. When this is a requirement, it may be better to share a small piece of the pie than fight for and lose the whole thing. The danger is that you may be setting up a future competitor in the importing country. In this time of rapidly changing technology, however, this may not be a problem for you. By the time the country is ready to produce the product competitively, you probably will have made sufficient technological improvements to it for the old version not be a threat to your business.

Some countries will simply require that you spend a certain percentage of the contract value in the country. You can do this via the methods mentioned above, or you can purchase other goods and services from the country. In some instances, even the cost of holding conventions in the country has counted as an industrial benefit.

Customer Payoffs

Whether you like it or not and whether it is illegal or not, customer payoffs do happen all over the world. The practice is rampant in most developing countries and former Communist countries and also goes on in Western Europe as well as some parts of the United States and Canada. It has been going on for centuries, and in many countries, it is part of their commerce. Do not be surprised when you are confronted with it. As a precaution, you should know the requirements of the U.S. government's Foreign Business Practices Act, which forbids bribing foreign officials to get a contract.

It is part of the agent's unwritten responsibility to handle all the details associated with this seedier side of international marketing, if it is required. You are kept completely out of it and unaware of it. The usual situation is that, in order for an agent to get a contract, officials who can influence the decision must be promised payment to be on the agent's side. Each of these officials is entitled to a certain percentage of the value of the transaction. Good agents know these officials and probably work with them on many projects. They must negotiate a percentage payoff with them and make the payoffs when the transaction is completed. The money for all of this is included in the agent's commission and included in the price paid for the goods or services.

A marketing friend of the author's was confronted with this issue very blatantly in a Latin American country. After two days of going around discussing the project with various government officials, the agent explained the facts of life to the marketer. He said there was strong competition from two European countries for the business, and the customer did not really care whose product was better or even whose price was less. What mattered was who had the better government contacts and how they were looked after.

Then he laid it all out.

"You have now met the men who, I think, will decide if we get the contract or not. Mr. ____, whose department will use the equipment wants five percent. His boss, Mr. ____, will get only three percent. Mr. ____, who does the purchasing will also get three percent. The Deputy Minister must get five percent as well because he has to share it with some others. And I need at least nine percent for myself. After all, it is I who can end up in jail."

Meet the Sales Challenges

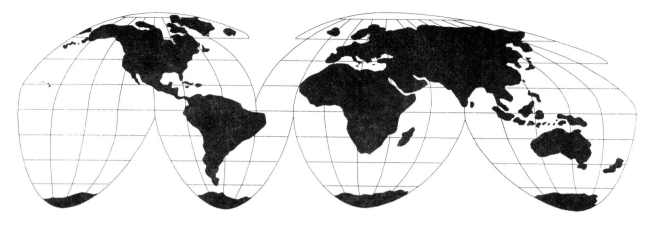

Chapter 26

Agent and Customer Issues

As in all marketing activities, there will be some problems with customers. In international marketing, there may be added problems caused by the agent. This chapter touches on some of these problems and makes recommendations about how to prevent and solve them.

Agent Inactivity

A common problem in international marketing is agent inactivity, when your agent in a country appears to be doing nothing on your behalf. There are many reasons for this. The agent may be too busy with other product lines, your product may be too difficult to sell, they may not be able to make enough money from your sales, or they may not sufficiently understand your product to promote it adequately. If you suspect they are not doing enough on your behalf, you should find out why as soon as possible and correct the problem. Otherwise, you could lose valuable marketing time in the country.

A major cause of agent inactivity is lack of support from the company they are representing. Many companies behave as though all you have to do is sign an agreement with an agent, then forget about them and let them make the sales on their own. You would not expect that from your own marketing department, so do not expect it from an agent. Both need company support in order to support the company.

Keep in touch regularly with the agent. Sending them new brochures or new product information is not enough, although some companies do not even do that. Telephone or fax regularly, either for an update on a hot customer they are working on or just to talk. For example, you can talk about contracts you have won in other countries. They can use this information in their own marketing. You may ask for their input on new brochures or new company gifts you are planning. All of this will make them feel part of your company, and they will be more active for you.

If the agent does have problems in promoting your product, get them to discuss the problems with you, even though they may be reluctant to do so. Quite often the problem will be the difficulty of pushing your product against an established competing product. If this is the case, you can help them to better understand and promote the differentiators that make your product more appealing or advantageous to a buyer. It is possible your agent is conscious of only those product attributes that relate to those of the product they already knew about and did not realize that there are other differences that could be significant selling points. The whole thing boils down to good communications between you and your agent.

If all else fails and your agent is still not representing you the way you expect, you must terminate your agreement and replace them with another agent. The cleanest way is to wait until your agent agreement terminates, if you can wait that long. Otherwise, you will have to use the termination clause in your contract. Whichever way you chose, get on with it as soon as possible. Otherwise you will be wasting valuable marketing time, and your product will be getting shop worn in the country.

Agent Overactivity

On the other hand, you do not want to goad an agent into setting you up to have to respond to unqualified leads. This can happen very easily if you push them too much. You may not hear from your agent for months, then shortly after you contact them, they will ask you for a detailed proposal for a customer. This may be based only on a telephone inquiry they received, rather than a qualified lead, and they are just trying to appease you. Watch for this pattern of agent behavior, and if you suspect it, ask the agent for more qualification of the opportunity. For example, ask him to find out when the customer plans to place a contract or order, what his desired deliver schedule is, and if there is an approved budget.

Political Issues

If your product is aimed at government or military customers, you will be involved with the politics of the country whether you want to be or not. Your first involvement will be during the agent selection process. As discussed in previous chapters, the agent's government and military contacts are a major factor in their selection in some countries, but these contacts can change with the politics, and your agent may become ineffective because of these changes.

The best example of this is close to home. The Mexican constitution requires that the president change every six years. When this happens, a large portion of the senior bureaucrats and military also change because these are political appointments, which is not unlike the aftermath of a U.S. presidential election. The difference is that your agent probably depends heavily on their contacts with these former appointees for their business and will then have to take time and resources to develop new relationships. This will, of course, slow your business. More astute agents will try to ease this transition problem by courting likely new appointees before the election.

Political relationships between countries can also seriously affect your business. This is particularly true if there is a political rift between your country and the country you are marketing to and if the rift has trade overtones. However, if the problem is with a country that is your trading competitor, it can be to your advantage. For example, a few years ago a political and trade disagreement developed between Malaysia and the United Kingdom. The Malaysians actually had a campaign within their country to buy British last. It got so bad that Margaret Thatcher, the Prime Minister of Britain, had to visit Malaysia to try to improve the situation. Needless to say, British companies had a problem doing business in Malaysia during this period, but the door was open wider than usual for other countries.

Understanding of Technology

If your product is heavily technological, problems can develop based on the lack of understanding of the technology by your agent and your customers. These are usually associated with the agent overselling the product's capabilities, creating expectations by the customer that are too high. The problem manifests itself after the product has been delivered, is being used by the customer, and has several negative results such as high warranty costs; loss of good relations between the customer, the agent, and your company; and loss of follow-up sales. The best solution is to prevent the problem in the first place by making sure your agent and customers understand the implications and limitations of the technology. This, unfortunately, is not always possible to convey during the exuberance of marketing.

The author sold some commercial fishing sonar equipment to a large fishing fleet in Chile, and the follow-up sales looked very good. Then the agent reported that the fishing company was very unhappy with the sonar because it did not have the range they were told it had. The author flew down to the northern Chile port of Iquique where the boat with the sonar was located and met with the fishing company officials and the boat's captain. Ironically, the captain thought the sonar was great and was using it regularly to out catch the other boats in the area. But the range was indeed limited.

The author suggested to the company that the problem may be an adverse affect of the water conditions around Iquique and then explained the technical details to them. One of the officials contacted a friend in the Chilean Navy to confirm this information. He was told that the sonar conditions around the area were so bad they were lucky to get anything on the sonar. It was all being caused by El Niño, the periodic increase in water temperature in the Pacific Ocean associated with variations in the world weather patterns. Although the customer did not fully understand the reason for the drop in the sonar's range, he understood there was a legitimate technological limitation to the equipment, something that should have been pointed out to him at the beginning.

Payoff Problems

Probably the worst agent and customer problem is when the agent fails to make the promised payoffs to the customer. You will probably not have known that this was required, but you will soon suspect something is wrong. The customer will cause problems in the contract, and you will not get any follow-up business. There is very little you can do about this, other than change agents and have the new agent correct the situation if possible.

A European marketer was caught up with this problem in an Asian country. The country was, and still is, heavily controlled by the military, though in a concealed way. The marketer had made a fairly large sale to the government, and his agent, who had excellent connections, was able to get them to make a very substantial down payment upon signing the contract. The down payment was sent to the company, which in turn sent a substantial percentage of the payment to the agent for his commission.

Then the problems began. The first indication was trouble in clearing the shipment through the country's customs. The agent was not available to help. Next, the milestone payment, due on delivery of the equipment, was not forthcoming. Again, the agent could not be contacted to help. The marketer had to visit the country to sort things out. Once there he discovered that the agent was no longer in business. During private discussions with some of the customers, he also discovered the agent had left with all the commission money before making the agreed payoffs to local officials. This was a foolish thing to do in a military-controlled country, as the agent was soon located. Presumably the payments were extracted from him, because the contract began to run smoothly again. Needless to say, the marketer never used that agent again. Probably nobody did.

———————————

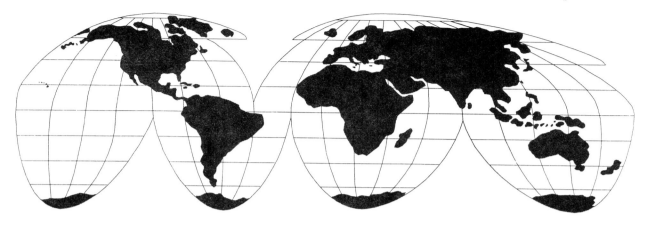

Chapter 27

Watching Out for Dirty Tricks

International marketing is such big business, with very high stakes at times, that companies and agents are not averse to resorting to dirty tricks to get contracts. This chapter outlines some of the underhanded activities you may encounter. Keep an eye out for them. As the economic battles intensify, so will the dirty tricks.

Agent Pressures for an Agreement

If you have a product that looks like a big seller in a country, you will be inundated with agents trying to represent you. As discussed previously, it is best not to sign an agreement with an agent until you are sure that agent is the right one for you and your product. The best way to test this is to have them introduce you to real customers to prove their worth.

If need be, you can give an agent a letter of intent stating that you will enter into an agreement with them if they are instrumental in getting some business going for you. Most agents will settle for this letter for a while, but soon they will pressure you for a full agency agreement.

In a developing country where the author was trying to sell equipment to the local military, an agent pulled a very high-pressure tactic to convince the author to engage him. The agent claimed to have good military connections but insisted on an agreement or letter of intent before he did anything. The author finally persuaded him to prove his connections. He reluctantly did so by having the author invited to demonstrate the equipment at a military base. There were to be two demonstrations on two consecutive days. On the first day, they set up the equipment in the morning and in the afternoon gave the demonstration to some potential customers. Everything went very well. The agent had made sure that key customers attended the demonstration, and they asked many questions that indicted serious interest. The author was elated at the sales possibilities and left the equipment set up inside the base for the next day's demonstration.

The next morning when he arrived at the entrance to the military base, the guards told him that he was not allowed on the base. He tried to make some phone calls to the military people who looked after him the previous day, but nobody would talk to him. Finally, the would-be agent drove up to the entrance gate from inside the base. He casually strode over and asked the author if he was having a problem. The sly smirk on his face said it all.

The author agreed to go back to the hotel with him, where they signed a letter of intent. Then they were all friends again. That afternoon the author was able to easily get on the base to do the demonstration. The attendees, who had to be rescheduled, acted as if nothing had happened, although some of them must have known of the incident. It was quite obvious this agent had a very strong influence with the military, which is what you want for this kind of business.

Competing Agent Influences

When selecting an agent, your objective is to select one who has influence with your prospective customers. Always remember, however, that your competition, no matter where they come from, have the same objective. It is therefore inevitable that you will get caught up in situations of competing influences as well as competing products.

For example, you and your agent may be briefing a group of customers when the briefing ends with a question and answer session. One of the audience will ask a number of embarrassing questions that highlight the shortcomings of your product. In all likelihood, the heckler is associated with a competing agent and product and is trying to make your product look inferior so his colleagues will buy from your competitor. If you know who the competition is, you can counter this heckling by mentioning the shortcomings of the competing product and explaining how yours is better.

There is another practice that is becoming popular in some countries and is even more underhanded. Foreign suppliers are paying agencies to block the business of other suppliers even when the agency is not contracted to make any sales. The income for the agency comes from preventing business, not getting it. If you do know it is happening, get your agent to deal with it, possibly by discretely discussing the situation with the customer.

Corrupt Government Officials

In some countries, government officials treat corruption and payoffs as a way of life and part of their income. This is particularly true in post-communist Russia. The stories are legion about how local officials must be bribed in order for the foreign companies to do business and how the local Mafia has to be paid off for the same reason. The standard approach is to affiliate with a local Russian partner who looks after this dirty part of the business. Instances have occurred, however, when this partner has turned against the foreigner and become one of the extortionists. Instances have also occurred where the local partner has been murdered because he would not go along with the Mafia. It is not easy doing business in Russia, as many American companies are learning the hard way.

Russia is not the only place with corrupt government officials. Nigeria has been documented as the most corrupt place to do business in the world. Your local U.S. Department of Commerce trade officials probably have file cabinets full of complaint letters from companies that have been ripped off trying to do business there.

Sucker Bids

Another customer dirty trick to watch out for that can cause you to waste a lot of time and resources is the sucker, or straw man, bids. This usually happens in conjunction with government contracts in countries that have fairly rigid government controls on purchasing. The situation is that an office in the government has decided they want to purchase a particular product from a particular company. Their regulations, however, require them to get and assess bids from a number of companies, usually at least three, before they can make the selection of who will get the contract. They try to get at least two other companies to put in a bid, knowing full well that these companies will never get the contract. They do this by giving the requirement to gullible agents and encouraging them to get bids from their foreign suppliers.

Industrial Espionage

Industrial espionage has become the successor to cold war spy activities. If you are involved with technologically advanced products, you could be targeted. The U.S. government has become quite concerned about this technology theft, because American technology is a prime target. Steps are being taken to cut these losses, but it is really up to the companies themselves to prevent it. One of the most likely times and places for it to happen is during an international marketing activity.

You may be particularly vulnerable at trade shows. There have been instances when, during the night, staff from a company displaying at a show went to the booth of a competitor, opened up the equipment, and took pictures of the electronics inside. This is a very amateurish activity. Nevertheless, it has happened, and forms of it will continue to happen. So be very careful about leaving your equipment unattended at trade shows.

On a higher level, a few years ago the U.S. government openly warned American companies that the French spy agency was tasked to get information on American technology during the Paris Air Show. This resulted in a number of big U.S. companies dropping out of the show before it started. If this is happening in Paris, think of what might go on at airshows in places like Singapore or Dubai.

Sabotage

Sabotage is another underhanded business practice you may encounter, perpetuated by your competitors. As previously discussed, in-country product demonstrations are often a requirement to make the sale. Sometimes these are in the form of a field trial contest between competing products, with the winner getting the contract. This is particularly true with military products when the competitors are from different countries. Some of these competing countries are not very ethical in their business practices.

A British company was involved with a sabotage attack from a competing French company. They were both trying to sell army radios to a developing country. The competition had gotten to the point of a field trial in the country, where the two products went head to head. One morning, the British radios would not work, and they had to drop out of the competition. Back at their facilities, they discovered the radios had been opened and a critical component was damaged in each one. Since the two companies were quartered in the same area during the field trial, it was easy to guess who had done the damage during the night.

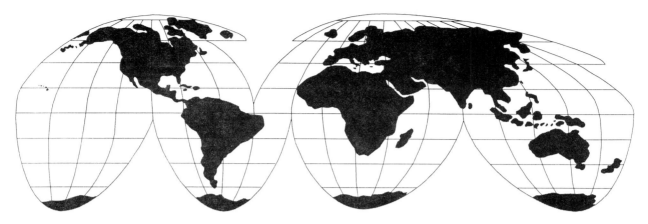

Chapter 28

Making the Sale

This is what it is all about, making the sale. This chapter addresses some of the aspects associated with an international sale that you may not have encounted in your domestic business.

Contracts

The first difference you are going to run across in international contracts is language. The buyer will usually insist that the contract be in their language, and you will probably have to agree to it. Be sure to insist that you receive a copy of the contract in plenty of time to have it translated and reviewed by your contracts people before the signing. It is also common for the buyer to insist the contract be governed by the laws of their country. You will probably have to agree to this as well.

The sales contract will have most of the usual terms and conditions. Because you are dealing with a foreign country, it should also include:

- Currency used in the transaction
- Law governing the contract
- Adequate descriptions of the goods or services being sold

- Detailed payment terms, for example Letter of Credit details
- Delivery terms
- Freight costs
- Insurance details and who pays the costs
- Shipping details

Payment Methods

The customer payment method will depend on the product and the business arrangement you have with your agent. If you are selling stock items through a distributor, the payment procedures are quite different than if you are providing and installing equipment over a period of time. The most common methods of payment for international transactions are:

- Advance payment. The importer pays for the goods prior to their being shipped. This method is obviously the best for the exporter but is not always achievable. The best you can usually hope for is a 25 to 30 percent down payment on signing the contract, then milestone payments after that.
- Open account. The account is settled on a regular basis, usually monthly. This method favors the importer and may be convenient for regular, high-volume shipments.
- Consignment. After the goods are shipped, the exporter owns them until they are sold, even when they are in the country of destination. You need a lot of faith in your agent or whoever you have looking after your goods to enter into this arrangement.
- Letters of Credit. This is the most usual method of settling international transactions. This subject is covered in more detail below.

Letters of Credit

A Letter of Credit (LC) is an agreement between your company, your bank, the purchaser's bank, and the purchaser. The terms of an LC can vary, but usually it works this way. The purchaser arranges with their bank to set aside the required amount of funds for the goods being purchased from you the exporter. Their bank then issues an LC with the terms required for you to get the money. Your bank confirms with the purchaser's bank that the LC and money are available, then informs you. When you receive the confirmation and terms, you can ship the goods and take the shipping and other documents required by the terms of the LC to your bank as proof of shipment. Your bank reports to the purchaser's bank that the terms of the LC have been met, and the purchaser's bank transfers the payment to your bank. Your bank then pays the money to you.

Unfortunately, the LC is not always as simple as it sounds. There are a number of different types of LC, and the shipping and payment terms can be quite involved. These are the most common LCs.

- Revocable Letter of Credit. This LC may be canceled or amended at any time after it is issued, without your consent and without notice to you, the exporter, or your bank. Fortunately, this type of LC is not very popular.

- Irrevocable Letter of Credit. The purchaser's bank issues an LC that cannot be canceled or amended before the expiration date without the express consent of all parties concerned. Because this LC still depends on the business practices of both banks, it may not be reliable in some situations.

- Irrevocable, Confirmed Letter of Credit. The issuing bank confirms the credit in the LC and undertakes to make the required payments to the exporter, provided that the exporter complies with the terms and conditions of the LC.

Needless to say, you should always try to get an Irrevocable, Confirmed Letter of Credit, or at least an Irrevocable Letter of Credit if you trust the issuing bank. Never accept a Revocable Letter of Credit unless you are confident of operating in a situation similar to an open account relationship with your importer.

There are some practical aspects about Letters of Credit that should be considered. Banks charge a fee for this service, usually a percentage of the value of the LC. The rate depends on a number of factors, such as the issuing country, the issuing bank, the terms and conditions, and other factors. In addition, despite what your banks may tell you, it can take months to get an LC organized, and it can take weeks to receive payment, even after you meet its terms and conditions. For some transactions, it may be to your advantage to use other methods of payment such as one of those previously mentioned.

Delivery Arrangements

Make sure the delivery arrangements are stipulated in the contract or purchase order. As discussed previously, there are several delivery options with varying costs. Pay particular attention to terms concerning where the customer will assume responsibility for the shipment. This will affect not only your delivery costs but your insurance as well. You do not want the goods sitting in a terminal in the customer's country until they decide to pick them up, while you pay the terminal fees and risk losing part of the shipment to pilferage.

You should also be aware that the customer may request delivery to an unexpected location. This could be because their end use of the product is in that location or because of other considerations. For example, many countries now have tax-free zones, locations where goods can be shipped into and out of the country without paying import or export duties. Companies that use the imported goods in other products that are exported can be set up in these locations and use local labor to produce the export product.

Setup and Training

If your product has to be set up for the customer or you have to train the customer to use it, be prepared for unexpected problems. The required caliber of work force may not be available to help you do the setup, and your staff may have to do all the work, at more time and expense to you. Another problem in some countries is that the labor or union laws will not allow your staff to do any work. You agent should have warned you about this, or you should have checked it out earlier with the embassy. All you can do is work around the situation, probably at additional cost to you.

Training can also be an issue if the people you are to train do not have the basic knowledge or skills to absorb the training. This is a very common problem. Your training approach may then have to go back to some basic instruction. If you allow for this in your pricing, you may even make some profit on it. If the basic training is not required, you will make even more.

Warranties

In addition to the usual warranty costs you normally incur with your domestic customers, be prepared for them to be higher overseas, particularly if your product is of a technical nature. The customer may have problems operating it and damage it in the process or complain that it doesn't work, not realizing that they do not know how to make it work. Either way, you end up with additional costs, so you will want to increase your warranty costs in your pricing.

The fact that your warranty is for only a year or two after delivery is often disregarded by foreign customers. They will still want you to make free repairs long after the warranty expires. If you don't, you run the risk of alienating the customer and jeopardizing your business in that country. The solution is usually to come to some compromise, such as the customer making additional purchases from you if you make the requested post-warranty repairs.

Subsequent Business

In many countries, once you make a few sales and establish yourself as a good company to deal with there, they will stay with you, so your future sales will be much easier. This is a happy state to get into, but you have to earn it. You must bend over backwards when dealing with any issues associated with your initial sales, such as timely delivery, setup, and warrantee work. Going the extra mile may seem difficult at the time, but the potential for subsequent business from good current relationships may be well worth the effort.

You will want to make sure your agent aggressively goes after potential business and does not simply rest on their laurels. You can help by discussing the possibilities with your agent and developing a plan to go after subsequent business. You may decide to do some in-country advertising. You may have identified another customer community that can use the product and an associate agent that your agent could work with to develop additional markets. You have worked hard to get where you are, so go after the added benefits.

In Conclusion

Now that you have worked your way through this book, even if you've only read it without attempting any markets, you should feel better about testing the international waters. If you have used the book to actually work the international scene, you have probably experienced some of the pitfalls encountered by those first venturing off-shore and the book enabled you to ease these problems.

You might also want read a companion publication from The Oasis Press entitled *Export Now: A Guide for Small Business* by Richard L. Liza. This book provides more details on the mechanics of exporting. Other sources of information include the many publications put out by the U.S. Department of Commerce. You can find out more about their services and publications from their web site <www.i-trade.com>.

The international marketplace should no longer scare you. Instead, you can now look at the world as a huge opportunity. So get out there and build on your knowledge. You will find it very rewarding and a lot of fun.

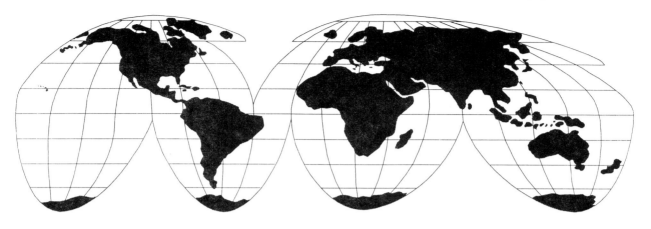

Predeparture Checklists

This appendix provides a handy checklist to help you prepare for a marketing visit to a foreign country. It is divided into long-lead issues that should be addressed several months prior to the trip and things that should be prepared a few days prior to leaving on the trip.

The checklist is by no means complete because you will want to add items specific to your particular business. It is good to get into the habit of adding to the list or jotting down a note whenever you think of something else to take with you or that must be done prior to the trip. Another helpful tool you can set up long before the trip is a travel basket or table where notes, files, or other items pertaining to the trip can be placed together. When it comes time to pack, you will have all the items in one place. Early preparation for a trip can help you avoid problems that result from forgetting essential information or items.

Marketing Trip Checklist

Several Months Prior To Trip

As soon as you know you will be making a marketing trip, consider the following activities.

☐ **Establish your objectives.** List what you want to accomplish on the trip. This may affect your overall preparations.

☐ **Do background reading.** Learn about the country you are going to visit, including its economy, climate, history, and customs.

☐ **Check out the country's holidays and working days.** You do not want to plan to visit a country during a prolonged local holiday or over a local weekend.

☐ **Identify potential agents.** Begin developing a list of potential agents to interview, if this is your purpose for the visit.

☐ **Check your passport expiration date.** Ensure your passport is up-to-date, or will not expire while you are traveling.

☐ **Obtain the necessary visas.** Identify visa requirements early, and make applications. It can sometimes take several weeks or even months to obtain a visa to visit some countries.

☐ **Identify required immunizations.** Some vaccinations must be given weeks or months prior to visiting a country.

☐ **Review your promotional literature.** Check over the brochures, video tapes, and company give-aways you will take with you, to ensure your have a sufficient supply. You may also want to get some translated into the language of the country you are visiting.

☐ **Check your business card supply.** Ensure you will have enough for the trip. You may also want to get them translated into the language of the country, printed with English on one side and the other language on the other.

☐ **Check your product samples and demonstration equipment.** Make sure you have the latest versions, and that they are functioning.

☐ **Have a carnet for demonstration equipment.** If you are taking demonstration equipment, ensure you have an up-to-date international carnet, or other appropriate documentation, that will allow you to take the equipment into the country and bring it back home without paying import duties.

☐ **Begin making appointments early.** People you wish to see may be absent during your planned visit, and you may have to rearrange your schedule.

☐ **Make your travel and hotel reservations early.** This way you can take advantage of any reduced fares and, more importantly, ensure space availability.

☐ **Get an international driver's license.** If you intend to rent a car on the trip, obtain an international driver's license from an automobile association.

☐ **Make rental car reservation and prepayment.** It is not always easy to rent cars in some countries. For many European countries, you can prepay for a rental car at considerably reduced rates prior to leaving the United States. Check with the major rental companies.

Marketing Trip Checklist

Several Days Prior To Trip

Begin packing or setting aside items for the trip several days prior to departure. In addition to your personal items, there are several things to remember.

☐ **Country information.** Take general information on the country that you will need while there, such as maps, conversion tables, and contact information.

☐ **Promotional literature.** Rather than carry a heavy load of company brochures, you may want to send some ahead.

☐ **Portable computer.** Load your portable computer or a travel disk with applicable files, price lists, proposals, and any other information you will need.

☐ **Business cards.** Take plenty because you will be passing them out frequently.

☐ **Company stationary.** Take blank stationary with the company letterhead for writing letters, quotations, and proposals to customers and agents.

☐ **Price lists.** Take up-to-date price lists, including the cost of insurance and freight to the country.

☐ **Samples and demonstration equipment.** Check the operation of samples and demonstration equipment you plan to take with you.

☐ **Carnet.** Check that the carnets are in order and are for the equipment your will be taking.

☐ **Passport.** Recheck your passport for expiration date, and make sure you take it.

☐ **Visas.** Ensure you have the proper visas for entry into the countries you plan to visit.

☐ **Passport photos.** Obtain and take extra passport photos for additional visas if required during the trip.

☐ **International certificates of vaccination.** Get the necessary vaccinations and inoculations, and have them entered in your International Certificate of Vaccination.

☐ **Medication for common diseases such as diarrhea and malaria.** Obtain recommended travel medication, and check expiration date on existing medications.

☐ **Hotel reservation confirmations.** Reconfirm hotel reservations.

☐ **Traveler's checks.** Obtain traveler's checks in U.S. dollars.

☐ **Currency of the country.** Obtain a small amount of the currency of the countries you are visiting to enable you to pay for immediate arrival expenses such as visas and taxis.

☐ **Inform embassy.** If appropriate, inform the trade officials at your embassy in the foreign countries of your itinerary.

☐ **Aircraft seat selection.** Make sure your travel agent has selected suitable seats for you, particularly if it is an overnight flight.

Notes

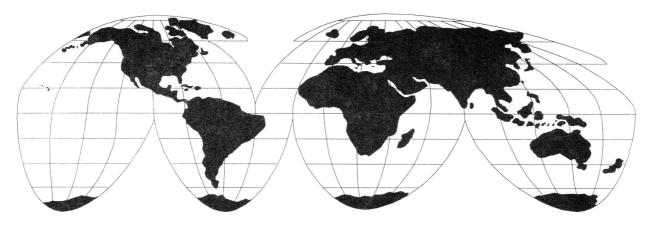

Information about 120 Countries

This appendix provides a handy reference to important marketing-related political, social, and economic information on the following countries. All references to dollars ($) are U.S. dollars unless otherwise stated, and all references to temperature are in degrees Fahrenheit. Political situations and health requirements change quickly, and travellers should check for the latest information. Some of the categories of information were not available for all countries, such as the crime rate, however, it is provided for most of the major trading countries. The gross domestic product (GDP) of each country is given, along with the GDP per capita. This will give you an idea of the wealth of the country and its people, that may affect your exporting decision. The currency exchange rates given are those at the time of writing, but they can change significantly with inflation and devaluation. Issues such as the Euro dollar (if and when it happens) will also affect exchange rates.

Much of the information in this appendix comes from the U.S. Central Intelligence Agency (CIA) *World Fact Book*. It can be accessed at their web site <www.odci.gov/cia/publications/factbook>. Market related information only is provided on the following countries.

Afghanistan	Honduras	Paraguay
Albania	Hong Kong	Peru
Algeria	Hungary	Philippines
Argentina	Iceland	Poland
Australia	India	Portugal
Austria	Indonesia	Puerto Rico
Bahrain	Iran	Qatar
Bangladesh	Iraq	Romania
Belarus	Ireland	Russia
Belgium	Israel	Rwanda
Bolivia	Italy	Saudi Arabia
Brazil	Jamaica	Singapore
Brunei	Japan	Slovakia
Bulgaria	Jordan	Slovenia
Burma (Myanmar)	Kazakhstan	Somalia
Cambodia	Kenya	South Africa
Cameroon	Kuwait	South Korea
Canada	Laos	Spain
Chile	Latvia	Sri Lanka
China	Lebanon	Sudan
Columbia	Liberia	Sweden
Costa Rica	Libya	Switzerland
Cote d'Ivoire (Ivory Coast)	Lithuania	Syria
Cuba	Madagascar	Taiwan (Republic of China)
Czech Republic	Malaysia	Tanzania
Denmark	Mexico	Thailand
Dominican Republic	Monaco	Trinidad and Tobago
Ecuador	Mongolia	Tunisia
Egypt	Morocco	Turkey
El Salvador	Mozambique	Uganda
Eritrea	Nepal	Ukraine
Estonia	Netherlands	United Arab Emirates
Ethiopia	New Zealand	United Kingdom
Finland	Nicaragua	United States of America
France	Nigeria	Uruguay
Georgia	North Korea	Venezuela
Germany	Norway	Vietnam (Viet Nam)
Ghana	Oman	Yemen
Greece	Pakistan	Zaire (Democratic
Guatemala	Panama	Republic of the Congo)
Haiti	Papua New Guinea	

Afghanistan

Official Name	Islamic State of Afghanistan.
Population	Approximately 24 million.
Main Cities	Kabul is the capital.
Government	New constitution still being developed.
Language	Official languages are Pushtu and Dari.
Religion	Islam 99%, other 1%.
Literacy Rate	29%
GDP	$18 billion. $800 per capita.
Currency	Afghani (Af). Approximately 17,000 to one U.S. dollar.
Exports	Natural gas, fruits, carpets.
Imports	Petroleum, foodstuffs.
Local Agent	Recommended.
Climate	Varies with altitude. In Kabul winter temperatures average 90 degrees.
Health	Vaccination certificates for cholera are mandatory if travelling from an infected area. Typhoid immunization and anti-malaria medication are recommended.
Local Holidays	Friday is the weekly holiday, and some places Thursday as well. The Muslim month of Ramadan is observed. Revolution Day (April 27), Worker's Day (May 1), Independence Day (August 18).
Local Time	9 A.M. EST is 6:30 P.M. in Afghanistan.
Travel Documents	Passport and visas required, obtained with an Afghan sponsor. It is not possible to obtain a tourist visa. Exit permits required.

Albania

Official Name	Republic of Albania.
Population	Approximately 3.3 million.
Main Cities	Tirane is the capital.
Government	Elected People's Assembly. New constitution being developed.
Language	Official language is Albanian. Greek is also spoken.
Religion	Islam 70%, Greek Orthodox 20%, Roman Catholic 10%.
Literacy Rate	72%
GDP	$4.4 billion. $1,290 per capita.
Currency	Lek (L). Approximately 150 to one U.S. dollar.
Exports	Metals, electricity, petroleum, vegetables, fruit.

Imports	Machinery, consumer goods, foodstuffs.
Local Agent	Recommended.
Climate	Hot and dry summers, cool and wet winters.
Local Holidays	Liberation Day (November 29).
Local Time	9 A.M. EST is 3 P.M. in Albania.
Travel Documents	Passport and visa required, obtained at Albanian diplomatic mission abroad.

Algeria

Official Name	Democratic and Popular Republic of Algeria.
Population	Approximately 30 million.
Main Cities	Algiers is the capital. Other major centers are Oran, Constantine, Annaba and Setif.
Government	Republic with elected president and National People's Assembly. Second round of elections in 1991 were canceled by the military.
Language	Arabic is the official language, but French is the language of business.
Religion	National religion is Islam.
Literacy Rate	57%
GDP	$116 billion. $4,000 per capita.
Currency	Algerian Dinar (AD). Approximately 57 to one U.S. dollar.
Exports	Petroleum and natural gas products.
Imports	Industrialized products, foodstuffs.
Regulations	The government controls the main industries and most imports.
Local Agent	Local agents are not permitted.
Business Tips	Avoid visiting during the month of Ramadan.
Health	International Certificate of Vaccination against smallpox may be required and against cholera and yellow fever if arriving from an infected area. Immunizations against cholera, typhoid, and polio, plus medication against malaria recommended.
Business Hours	8 A.M. to 5 P.M. Saturday through Wednesday.
Climate	Along the coast the summers are hot and dry with temperatures from about 80 to 95 degrees. The winter is cool and wet with temperatures from about 45 to 60 degrees.
Local Holidays	The Muslim weekend of Thursday and Friday is observed. Muslim holidays, including the month of Ramadan, are observed. New Year's Day (January 1), Anniversary Day (June 19), Independence Day (July 5), Anniversary of the Revolution (November 10).
Local Time	9 A.M. EST is 3 P.M. in Algeria.
Travel Documents	Passport and visa valid for 90 days.

Argentina

Official Name	Argentine Republic.
Population	Approximately 36 million.
Main Cities	Buenos Aires is the capital. Other main cities are Cordoba, Rosario, Mendoza and La Plata.
Government	Elected president with a congress consisting of a senate and a house of deputies.
Language	Spanish.
Religion	Roman Catholic 90%, Protestant 2%, other 8%.
Literacy Rate	95%
Crime Rate	1,573 total offenses per 100,000 persons, 6.7 murders per 100,000 persons, 343 thefts per 100,000 persons.
GDP	$297 billion. $8,600 per capita.
Currency	Peso. Approximately equal to the U.S. dollar.
Exports	Cereal grains, meat, leather.
Imports	Fuel, industrialized products.
Regulations	Imports require a declaration of need. Special certificates are required for a number of products.
Local Agent	Highly recommended.
Health	Risk of malaria in northern area.
Business Hours	8:30 A.M. to 5:30 P.M.
Climate	Varies from subtropical in the north to subantarctic in the south. Buenos Aires maximum summer temperature is about 90 degrees. Winters are mild with occasional frost and snow, except in the south.
Local Holidays	Revolution Day (May 25).
Local Time	9 A.M. EST is 7 A.M. in Buenos Aires.
Travel Documents	Passport only required for non-working visits up to 3 months.

Australia

Official Name	Commonwealth of Australia.
Population	Approximately 18 million.
Main Cities	Sydney and Melbourne are the main centers of financial and industrial activity. Canberra is the capital city.
Government	Federation of six states. Elected Senate, House of Representatives, and independent judiciary.
Language	English.

Religion	Anglican 26%, Roman Catholic 26%, other Christian 24%, other 24%.
Literacy Rate	99%
Crime Rate	6,773 total offenses per 100,000 persons, 4.48 murders per 100,000 persons, 5,491 thefts per 100,000 persons.
GDP	$430 billion. $23,600 per capita.
Currency	Australian Dollar ($A). Approximately 1.28 to one U.S. dollar.
Exports	Meat, dairy products, cereal, fruit, honey, wool.
Imports	Petroleum products, chemicals, paper, textiles, electric machinery, transportation equipment.
Regulations	Many regulations controlling the quality, safety and purity of a wide variety of goods.
Local Agent	Advisable, but better to establish a local subsidiary and become Australian.
Business Tips	During the summer months of December and January, many businesspeople are on vacation.
Health	International Certificate of Vaccination against smallpox and yellow fever is required in some areas.
Climate	The coastal cities of Perth, Adelaide, Melbourne, and Hobart, and the inland city of Canberra usually have dry summer heat, while Darwin, Sydney, and Brisbane have subtropical climates with damp heat. These cities have mild winters with no snow, while in the interior the climate is more extreme.
Clothing	Lightweight clothes may be worn year round in the tropical regions and from October to April in the southern regions. During the winter in the south, heavier clothing is usually needed.
Local Holidays	New Year's Day (January 1), Australia Day (January 26), Good Friday (variable), Easter Monday (variable), ANZAC Day (April 25), Queen's Birthday (June 12), Christmas (December 25), Boxing Day (December 26).
Local Time	9 A.M. EST is midnight in Canberra.
Travel Documents	Passport and visa required, obtained at a Australian diplomatic office in a foreign country.

Austria

Official Name	Republic of Austria.
Population	Approximately 8 million.
Main Cities	Vienna is the capital and a main international trading center. Linz is a major industrial center. Other major centers are Saltzburg, Innsbruck, Graz, and Klagenfurt.
Government	Parliamentary democracy.
Language	German, but English and some French is spoken by most businesspeople.

Religion	Roman Catholic 85%, Protestant 6%, other 9%.
Literacy Rate	99%
Crime Rate	5,288 total offenses per 100,000 persons, 1.8 murders per 100,000 persons, 2,505 thefts per 100,000 persons.
GDP	$157 billion. $19,700 per capita.
Currency	Austrian shilling (S). Approximately 11.3 to one U.S. dollar.
Exports	Iron, steel, lumber, paper, machinery.
Imports	Petroleum, foodstuffs, chemicals, clothing.
Regulations	There are few import restrictions, other than for agricultural items.
Local Agent	Recommended, either from within the country or from other countries such as Germany.
Business Tips	Austria is the headquarters of a number of United Nations organizations that purchase products and services.
Business Hours	8:30 A.M. to 5 P.M. Monday through Friday.
Climate	Warm days and cool nights in summer. Winters are cold with snow. Average temperatures in Vienna in summer are about 65 degrees, and in winter about 30 degrees.
Clothing	Usual business dress.
Local Holidays	National Day (October 26).
Local Time	9 A.M. EST is 3 P.M. in Austria.
Travel Documents	Passport only for less than 90-day visit.

Bahrain

Official Name	State of Bahrain.
Population	Approximately 603,000.
Main Cities	Manama is the capital.
Government	Constitutional state ruled by an Emir, with a cabinet.
Language	Arabic, but English is widely spoken in business.
Religion	Islam.
Literacy Rate	77%
Crime Rate	4,374 total offenses per 100,000 persons, 0.57 murders per 100,000 persons, 732 thefts per 100,000 persons.
GDP	$7.7 billion. $13,000 per capita.
Local Customs	Muslim customs are predominant, in which alcohol and pork are forbidden. Food and other items should be taken and passed with the right hand.
Currency	Bahrain dinar (BD). Approximately 0.37 to one U.S. dollar.

Exports	Petroleum.
Imports	Industrialized products, foodstuffs, automobiles.
Local Agent	Agent (a national) required by law, except for government and military business where agent is not allowed.
Business Tips	Business depends heavily on frequent personal contact. Avoid visits during the month of Ramadan.
Health	Immunizations against typhoid, tetanus, polio, and meningococcal meningitis are recommended.
Business Hours	8 A.M. to 12:30 P.M., then 4 P.M. to 7 P.M., Saturday through Wednesday.
Climate	Hot and humid in summer with temperatures over 100, milder in winter.
Clothing	Lightweight business clothes.
Health	Certificate of vaccination against yellow fever and cholera if travelling from an infected area.
Local Holidays	The Muslim weekend (Thursday and Friday), Muslim holidays, and the month of Ramadan are observed. New Year's Day (January 1), National Day (December 16).
Local Time	9 A.M. EST is 5 P.M. in Bahrain.
Travel Documents	Passport and visa is required. Visa obtained at a Bahrain diplomatic mission abroad. A 72-hour transit visa can be obtained at the airport on entry with a valid passport and proof of onward transportation.

Bangladesh

Official Name	People's Republic of Bangladesh.
Population	Approximately 125 million.
Main Cities	Dhaka is the capital city. Chittagong is the main port.
Government	Elected president, vice president, and 300-member Parliament.
Language	Bangla is the official language, but English is widely spoken and used in business.
Religion	Islam 83%, Hindu 16%, other 1%.
Literacy Rate	35%
GDP	$155 billion. $1,260 per capita.
Currency	Taka (Tk). Approximately 42 to one U.S. dollar.
Exports	Clothing, jute, shrimp.
Imports	Petroleum, textiles, machinery, foodstuffs.
Regulations	All imports are controlled by the Chief Controller of Import and Export at the Ministry of Commerce.
Local Agent	Essential.

Business Tips	Eating pork and drinking alcohol are frowned upon.
Climate	Tropical monsoon climate with warm to hot temperatures and high humidity. Winter temperatures drop to 55 degrees, and summer temperatures are up to 95 degrees.
Clothing	Shirt and tie in summer, with jacket in winter. Frequent clothing changes may be necessary because of heat and humidity.
Health	Visitors should have cholera, tetanus, polio, typhoid, and gamma globulin inoculations before entering Bangladesh. Medication for malaria and stomach problems should also be taken.
Local Holidays	Friday is the weekly holiday in Bangladesh, and the month of Ramadan is observed. Independence Day (March 26), Eid-ul-Fitre (variable), May Day (May 1), Eid-ul-Azha (variable), National Revolution Day (November 7), Christmas Day (December 25).
Local Time	9 A.M. EST is 8 P.M. in Bangladesh.
Travel Documents	Passport and onward transportation ticket required for stay up to 14 days. Visa required for stay over 14 days, issued by a Bangladesh diplomatic mission abroad.

Belarus

Official Name	Republic of Belarus.
Population	Approximately 10 million.
Main Cities	Minsk in the capital city.
Government	Republic. Most of the power is in the hands of the President, who appoints the prime minister.
Language	Byelorussian, Russian, other.
Religion	Eastern Orthodox 80%, Roman Catholic, Protestant, Jewish, and Muslim 20%.
Literacy Rate	98%
GDP	$52 billion. $5,000 per capita.
Currency	Belarusian (BR). Approximately 16,600 to one U.S. dollar.
Exports	Machinery and transport equipment, chemicals, foodstuffs.
Imports	Fuel, industrial raw materials, textiles, sugar.
Local Agent	Highly recommended.
Climate	Cold winters, cool and moist summers.
Clothing	Standard business attire.
Local Holidays	Independence Day (July 3).
Local Time	9 A.M. EST is 4 P.M. in Belgium.
Travel Documents	Passport and visa required.

Belgium

Official Name	Kingdom of Belgium.
Population	Approximately 10 million.
Main Cities	Brussels in the capital. Other major centers are Antwerp, Liege, Gent, and Charleroi.
Government	Constitutional monarchy.
Language	Flemish in the north and French in the south. Other business languages are English and German.
Religion	Roman Catholic 75%, Protestant and other 25%.
Literacy Rate	99%
Crime Rate	3,045 total offenses per 100,000 persons, 2.8 murders per 100,000 persons, 2,419 thefts per 100,000 persons.
GDP	$206 billion. $20,590 per capita.
Currency	Belgium franc (BF). Approximately 33 to one U.S. dollar.
Exports	Machinery, steel, chemicals, textiles.
Imports	Raw materials, petroleum, machinery.
Regulations	Special regulations apply to many food imports.
Local Agent	Recommended.
Business Tips	For sales to the government, be prepared to offer some offsetting work in Belgium.
Climate	Temperature rarely falls below 32 degrees in winter and rarely goes over 75 degrees in summer.
Clothing	Usual business wear.
Local Holidays	Christian holidays, National Day (July 21).
Local Time	9 A.M. EST is 3 P.M. in Belgium.
Travel Documents	Passport only required for stay up to 90 days.

Bolivia

Official Name	Republic of Bolivia.
Population	Approximately 7.6 million.
Main Cities	La Paz is the capital and commercial center. Santa Cruz, where petroleum industry is located, is second most important city.
Government	Based on the U.S. system.
Language	Spanish is the official and commercial language.
Religion	Roman Catholic 95%, other 5%.

Literacy Rate	78%
GDP	$22 billion. $3,000 per capita.
Currency	Boliviano (Bs). Approximately 5 to one U.S. dollar.
Exports	Tin, natural gas.
Imports	Industrialized products, foodstuffs.
Regulations	Many items are subject to import regulations.
Local Agent	Essential.
Business Tips	Legal procedures are slow and complicated.
Health	International Certificate of Vaccination against smallpox and yellow fever are recommended. The altitude of La Paz can cause discomfort and health problems for those with heart or lung ailments.
Climate	Climate varies with altitude. Average temperature is La Paz is about 45 degrees, but the lower, eastern part of the country is hot and humid.
Local Holidays	New Year's Day (January 1), Carnival (variable), Good Friday (variable), Labor Day (May 1), National Day (August 6), All Saints Day (November 1), Christmas (December 25).
Local Time	9 A.M. EST is 10 A.M. in Bolivia.
Travel Documents	Passport required for tourist stay up to 30 days. Business visa required, issued at Bolivian missions abroad.

Brazil

Official Name	Federative Republic of Brazil.
Population	Approximately 165 million.
Main Cities	Sao Paulo is the industrial center. Brazilia is the capital. Other major cities are Rio de Janeiro, Belo Horizonte, Porto Alegre, and Salvador.
Government	Federal republic with president elected every 6 years. Consists of 26 states and one federal district.
Language	Portuguese is official language. English not widely used commercially. Spanish is widely understood, but Spanish business literature is not acceptable.
Religion	90% Roman Catholic.
Literacy Rate	81%
GDP	$1.022 trillion. $6,300 per capita.
Local Customs	Personal business relations are important. Coffee is an important aspect of life, and it is considered discourteous to decline it.
Currency	Real (R). Approximately 1.04 to one U.S. dollar.
Exports	Coffee, fruits, leather, motor vehicles, textiles.
Imports	Cereal grains, newsprint, industrialized products.

Regulations	Import certificates are required for almost all goods. Import quotas are applicable to most goods.
Local Agent	Not a legal requirement but highly recommended. Commissions are normally required to be shown on documents.
Business Tips	Hotel accommodation is heavily booked from December until Carnival in February or March, because of holidays and school vacations. No business is done during Carnival week.
Health	Inoculation against typhoid is recommended. For the Amazon region, should have inoculation against yellow fever and take anti-malaria medication.
Business Hours	8:30 A.M. to 6 P.M. Monday to Friday, with a two-hour break for lunch.
Climate	The equatorial region, average temperature of 81 degrees. The middle region, average temperatures of 74 to 80 degrees in the lowlands and 64 to 70 in higher locations. The southern region, average temperatures of 62 to 66 degrees.
Clothing	Tropical clothing is necessary, but evenings in Sao Paulo and the south can be cool. Business suits are normally worn.
Local Holidays	New Year's day (January 1), Epiphany (January 6), Carnival (3 days up to Ash Wednesday), Good Friday (variable), Labor Day (May 1), Independence Day (September 7), All Saints Day (November 1), Proclamation of the Republic (November 15), Christmas (December 25).
Local Time	9 A.M. EST is 7 A.M. in eastern Brazil and 8 A.M. in western Brazil.
Travel Documents	Passport and visa required, obtained at Brazil diplomatic mission abroad.

Brunei

Official Name	Negara Brunei Darussalam.
Population	Approximately 307,600.
Main Cities	Capital is Bandar Seri Begawan.
Government	Sultanate. Former British protectorate until 1984.
Language	Malay, Chinese, and English.
Religion	Islam 63%, Buddhist 14%, Christian 8%, other 15%.
Literacy Rate	88%
Crime Rate	358 total offenses per 100,000 persons, 0.41 murders per 100,000 persons, 170 thefts per 100,000 persons.
GDP	$4.6 billion. $15,800 per capita.
Currency	Brunei Dollar ($), which is approximately 1.40 to the U.S. dollar.
Exports	Petroleum. World's second largest exporter of liquified natural gas (LNG).
Imports	Industrialized products, foodstuffs, consumer goods.
Regulations	Some items such as used vehicles require special import licenses. Non-Bruneis are prohibited from owning land.

Local Agent	Recommended.
Climate	Hot and humid, with average daytime temperatures about 85 degrees and 75 degrees at night.
Local Holidays	National Day (February 23).
Local Time	9 A.M. EST is 10 P.M. in Brunei.
Travel Documents	Passport and visa required. They can be obtained from Brunei diplomatic mission abroad.

Bulgaria

Official Name	Republic of Bulgaria.
Population	Approximately 8.3 million.
Main Cities	Sofia is the capital.
Government	Elected president and National Assembly.
Language	Bulgarian is official language.
Religion	Bulgarian Orthodox 85%, Islam 13%, other 2%.
Literacy Rate	93%
GDP	$40 billion. $4,630 per capita.
Currency	Lev (Lv). Approximately 483 to one U.S. dollar.
Exports	Machinery, consumer goods, agricultural products, raw materials.
Imports	Fuels, machinery, consumer goods, foodstuffs.
Local Agent	Recommended.
Climate	Hot, dry summers. Cold, wet winters.
Local Holidays	National Day (March 3).
Local Time	9 A.M. EST is 4 P.M. in Bulgaria.
Travel Documents	Passport only required for tourist visit up to 30 days. Business visa required, obtained at Bulgarian diplomatic mission abroad.

Burma (Myanmar)

Official Name	Union of Myanmar.
Population	Approximately 47 million.
Main Cities	Rangoon is the capital.
Government	Military regime.
Language	Burmese.

Religion	Buddhist 89%, Christian 4%, other 7%.
Literacy Rate	81%
Crime Rate	200 total offenses per 100,000 persons, 5.94 murders per 100,000 persons, 58 thefts per 100,000 persons.
GDP	$51 billion. $1,120 per capita.
Currency	Kyat (K). Approximately 6 to one U.S. dollar.
Exports	Teak, rice, metals, gems.
Imports	Machinery, chemicals, foodstuffs.
Local Agent	Recommended.
Climate	Hot and humid summers, milder in winter. Monsoon season is December to April.
Health	Cholera, tuberculosis, plague, leprosy, malaria, and typhoid are common.
Local Holidays	Independence Day (January 4).
Local Time	9 A.M. EST is 8:30 P.M. in Burma.
Travel Documents	Passport and visa required, good for stay up to 14 days. Obtained at Burmese diplomatic mission abroad.

Cambodia

Official Name	Kingdom of Cambodia.
Population	Approximately 11 million.
Main Cities	Phnom Penh is the capital.
Government	Transitional government under the auspices of the United Nations.
Language	Khmer is official language. French is also spoken.
Religion	Buddhism 95%, other 5%.
Literacy Rate	35%
GDP	$7.7 billion. $710 per capita.
Currency	Riel (CR). Approximately 3,000 to one U.S. dollar.
Exports	Rubber, rice, spices.
Imports	Fuel, machinery, consumer goods, foodstuffs.
Local Agent	Recommended.
Climate	Hot and humid. Monsoon season is May to October.
Health	Anti-malaria medication is recommend.
Local Holidays	Liberation Day (January 7), Independence Day (April 17).
Local Time	9 A.M. EST is 9 P.M. in Cambodia.
Travel Documents	U.S. citizens require special U.S. government documentation to visit Cambodia.

Cameroon

Official Name	Republic of Cameroon.
Population	Approximately 15 million.
Main Cities	Yaounde is the capital.
Government	Elected president and National Assembly.
Language	English and French are official languages, but there are numerous African languages spoken.
Religion	Local religions 51%, Christian 33%, Islam 16%.
Literacy Rate	54%
Crime Rate	0.21 murders per 100,000 persons, 2.29 thefts per 100,000 persons.
GDP	$17 billion. $1,230 per capita.
Currency	CFA franc (CFAF). Approximately 542 to one U.S. dollar.
Exports	Petroleum, coffee, cocoa, aluminum, timber.
Imports	Machinery, consumer goods, foodstuffs.
Local Agent	Recommended.
Climate	Tropical along the coast, hot and dry inland.
Health	Anti-malaria medication is recommended.
Local Holidays	National Day (May 20).
Local Time	9 A.M. EST is 3 P.M. in Cameroon.
Travel Documents	Passport and visa required.

Canada

Official Name	Canada.
Population	Approximately 30 million.
Main Cities	Ottawa is the capital. Toronto, Montreal, and Vancouver are the main business centers.
Government	Parliamentary democracy with ten provinces and two territories. Elected House of Commons and appointed Senate. Prime minister is leader of majority party in House of Commons.
Language	English and French are official languages.
Religion	Roman Catholic 46%, United Church 16%, Anglican 10%, other 28%.
Literacy Rate	99%
Crime Rate	11,414 total offenses per 100,000 persons, 5.45 murders per 100,000 persons, 5,133 thefts per 100,000 persons.

GDP	$721 billion. $25,000 per capita.
Currency	Canadian dollar (Can$). Approximately 1.42 to one U.S. dollar.
Exports	Petroleum, natural gas, newsprint, timber products, metals, motor vehicles, electronic equipment, foodstuffs.
Imports	Motor vehicles, chemicals, electronic equipment.
Regulations	Canada is part of the North American Free Trade Agreement.
Local Agent	Usually not required.
Climate	Temperate in populated south, subarctic and arctic in north.
Clothing	Usual business dress.
Health	No major health problems.
Local Holidays	New Year's Day (January 1), Easter (variable), Victoria Day (May 21), Canada Day (July 1), Labor Day (September 4), Thanksgiving Day (October 9), Christmas Day (December 25), Boxing Day (December 26).
Local Time	Time zones similar to the United States.
Travel Documents	Passport only required for most nationals.

Chile

Official Name	Republic of Chile.
Population	Approximately 14 million.
Main Cities	Santiago is the capital and commercial center. Valparaiso is another major city.
Government	Republic with elected president and Chamber of Deputies.
Language	Spanish is the official language, but many businesspersons speak English.
Religion	Roman Catholic 89%, Protestant 11%.
Local Customs	Business activities are similar to North America.
Literacy Rate	93%
Crime Rate	1,309 total offenses per 100,000 persons, 6.54 murders per 100,000 persons, 748 thefts per 100,000 persons.
GDP	$120 billion. $8,400 per capita.
Currency	Chilean peso (Ch$). Approximately 423 to one U.S. dollar.
Exports	Copper, other minerals, wood products, fish products.
Imports	Industrialized products, petroleum, foodstuffs.
Regulations	Import licenses are not required, but imports must be reported. There are free trade zones that allow processing of goods duty free.
Local Agent	Specialized agent is recommended.
Business Tips	Businesspeople rely on good personal relations.

Health	No major problems.
Business Hours	9 A.M. to 6 P.M. Monday through Friday, and 9 A.M. to 1 P.M. on Saturday.
Climate	The north has warm weather summer and winter. The south has short cool summers and long, cold, and wet winters. The average summer temperature in Santiago is about 83 degrees and the average winter temperature about 54 degrees.
Clothing	Light tropical clothing for the northern areas, medium weight for the central regions, and heavy winter clothing in the south.
Local Holidays	Independence Day (September 18).
Local Time	9 A.M. EST is 10 A.M. in Chile.
Travel Documents	Passport allows 90-day visit.

China

Official Name	People's Republic of China.
Population	Approximately 1.2 billion.
Main Cities	Beijing is the capital. Shanghai is the largest city and main port. Other major centers are Wuhan, Shenyang, Changchun, Tianjin, Qingdao, Dalian, Shantou, and Guangzhou (Canton).
Government	Socialist republic with the Communist party as the overall authority.
Language	National language is Mandarin Chinese.
Local Customs	Tipping is not done, but service people should be thanked for their efforts.
Literacy Rate	73%
GDP	$3.39 trillion. $2,800 per capita.
Currency	Yuan (Y) or Renminbi (Rmb). Approximately 8.5 to one U.S. dollar.
Exports	Rice, cotton textiles, silk, fruit, coal, petroleum, consumer goods.
Imports	Industrial products, machinery, chemicals, fertilizer, cotton, cereals.
Regulations	No Chinese money can be taken out of the country. Foreign visitors must declare all foreign money (including travelers' checks) and valuables on entering the country and must exchange Chinese money for foreign money when leaving.
Local Agent	State corporations handle all imports.
Business Tips	Import decisions are made by officials in Beijing. Always use the address "People's Republic of China." Tips should not be offered.
Business Hours	8 A.M. to 11:30 A.M., then 1:30 P.M. to 5 P.M., Monday through Saturday.
Climate	The climate varies across the country. In Beijing the average winter temperature is about 25 degrees and the average summer temperature about 80 degrees. In Guangzhou the average winter temperature is about 55 degrees and the average summer temperature about 85 degrees.

Clothing	Business suits are standard.
Local Holidays	May Day (May 1), National Day (October 1).
Local Time	9 A.M. EST is 10 P.M. in China.
Travel Documents	Visa required.

Columbia

Official Name	Republic of Columbia.
Population	Approximately 37 million.
Main Cities	Bogota is the capital and the major commercial center. Other major cities are Medellin, Cali, Barranquilla, and Bucaramanga.
Government	Presidential democracy structured similar to the U.S.A.
Language	Spanish is the main language. Many businesspeople speak English.
Religion	Almost 100% Roman Catholic.
Local Customs	Current drug-related problems can cause dangerous personal situations to arise.
Literacy Rate	87%
GDP	$201 billion. $5,400 per capita.
Currency	Columbian peso (Col$). Approximately 1,028 to the U.S. dollar.
Exports	Petroleum, coffee, fresh-cut flowers.
Imports	Industrialized products, consumer goods, chemicals.
Regulations	All imports must be registered with the government.
Local Agent	Agency agreement must be in Columbian law and certified by the Columbian embassy or consulate.
Business Tips	December and January are holiday months.
Health	The thin and polluted air of Bogota may cause problems to some people. Cholera and yellow fever immunizations are recommended, as well as anti-malaria medication.
Business Hours	8:30 A.M. to noon, then 2 P.M. to 5:30 P.M.
Climate	Climate varies due to altitude. Bogota has an average temperature of 57 degrees while coastal areas are hot and humid.
Clothing	Business suits are usually worn. Warmer clothing is advisable for Bogota, but lighter clothing is required in the hot and humid lower altitudes.
Local Holidays	Independence Day (July 20).
Local Time	Eastern Standard Time.
Travel Documents	Tourist visa only is required for most business visits. A business visa may be required for some business activities such as writing up orders.

Costa Rica

Official Name	Republic of Costa Rica.
Population	Approximately 3.3 million.
Main Cities	San Jose is the capital.
Government	Democratic republic with elected president and Legislative Assembly.
Language	Spanish is the official language. English also spoken.
Religion	Predominantly Roman Catholic.
Literacy Rate	93%
Crime Rate	839 total offenses per 100,000 persons, 5.68 murders per 100,000 persons, 513 thefts per 100,000 persons.
GDP	$19 billion. $5,500 per capita.
Currency	Costa Rican colones (C). Approximately 219 to one U.S. dollar.
Exports	Coffee, bananas, sugar, textiles.
Imports	Machinery, petroleum, consumer goods.
Local Agent	Recommended.
Climate	Tropical climate.
Health	Immunization against typhoid is recommended, as well as anti-malaria medication.
Local Holidays	Independence Day (September 15).
Local Time	9 A.M. EST is 8 A.M. in Costa Rica.
Travel Documents	Passport only required.

Cote d'Ivoire

Official Name	Republic of Cote d'Ivoire. (Formerly Ivory Coast.)
Population	Approximately 14 million.
Main Cities	Yamoussoukro is the capital.
Government	Republic with elected president and National Assembly.
Language	French is the official language. Many African languages spoken.
Religion	Local 63%, Islam 25%, Christian 12%.
Literacy Rate	54%
Crime Rate	310 total offenses per 100,000 persons, 4.05 murders per 100,000 persons, 185 thefts per 100,000 persons.
GDP	$24 billion. $1,620 per capita.

Currency	Communaute Financiere Africaine franc (CFAF). Approximately 542 to one U.S. dollar.
Exports	Cocoa, coffee, lumber, fruits.
Imports	Machinery, fuel, consumer goods, foodstuffs.
Local Agent	Recommended.
Climate	Tropical along the coast. Hot and dry inland.
Local Holidays	National Day (December 7).
Local Time	9 A.M. EST is 2 P.M. in Cote d'Ivoire.
Travel Documents	Passport and visa required, obtained at a Cote d'Ivoire diplomatic mission abroad.

Cuba

Official Name	Republic of Cuba.
Population	Approximately 11 million.
Main Cities	Havana is the capital. Santiago de Cuba is also a major city.
Government	Centralized government and economy, with Fidel Castro as President of the Council of State, President of the Council of Ministers, Commander-in-Chief of the Armed Forces, and First Secretary of the Central Committee of the Cuban Communist Party.
Language	Spanish is the official language.
Religion	Main religion is Roman Catholic.
Literacy Rate	94%
GDP	$16.2 billion. $1,480 per capita.
Currency	Cuban peso (Cu$). Approximately 1.00 to one U.S. dollar.
Exports	Sugar, tobacco.
Imports	Industrialized products, petroleum, fertilizers.
Regulations	Special regulations apply to animal and vegetable products.
Local Agent	There are no local agents in Cuba. The government deals directly with foreign suppliers.
Business Tips	All purchasing is handled by the state.
Health	No special regulations.
Business Hours	8:30 A.M. to 12:30 P.M., then 1:30 P.M. to 5:30 P.M.
Climate	Average temperature varies from about 82 degrees in summer to about 71 degrees in winter.
Clothing	Lightweight suits are worn all year.
Local Holidays	May Day (May 1), Rebellion Day (July 26).

Local Time	EST.
Travel Documents	Passport and visa are required.

Czech Republic

Official Name	Czech Republic. (Part of the former Czechoslovakia.)
Population	Approximately 10 million.
Main Cities	Prague is the capital.
Government	Parliamentary democracy with elected president and Chamber of Deputies.
Language	Czech and Slovak.
Religion	Atheist 40%, Roman Catholic 40%, Protestant 5%, other 15%.
GDP	$114 billion. $11,100 per capita.
Currency	Koruna (Kc). Approximately 28 to one U.S. dollar.
Exports	Manufactured goods, machinery, raw materials.
Imports	Fuels, machinery, chemicals, agricultural products, consumer goods.
Local Agent	Recommended.
Climate	Cool summers. Cold and wet winters.
Local Time	9 A.M. EST is 3 P.M. in the Czech Republic.
Travel Documents	Passport only required.

Denmark

Official Name	Kingdom of Denmark.
Population	Approximately 5.3 million.
Main Cities	Copenhagen is the capital. Other main centers are Aarhus, Odense and Aalborg.
Language	Danish, and English is widely spoken.
Literacy Rate	99%
Crime Rate	10,500 total offenses per 100,000 persons, 5.17 murders per 100,000 persons, 8,525 thefts per 100,000 persons.
GDP	$118 billion. $22,700 per capita.
Currency	Danish krone (DKr). Approximately 6.1 to the U.S. dollar.
Exports	Industrialized products, foodstuffs.
Imports	Petroleum, raw materials.
Regulations	Imports competing with domestic products are restricted or controlled.

Local Agent	Recommended.
Business Tips	Avoid visits during the summer vacation months.
Climate	The average temperature in July is about 60 degrees, and the average temperature in January is about 32 degrees.
Clothing	Usual business wear.
Local Holidays	Birthday of the Queen (April 16).
Local Time	9 A.M. EST is 3 P.M. in Denmark.
Travel Documents	Passport only required for stay up to 3 months.

Dominican Republic

Official Name	Dominican Republic.
Population	Approximately 7.7 million.
Main Cities	Santo Domingo is the capital and main commercial center. Other centers are Santiago and La Vega.
Government	Republic with elected president and Congress.
Language	Spanish is the main language, but English is spoken by most business people and government officials.
Religion	Roman Catholic is the major religion.
Literacy Rate	83%
Crime Rate	946 total offenses per 100,000 persons, 11.93 murders per 100,000 persons, 438 thefts per 100,000 persons.
GDP	$30 billion. $3,670 per capita.
Currency	Dominican peso (RD$). Approximately 14 to one U.S. dollar.
Exports	Sugar, coffee, metals.
Imports	Petroleum, foodstuffs, chemicals.
Local Agent	Highly recommended. The Agent Distributor Law makes it almost impossible to change agents once they are appointed.
Business Tips	Freight insurance must be through a local insurance company.
Climate	Daily highs between 80 and 90 degrees. Humid in summer.
Clothing	Lightweight suits.
Health	Anti-malaria medication recommend.
Local Holidays	New Year's Day (January 1), Three King's Day (January 6), Independence Day (February 27), Good Friday (variable), Labor Day (May 1), Restoration Day (August 16), Mercedes Day (September 24), Christmas Day (December 25).
Local Time	9 A.M. EST is 9 A.M. in the Dominican Republic.
Travel Documents	Valid passport only required.

Ecuador

Official Name	Republic of Ecuador.
Population	Approximately 12 million.
Main Cities	Quito in the capital. Other main cities are Cuenca and Guayaquil.
Language	Spanish is the official language.
Literacy Rate	86%
GDP	$47 billion. $4,100 per capita.
Currency	Sucre (S/). Approximately 3,670 to one U.S. dollar.
Exports	Petroleum, bananas, shrimp, coffee.
Imports	Industrialized products, machinery, chemicals.
Local Agent	Highly recommended. Under Ecuador law, a principal may not terminate or refuse to renew an agency agreement except for a judicially determined just cause.
Business Tips	All imports into Ecuador require an import license issued by the Central Bank.
Climate	Climate is quite variable, from tropical on the coast to temperate in the highlands.
Clothing	Light suits during the day, dark suits at social functions.
Health	Tap water is the main health risk. Precautions against malaria and other tropical diseases recommended.
Local Holidays	Independence Day (August 10).
Local Time	Eastern Standard Time.
Travel Documents	Passport and proof of onward travel required.

Egypt

Official Name	Arab Republic of Egypt.
Population	Approximately 65 million.
Main Cities	Cairo is the capital.
Government	Democratic state with elected president and People's Assembly.
Language	Arabic is official language.
Religion	Islam 94%, other 6%.
Literacy Rate	63%
Crime Rate	2,939 total offenses per 100,000 persons, 1.53 murders per 100,000 persons, 39 thefts per 100,000 persons.
GDP	$184 billion. $2,900 per capita.

Currency	Egyptian Pound (£E). Approximately 3.4 to one U.S. dollar.
Exports	Petroleum, cotton, chemicals.
Imports	Machinery, foodstuffs, fertilizers, consumer goods.
Local Agent	Highly recommended.
Climate	Hot and dry with average temperatures about 100.
Health	Immunizations against cholera, typhoid, tetanus, polio, and hepatitis recommended.
Local Holidays	The Muslim weekend (Thursday and Friday), Muslim holidays, and the month of Ramadan are observed. New Year's Day (January 1), Sinai Liberation Day (April 25), Evacuation Day (June 18), Revolution Day (July 23), Popular Resistance Day (October 24).
Local Time	9 A.M. EST is 4 P.M. in Egypt.
Travel Documents	Transit visa for up to seven days can be obtained at the Cairo airport with a valid passport.

El Salvador

Official Name	Republic of El Salvador.
Population	Approximately 5.6 million.
Main Cities	San Salvador is the capital.
Government	Republic with elected president and Legislative Assembly.
Language	Spanish is the main language.
Religion	Roman Catholic 75%, other 25%.
Literacy Rate	73%
GDP	$12 billion. $2,080 per capita.
Currency	Salvadoran colon (C). Approximately 9 to one U.S. dollar.
Exports	Coffee, sugar, cotton, shrimp.
Imports	Consumer goods.
Local Agent	Highly recommended.
Climate	Tropical climate.
Health	Immunizations against typhoid, hepatitis, polio, and tetanus recommended.
Local Holidays	Christian holidays, Independence Day (September 15).
Local Time	9 A.M. EST is 8 A.M. in El Salvador.
Travel Documents	Passport and visa required, obtained from El Salvador diplomatic mission abroad.

Eritrea

Official Name	State of Eritrea.
Population	Approximately 3.5 million.
Main Cities	Asmara is the capital.
Government	Provisional government in aftermath of independence from Ethiopia.
Language	Tigre is the main language.
Religion	Islam and Christian.
GDP	$2 billion. $570 per capita.
Local Agent	Highly recommended.
Climate	Hot and dry along coast. Cooler and wetter inland.
Local Holidays	National Day (May 24).
Local Time	9 A.M. EST is 5 P.M. in Eritrea.
Travel Documents	Passport and visa required.

Estonia

Official Name	Republic of Estonia.
Population	Approximately 1.4 million.
Main Cities	Tallinn is the capital.
Government	Republic with elected president and Parliament.
Language	Estonian is the official language. Other languages spoken are Russian, Latvian and Lithuanian.
Religion	Lutheran is the main religion.
Literacy Rate	100%
Currency	Estonian kroon (EEK). Approximately 12 to one U.S. dollar.
Exports	Textiles, wood products, dairy products.
Imports	Fuel, machinery, chemicals.
Local Agent	Recommended.
Climate	Temperate summers, moderate winters.
Local Holidays	Christian holidays, Independence Day (February 24).
Local Time	9 A.M. EST is 4 P.M. in Estonia.
Travel Documents	Passport only required.

Ethiopia

Official Name	Ethiopia.
Population	Approximately 59 million.
Main Cities	Addis Ababa in the capital.
Government	Transitional government following civil war.
Language	Amharic is the official language. Arabic, English and other languages also spoken.
Religion	Islam 50%, Greek Orthodox 40%, other 10%.
Literacy Rate	62%
Crime Rate	94 total offenses per 100,000 persons, 6.73 murders per 100,000 persons, 21 thefts per 100,000 persons.
GDP	$25 billion. $430 per capita.
Currency	Birr (Br). Approximately 6.4 to one U.S. dollar.
Exports	Petroleum, coffee.
Imports	Fuel, consumer goods.
Local Agent	Highly recommended.
Climate	Tropical climate with areas of drought.
Local Holidays	National Day (May 28).
Local Time	9 A.M. EST is 5 P.M. in Ethiopia.
Travel Documents	Passport and visa required.

Finland

Official Name	Republic of Finland.
Population	Approximately 5 million.
Main Cities	Helsinki is the capital and business center. Other major centers are Tampere, Turku, Espoo, Vantaa, Lahti, and Oulu.
Government	Republic, with a Parliament elected every four years and a president elected for a six-year period.
Language	Finnish, but most businesspeople speak Swedish or English.
Religion	Predominantly Lutheran.
Literacy Rate	100%
Crime Rate	7,669 total offenses per 100,000 persons, 0.7 murders per 100,000 persons, 2,310 thefts per 100,000 persons.
GDP	$97 billion. $19,000 per capita.
Currency	Markka (FMk). Approximately 4.6 to one U.S. dollar.

Exports	Lumber, pulp and paper, ships, machinery.
Imports	Oil, raw materials, foodstuffs.
Local Agent	Essential, because tenders are not well publicized.
Business Tips	Avoid visiting in July which is summer vacation month.
Business Hours	8 A.M. to 4:30 P.M. Monday through Friday.
Climate	Summer temperatures range from 55 to 85 degrees, and winter temperatures range from –5 to 25 degrees.
Clothing	Usual business wear.
Local Holidays	Independence Day (December 6).
Local Time	9 A.M. EST is 4 P.M. in Finland.
Travel Documents	Passport only for stay up to 3 months.

France

Official Name	French Republic.
Population	Approximately 58 million.
Main Cities	Paris is the capital. Other main centers are Lyon, Marseilles, Lille, Bordeaux and Toulouse.
Government	Republic with elected president and national assembly. Consists of 22 regions divided into 96 departments.
Language	French.
Religion	Predominately Roman Catholic.
Literacy Rate	99%
Crime Rate	5,619 total offenses per 100,000 persons, 4.6 murders per 100,000 persons, 3,569 thefts per 100,000 persons.
GDP	$1.24 trillion. $21,379 per capita.
Currency	Franc (F). Approximately 5.4 to one U.S. dollar.
Exports	Machinery, automobiles, electronic products, steel, foodstuffs, chemicals, textiles.
Imports	Petroleum, foodstuffs, chemicals.
Regulations	Strict sanitary regulations apply to many products.
Local Agent	Local agent is recommended, but be aware that canceling an agreement can be a legal problem.
Business Tips	Punctuality is an important issue. Many companies shut down for holiday in August.
Climate	Southern France is warm, dry, and sunny. Northern France gets snow in winter. Average high temperature in Paris in January is about 42 degrees, and the average high temperature in July is about 75 degrees.

Clothing	Usual business wear.
Local Holidays	Christian holidays, Bastille Day (July 14).
Local Time	9 A.M. EST is 3 P.M. in France.
Travel Documents	Passport only required for stay up to 3 months.

Georgia

Official Name	Republic of Georgia.
Population	Approximately 5.1 million.
Main Cities	Tbilisi is the capital.
Government	Republic with elected Parliament. Newly independent state of former U.S.S.R.
Language	Georgian is the official language. Other languages are Armenian, Azerbaijani, and Russian.
Religion	Orthodox 83%, Islam 11%, other 6%.
Literacy Rate	100%
Currency	Russian ruble until new lari currency established.
Exports	Fruits, agricultural products, raw materials.
Imports	Fuel, machinery, consumer goods.
Local Agent	Highly recommended.
Climate	Warm, Mediterranean climate.
Local Holidays	Independence Day (April 9).
Local Time	9 A.M. EST is 4 P.M. in Georgia.
Travel Documents	Passport and visa required.

Germany

Official Name	Federal Republic of Germany.
Population	Approximately 82 million.
Main Cities	Berlin is the designated capital city, but Bonn still retains many government functions.
Government	Federal republic, with elected upper chamber (Bundesrat) and lower chamber (Bundestag). Unification of former East and West Germany took place on October 3, 1990.
Language	German. English widely spoken.
Religion	Protestant 45%, Roman Catholic 37%, other 18%.

Literacy Rate	99%
Crime Rate	71,140 total offenses per 100,000 persons, 4.2 murders per 100,000 persons, 4,383 thefts per 100,000 persons.
GDP	$1.7 trillion. $20,400 per capita.
Currency	Deutsche mark (DM). Approximately 1.6 DM to one U.S. dollar.
Exports	Machinery, chemicals, motor vehicles, iron and steel, agricultural products, raw materials.
Imports	Agricultural products, fuels, raw materials.
Local Agent	Recommended.
Climate	Temperate. Cool, wet winters, with warm and humid summers.
Clothing	Standard business dress.
Local Holidays	German Unity Day (October 3).
Local Time	9 A.M. EST is 3 P.M. in Germany.
Travel Documents	Passport only required for stay up to 3 months.

Ghana

Official Name	Republic of Ghana.
Population	Approximately 17 million.
Main Cities	Accra is the capital.
Government	Constitutional democracy with elected president and National Assembly.
Language	English is the official language. Several African languages spoken.
Religion	Local religions 38%, Islam 30%, Christian 24%, other 8%.
Literacy Rate	60%
Crime Rate	768 total offenses per 100,000 persons, 1.91 murders per 100,000 persons, 290 thefts per 100,000 persons.
GDP	$27 billion. $1,530 per capita.
Currency	Cedi (C). Approximately 1,718 to one U.S. dollar.
Exports	Cocoa, raw materials, tuna.
Imports	Petroleum, consumer goods, foodstuffs, machinery.
Local Agent	Highly recommended.
Climate	Warm along coastline, hot and humid inland.
Health	Immunization against yellow fever recommended.
Local Holidays	Independence Day (March 6), Labor Day (May 1).
Local Time	9 A.M. EST is 2 P.M. in Ghana.
Travel Documents	Passport and visa required. Visa good for 30 days.

Greece

Official Name	Hellenic Republic.
Population	Approximately 10 million.
Main Cities	Athens is the capital. Other major centers are Thessaloniki, Patras, Heraklion, and Volos.
Government	Republic with elected president and Chamber of Deputies.
Language	Greek is the official language, but most businesspeople speak English.
Religion	Greek Orthodox 98%, Islam 1%, other 1%.
Literacy Rate	93%
Crime Rate	3,119 total offenses per 100,000 persons, 1.76 murders per 100,000 persons, 447 thefts per 100,000 persons.
GDP	$107 billion. $10,000 per capita.
Currency	Drachma (Dr). Approximately 250 to the U.S. dollar.
Exports	Cotton, fruits, metal products.
Imports	Petroleum, machinery, industrialized products, foodstuffs.
Regulations	Import license required for luxury items, and many other items are subject to import regulations.
Local Agent	Highly recommended.
Climate	Weather in coastal areas is mild, with hot summers. Average summer temperature in Athens is about 80 degrees. Cold winters in the mountains with temperatures ranging from 15 to 30 degrees.
Clothing	Usual business wear.
Local Holidays	Christian holidays, New Year's Day (January 1), Independence Day (March 25), May Day (May 1).
Local Time	9 A.M. EST is 4 P.M. in Greece.
Travel Documents	Passport only required for stay up to 3 months.

Guatemala

Official Name	Republic of Guatemala.
Population	Approximately 12 million.
Main Cities	Guatemala City is the capital, and Quetzaltenango is another major city.
Government	Republic.
Language	Official language is Spanish, but most businesspeople speak English.
Religion	Predominantly Roman Catholic.

Literacy Rate	55%
GDP	$39 billion. $3,460 per capita.
Currency	Quetzal (Q). Approximately 6.0 to one U.S. dollar.
Exports	Coffee, cotton.
Imports	Industrialized products.
Regulations	Foreign firms and their agents must register with the government to do business with the government.
Local Agent	Recommended; however, by law foreign companies may have to pay the agent an indemnity if they terminate the agency contract.
Business Tips	Avoid visits around Christmas and Easter because of extended holidays.
Health	Immunization against typhoid and tetanus are recommended, and anti-malaria medication should be taken.
Business Hours	Monday through Friday 9 A.M. to 1 P.M., then 3 P.M. to 7 P.M. Saturday 9 A.M. to 1 P.M.
Climate	Coastal areas are hot and humid, but higher elevations are temperate. Guatamala City, at about 5,000 foot altitude, has an average yearly temperature of about 68 degrees.
Clothing	Lightweight clothing during the day, something warmer for the evening.
Local Holidays	Christian holidays, Independence Day (September 15).
Local Time	9 A.M. EST is 8 A.M. in Guatemala.
Travel Documents	Passport and tourist visa issued by airline only required for stays up to 30 days.

Haiti

Official Name	Republic of Haiti.
Population	Approximately 6.6 million.
Main Cities	Port-au-Prince is the capital.
Government	Transitioning from military rule to civilian rule, with an elected president and Chamber of Deputies.
Language	French is the official language, but Creole is the predominant language.
Religion	Roman Catholic 80%, Protestant 16%, other 4%. A large portion of the population also practices Voodoo.
Literacy Rate	53%
GDP	$6.8 billion. $1,000 per capita.
Currency	Gourde (G). Approximately 16 to one U.S. dollar.
Exports	Manufactured goods, coffee.
Imports	Machinery, petroleum, foodstuffs.

Local Agent	Highly recommended.
Climate	Tropical climate.
Health	Health facilities are very limited.
Local Holidays	Independence Day (January 1), All Saints Day (November 1).
Local Time	9 A.M. EST is 9 A.M. in Haiti.
Travel Documents	Passport only required.

Honduras

Official Name	Republic of Honduras.
Population	Approximately 5 million.
Main Cities	Tegucigalpa is the capital.
Government	Republic.
Language	Spanish is the official language.
Religion	Mainly Roman Catholic.
Literacy Rate	73%
GDP	$11.5 billion. $2,000 per capita.
Currency	Lempira (L). Approximately 13 to one U.S. dollar.
Exports	Coffee, bananas.
Imports	Industrialized products, fuel, foodstuffs.
Regulations	Import of nonessential products may require prior approval.
Local Agent	Highly recommended and required by law for some imports. Agents must be a citizen of Honduras. By law, foreign companies may have to pay the agent an indemnity if they terminate the agency contract.
Business Tips	Avoid visits around Christmas and Easter because of extended holidays.
Health	Immunization against typhoid and tetanus are recommended, and anti-malaria medication should be taken.
Business Hours	Monday through Friday 9 A.M. to 1 P.M., then 3 P.M. to 7 P.M. Saturday 9 A.M. to noon.
Climate	Hot and humid on the coast, temperate in the higher altitudes of the interior. The rainy season is May to October.
Clothing	Lightweight clothing during the day, something warmer for the evening.
Local Holidays	Christian holidays, New Year's Day (January 1), Labor Day (May 1), Independence Day (September 15), Columbus Day (October 12).
Local Time	9 A.M. EST is 8 A.M. in Honduras.
Travel Documents	Passport and tourist visa for stay up to 30 days.

Hong Kong

Official Name	Hong Kong. Became part of China on July 1, 1997.
Population	Approximately 6.5 million.
Main Cities	Victoria is the actual name of Hong Kong island. Other main city is Kowloon on the mainland.
Government	Part of China.
Language	Chinese (Cantonese) and English are both official languages. English is the main language spoken.
Local Customs	Hong Kong people are aggressive businesspersons.
Literacy Rate	77%
Crime Rate	1,479 total offenses per 100,000 persons, 1.5 murders per 100,000 persons, 903 thefts per 100,000 persons.
GDP	$164 billion. $26,000 per capita.
Currency	Hong Kong dollar (HK$). Approximately 7.73 to one U.S. dollar.
Exports	Clothing, textiles, electronic products, consumer goods.
Imports	Foodstuffs, raw materials, petroleum.
Regulations	The major free enterprise system in the world, with very little government regulation. Hong Kong is a free port with no tariffs on imported goods.
Local Agent	Highly recommended.
Business Tips	Avoid the summer tourist season.
Health	No major problems.
Business Hours	Monday through Friday 8:30 A.M. to 5 P.M. Saturday 8:30 A.M. to 12:30 P.M.
Climate	Hot and humid summers (86 degrees), comfortable winters.
Clothing	Lightweight suits.
Local Holidays	New Year's Day (January 1), Chinese New Year (3 days in January or February), Good Friday and Easter Monday (March or April, varies), Ching Ming Festival (March or April, varies), Queen's Birthday (June, varies), Dragon Boat Festival (June), Mid-Autumn Festival (September), Chung Yeung Festival (October), Christmas (December 25), Boxing Day (December 26).
Local Time	9 A.M. EST is 10 P.M. in Hong Kong.
Travel Documents	Passport only required.

Hungary

Official Name	Republic of Hungary.
Population	Approximately 10 million.

Main Cities	Budapest is the capital.
Government	Republic with elected president and National Assembly.
Language	Hungarian.
Religion	Roman Catholic 67%, Protestant 25%, other 8%.
Literacy Rate	99%
Crime Rate	1,748 total offenses per 100,000 persons, 3.8 murders per 100,000 persons, 1,022 thefts per 100,000 persons.
GDP	$75 billion. $7,500 per capita.
Currency	Forint (F). Approximately 166 to one U.S. dollar.
Exports	Raw materials, chemicals, semi-finished goods, food, agricultural products.
Imports	Fuels, machinery, consumer goods, foodstuffs.
Local Agent	Recommend.
Climate	Warm summers, mild winters with some snow.
Local Holidays	Christian holidays, New Year's Day (January 1), National Day (March 15), Labor Day (May 1), Constitution Day (August 20).
Local Time	9 A.M. EST is 3 P.M. in Hungary.
Travel Documents	Passport only required for stay up to 30 days.

Iceland

Official Name	Republic of Iceland.
Population	Approximately 270,000.
Main Cities	Reykjavik is the capital. Other major centers are Akureyri and Keflavik.
Government	Republic with elected president parliament (Althing).
Language	Icelandic, but most businesspersons speak English.
Religion	Lutheran 96%, other 4%.
Local Customs	People's names are based on their father's and mother's name. If a man's father's first name is Richard, the man's last name will be Richardson. If a woman's mother's first name was Sigrun, the woman's last name will be Sigrundottir.
Literacy Rate	100%
GDP	$5.3 billion. $19,800 per capita.
Currency	Icelandic krona (IKr). Approximately 66 to one U.S. dollar.
Exports	Fish products, aluminum, wool.
Imports	Petroleum, industrialized products, foodstuffs, consumer goods.
Regulations	Government-owned companies have monopoly over liquor, fertilizer, and some other products.

Local Agent	Essential.
Business Tips	The standard of living is high, with an abundance of electrical and electronic products in each household.
Business Hours	9 A.M. to 5 P.M. Monday through Friday.
Climate	The Gulf Stream moderates the climate. Average July temperature is about 52 degrees, and average January temperature is about 35 degrees.
Clothing	Usual business wear.
Local Holidays	Christian holidays, New Year's Day (January 1), First Day of Summer (April 25), Labor Day (May 1), Independence Day (June 17), Bank Holiday (August 5).
Local Time	9 A.M. EST is 2 P.M. in Iceland.
Travel Documents	Passport only required for stay up to 3 months.

India

Official Name	Republic of India.
Population	Approximately 967 million.
Main Cities	New Delhi is the capital. Other main centers are Bombay, Calcutta, Madras and Bangalore.
Government	Federal republic with elected People's Assembly. Made up of 25 states and 7 territories.
Language	There are numerous official languages. Hindi is the national language, and English is widely used in business and government.
Religion	Hindu 83%, Islam 11%, Christian 2%, Sikh 2%, other 2%.
Literacy Rate	48%
GDP	$1,538 billion. $1,600 per capita.
Currency	Indian rupee (Rs). Approximately 35 to one U.S. dollar.
Exports	Textiles, clothing, jewelry, manufactured goods.
Imports	Petroleum, machinery, fertilizer, chemicals, and consumer goods.
Local Agent	Highly recommended.
Climate	Varies from tropical in the south to temperate in the north.
Clothing	Standard business suits.
Health	Immunizations against typhoid, tetanus, hepatitis, and diphtheria are recommended, as well as anti-malaria medication. AIDS test required for stay in excess of 1 year.
Local Holidays	Proclamation Day (January 26).
Local Time	9 A.M. EST is 7:30 P.M. in India.
Travel Documents	Passport and visa required, obtained from Indian diplomatic missions abroad, good for 4-month stay.

Indonesia

Official Name	Republic of Indonesia.
Population	Approximately 210 million.
Main Cities	Capital is Jakarta. Other major cities are Surabaya, Medan, Bandung, and Semarang.
Government	President, a 1000-member People's Consultative Assembly, and a 500-member House of Representatives in which 100 are appointed from the Armed Forces.
Language	Indonesian is the official language, but English is widely spoken in business.
Religion	Moslem 87%, Christian 9%, Hindu 2%, others 2%.
Local Customs	Moslem customs are observed.
Literacy Rate	77%
Crime Rate	152 total offenses per 100,000 persons, 0.8 murders per 100,000 persons, 48 thefts per 100,000 persons.
GDP	$780 billion. $3,770 per capita.
Currency	Indonesian rupiah (Rp). Approximately 2,400 to one U.S. dollar.
Exports	Petroleum, natural gas, wood products, rubber, textiles, clothing.
Imports	Industrialized products, consumer goods.
Regulations	No import licenses are required. Some foodstuffs can only be imported by the government.
Local Agent	In general, foreign companies are not allowed to do business directly in the country. Law requires the appointment of a government-approved agent.
Business Tips	Business is slow paced and often not discussed at the first meeting. Gifts are often given when visiting.
Health	Immunizations against cholera, tetanus, polio, and typhoid are recommended, as well as anti-malaria medication. Immunization against yellow fever is required for those arriving from an infected area.
Business Hours	8 A.M. to 4 P.M. Monday through Friday. 8 A.M. to 1 P.M. on Saturday.
Climate	Tropical with high humidity and temperatures in the 90-degree range.
Clothing	Lightweight trousers, shirt, and tie are usual business dress, except when calling on senior officials when a suit is more appropriate.
Local Holidays	Muslim holidays and the month of Ramadan are observed. New Year's Day (January 1), Independence Day (August 17).
Local Time	There are three time zones. 9 A.M. EST is 9 P.M. in the western zone that includes Jakarta.
Travel Documents	Passport only required for visits under two months.

Iran

Official Name	Islamic Republic of Iran.
Population	Approximately 68 million.
Main Cities	Tehran is the capital.
Government	An Islamic republic, with elected president and parliament called Majilis, and an appointed upper chamber.
Language	Farsi.
Religion	Islam 99%, other 1%.
Literacy Rate	54%
GDP	$344 billion. $5,200 per capita.
Currency	Iranian rial (IR). Approximately 1,755 to one U.S. dollar.
Exports	Petroleum, carpets, fruits.
Imports	Machinery, foodstuffs.
Local Agent	Highly recommend.
Business Tips	Muslim law is strictly adhered to. Always refer to the Gulf as the Persian Gulf.
Climate	The climate varies from the southern desert region to the mountains in the west. Average temperatures vary from 40 degrees in January to 90 degrees in July.
Health	Cholera and yellow fever certificates required if travelling from an infected area. Typhoid and cholera immunization recommended. AIDS certificate required if staying more than three months.
Local Holidays	The Muslim weekend (Thursday and Friday), Muslim holidays, and the month of Ramadan are observed. New Year's Day (January 1), National Day (February 11), Petrol Nationalization Day (March 19), Nowruz, the Iranian New Year (March 21–24), Republic Day (April 1), Revolution Day (June 5).
Local Time	9 A.M. EST is 5:30 P.M. in Iran.
Travel Documents	Passport and visa required, obtained from an Iranian diplomatic mission abroad.

Iraq

Official Name	Republic of Iraq.
Population	Approximately 22 million.
Main Cities	Baghdad is the capital. Other centers are Basra, Mosul, Kirkuk, and Sulaymaniyah.
Government	Republic governed by the Ba'ath party in which Saddam Hussein is secretary general. He is also president and prime minister. There is an elected National Assembly with limited powers.

Language	Arabic is the official language. French and English are spoken in business.
Religion	Islam 97%, other 3%.
Literacy Rate	60%
GDP	$42 billion. $2,000 per capita.
Currency	Iraqi dinar (ID). Officially 3.2 to one U.S. dollar. Black-market rate approximately 1,200 to one U.S. dollar. Fluctuates widely.
Exports	Petroleum, fertilizer, sulfur.
Imports	Manufactured goods, foodstuffs.
Local Agent	Highly recommended.
Climate	Very hot. Summer temperatures up to 120 degrees and winter temperatures around 75 degrees.
Health	Within five days of arrival, visitors must arrange for an AIDS test. Malaria and hepatitis medication recommended.
Local Holidays	The Muslim weekend (Thursday and Friday), Muslim holidays, and the month of Ramadan are observed. New Year's Day (January 1), Labor Day (May 1), Republic Day (July 14), Revolution Anniversary (July 17), Iran/Iraq War Cease Fire Day (August 8).
Local Time	9 A.M. EST is 5:30 P.M. in Iraq.
Travel Documents	Passport and visa required, obtained from an Iraq diplomatic mission abroad with a letter of sponsorship from an Iraqi. After 15 days in the country, all visitors must register, and they require an exit visa to leave.

Ireland

Official Name	Ireland.
Population	Approximately 3.5 million.
Main Cities	Dublin is the capital.
Government	Republic with elected president, Senate and House of Representatives.
Language	English is the main language, but Gaelic is widely spoken.
Religion	Roman Catholic 93%, other 7%.
Literacy Rate	98%
Crime Rate	2,529 total offenses per 100,000 persons, 0.96 murders per 100,000 persons, 2,238 thefts per 100,000 persons.
GDP	$60 billion. $16,800 per capita.
Currency	Irish pound (£Ir). Approximately 0.62 to one U.S. dollar.
Exports	Machinery, chemicals, electronic equipment.
Imports	Foodstuffs, petroleum, machinery, textiles and clothing, consumer goods.

Local Agent	Advisable.
Climate	Temperate climate modified by the North Atlantic Current. Cool summers, cool and damp winters.
Local Holidays	Christian holidays, New Year's Day (January 1), St. Patrick's Day (March 17).
Local Time	9 A.M. EST is 2 P.M. in Ireland.
Travel Documents	Passport only required for stays up to 90 days.

Israel

Official Name	State of Israel.
Population	Approximately 5 million.
Main Cities	Jerusalem is the capital. Other centers are Tel Aviv, Jaffa, and Haifa.
Government	Parliamentary democracy, with a parliament or Knesset elected for four years.
Language	Official languages are Hebrew and Arabic, but English is widely spoken.
Religion	Judaism 83%, Islam 13%, Christianity, and other 4%.
Literacy Rate	92%
GDP	$86 billion. $16,400 per capita.
Currency	New Israeli shekel (NIS). Approximately 3.3 to one U.S. dollar.
Exports	Fruits, chemicals, machinery, textiles and clothing, electronics, military equipment.
Imports	Fuel, machinery, military equipment, raw materials, foodstuffs.
Regulations	Import licenses are required for many items.
Local Agent	Over 90% of the imports are handled by agents.
Business Tips	Government foreign purchases usually require matching purchases by the exporting country.
Business Hours	8 A.M. to 3 P.M. Sunday through Thursday. 8 A.M. to 1 P.M. Friday.
Climate	Hot dry summers and mild winters. In summer temperatures in Tel Aviv range from about 72 to 88 degrees and in winter from about 48 to 64 degrees.
Clothing	Business suits.
Local Holidays	Saturday, the Sabbath, is the official weekly holiday, but Muslims and Christians celebrate their respective holidays. First Day of Passover (April), Last Day of Passover (April), Independence Day (April 30), Shavout (May, 2 days), Rosh Hashanah (September), Yom Kippur Day (September), First Day of Succoth (October), Last Day of Succoth (October).
Local Time	9 A.M. EST is 2 P.M. in Israel.
Travel Documents	Passport good for 90-day visit.

Italy

Official Name	Republic of Italy.
Population	Approximately 58 million.
Main Cities	Rome is the capital. Other major centers are Milan, Naples, and Turin.
Government	Republic, with elected Senate and Chamber of Deputies.
Language	Italian, with German and French spoken in some regions.
Religion	Predominantly Roman Catholic.
Literacy Rate	98%
Crime Rate	3,298 total offenses per 100,000 persons, 2.18 murders per 100,000 persons, 2,085 thefts per 100,000 persons.
GDP	$1.12 trillion. $19,600 per capita.
Currency	Italian Lira (Lit). Approximately 1,570 to one U.S. dollar.
Exports	Textiles, clothing and footwear, motor vehicles, chemicals, industrialized products.
Imports	Petroleum, raw materials, chemicals, agricultural products.
Regulations	Food imports are subject to strict regulations. For example, the meat of animals that have been fed estrogens is forbidden. Many other products are also under import controls.
Local Agent	Recommended.
Business Tips	Avoid visits during the summer holiday months. Be prepared to wait for meetings. Business does not happen quickly in Italy.
Climate	Hot, dry summers and mild, humid winters. The average temperature throughout the year in Rome is about 61 degrees.
Clothing	Usual business wear.
Local Holidays	Christian holidays, Anniversary of the Republic (June 2).
Local Time	9 A.M. EST is 3 P.M. in Italy.
Travel Documents	Passport only required for stays up to 3 months.

Jamaica

Official Name	Jamaica.
Population	Approximately 2.5 million.
Main Cities	Kingston is the capital.
Government	Parliamentary democracy with elected House of Representatives.
Language	English and Creole.
Religion	Protestant 56%, Roman Catholic 5%, other 39%.

Literacy Rate	98%
Crime Rate	1,774 total offenses per 100,000 persons, 16.56 murders per 100,000 persons, 791 thefts per 100,000 persons.
GDP	$8.4 billion. $3,260 per capita.
Currency	Jamaican dollar (J$). Approximately 35 to one U.S. dollar.
Exports	Bauxite (aluminum ore), sugar, fruit, rum.
Imports	Fuel, machinery, foodstuffs, consumer products.
Local Agent	Recommended.
Climate	Hot and humid.
Local Holidays	Christian holidays, Independence Day (August 6).
Local Time	9 A.M. EST is 9 A.M. in Jamaica.
Travel Documents	Passport only required for stay up to 6 months.

Japan

Official Name	Japan.
Population	Approximately 125 million.
Main Cities	Tokyo is the capital. Other main centers are Yokohama, Osaka, Nagoya, Kyoko, Kobe, Sapporo, and Kawasaki.
Government	Constitutional monarchy, with an elected House of Representatives and House of Councilors, jointly referred to as the Diet.
Language	Japanese, with some English used commercially.
Religion	Shinto 96%, Buddhist 76%, other 13%. (Most Japanese observe both Shintoism and Buddhism.)
Local Customs	Bowing stiffly from the waist is the standard form of greeting, which may be followed with a handshake. Do not address Japanese people by their first names unless asked to do so. Use the surname with "san" added on.
Literacy Rate	99%
Crime Rate	1,430 total offenses per 100,000 persons, 1.2 murders per 100,000 persons, 1,160 thefts per 100,000 persons.
GDP	$2.85 trillion. $22,700 per capita.
Currency	Yen (Y). Approximately 118 to one U.S. dollar.
Exports	Automobiles, steel, electronics, chemicals, consumer goods.
Imports	Raw materials, foodstuffs, fuel.
Regulations	Import controls are surreptitiously carried out by imposing product standards.
Local Agent	Very large trading firms with wide distribution networks are often more suitable than smaller, specialized firms, depending on the product.

Business Tips	Exchanging business cards is a ritual, and it is considered disrespectful to write on them.
Health	International Certificate of Vaccination against smallpox, typhoid, and cholera, if arriving from infected areas.
Business Hours	9 A.M. to 5 P.M. Monday through Friday.
Climate	Hot and humid in summer with average temperature around 80 degrees, and cool winters with average temperature around 40 degrees.
Local Holidays	New Year's Day (January 1), Adults' Day (January 15), National Foundation Day (February 11), Vernal Equinox (March 20 or 21), Greenery Day (April 29), Constitution Day (May 3), Children's Day (May 5), Senior Citizens' Day (September 15), Autumnal Equinox (September 23 or 24), Sports Day (October 10), Cultural Day (November 3), Labor Day (November 23), Emperor's Birthday (December 23).
Local Time	9 A.M. EST is 11 P.M. in Japan.
Travel Documents	Passport only for 90-day visit.

Jordan

Official Name	Hashemite Kingdom of Jordan.
Population	Approximately 4 million.
Main Cities	Amman is the capital.
Government	Constitutional monarchy with an elected House of Representatives and an appointed Senate.
Language	Arabic is the official language. English widely spoken.
Religion	Islam 92%, Christian 8%.
Literacy Rate	80%
Crime Rate	486 total offenses per 100,000 persons, 1.96 murders per 100,000 persons, 125 thefts per 100,000 persons.
GDP	$21 billion. $5,000 per capita.
Currency	Jordanian dinar (JD). Approximately 0.69 to one U.S. dollar.
Exports	Fertilizers, agricultural products.
Imports	Petroleum, machinery, foodstuffs, manufactured goods, consumer goods.
Local Agent	Essential.
Climate	Varies with altitude. Hot and dry summers, mild and wet winters.
Local Holidays	The Muslim weekend (Thursday and Friday), Muslim holidays, and the month of Ramadan are observed. Labor Day (May 1), Independence Day (May 25), King Hussein's Accession (August 11), King Hussein's Birthday (November 14).
Local Time	9 A.M. EST is 4 P.M. in Jordan.
Travel Documents	Passport and visa required.

Kazakhstan

Official Name	Republic of Kazakhstan.
Population	Approximately 18 million.
Main Cities	Almaty is the capital.
Government	Recently independent state of former U.S.S.R.
Language	Kazakh is the official language. Russian is the business language.
Religion	Islam 47%, Christian 17%, other 36%.
Literacy Rate	100%
GDP	$49 billion. $2,880 per capita.
Currency	Tenga. Approximately 75 to one U.S. dollar.
Exports	Raw materials (provides 40% of world's chrome), petroleum, chemicals.
Imports	Machinery.
Local Agent	Highly recommended.
Climate	Varies from north to south. In Almaty temperatures range from 27 degrees in winter to 95 in summer.
Health	Immunization against all diseases recommended. Take maximum protection with drinking water and food. Take sterilized needles in case of requirement.
Local Time	9 A.M. EST is 8 P.M. in Kazakhstan.
Travel Documents	Passport and visa required, obtained from Russian diplomatic missions abroad that represent Kazakhstan. All areas to be visited must be listed.

Kenya

Official Name	Republic of Kenya.
Population	Approximately 29 million.
Main Cities	Nairobi is the capital.
Government	Republic with elected president and National Assembly.
Language	English and Swahili are the official languages. Numerous other languages are spoken.
Religion	Roman Catholic 28%, Protestant 26%, Islam 6%, other 40%.
Literacy Rate	69%
Crime Rate	486 total offenses per 100,000 persons, 4.85 murders per 100,000 persons, 86 thefts per 100,000 persons.
GDP	$39 billion. $1,400 per capita.
Currency	Kenyan shilling (KSh). Approximately 55 to one U.S. dollar.

Exports	Tea, coffee.
Imports	Machinery, petroleum, raw materials, foodstuffs, consumer goods.
Local Agent	Recommended.
Climate	Tropical climate along the coast. Arid in the interior.
Health	Immunizations for yellow fever, typhoid, polio, and hepatitis are recommended.
Local Holidays	Christian holidays, New Year's Day (January 1), Labor Day (May 1), Madaraka Day (June 1), Kenyatta Day (October 20), Independence Day (December 12).
Local Time	9 A.M. EST is 5 P.M. in Kenya.
Travel Documents	Passport and visa required. Transit visa for stay up to 7 days issued at airport. Other visas must be obtained from Kenyan diplomatic mission abroad.

Kuwait

Official Name	State of Kuwait.
Population	Approximately 1.8 million.
Main Cities	Kuwait City is the capital.
Government	Governed by a ruling family, with an elected National Assembly.
Language	Arabic is official language, but English is widely spoken in business.
Religion	Islam 85%, other 15%.
Local Customs	Muslim customs are predominant, in which alcohol and pork are forbidden. Alcohol is forbidden by law. Food and other items should be taken and passed with the right hand.
Literacy Rate	73%
Crime Rate	695 total offenses per 100,000 persons, 6.64 murders per 100,000 persons, 171 thefts per 100,000 persons.
GDP	$33 billion. $16,700 per capita.
Currency	Kuwaiti dinar (KD). Approximately 0.30 to one U.S. dollar.
Exports	Petroleum.
Imports	Industrialized products, foodstuffs, automobiles, consumer goods.
Local Agent	Agent required by law, and they must be a national.
Business Tips	Business depends heavily on frequent personal contact. Avoid visits during the month of Ramadan.
Health	Immunizations against typhoid, tetanus, polio, and meningococcal meningitis are recommended.
Business Hours	8 A.M. to 12:30 P.M., then 4 P.M. to 7 P.M., Saturday through Wednesday.
Climate	Extremely hot in summer with temperatures up to 120 degrees, milder in winter.
Clothing	Lightweight business clothes.

Local Holidays	The Muslim weekend (Thursday and Friday), Muslim holidays, and the month of Ramadan are observed. New Year's Day (January 1), National Day (February 25).
Local Time	9 A.M. EST is 5 P.M. in Kuwait.
Travel Documents	Passport and visa are required, obtainable only by a letter of invitation from a national sponsor. Visa can be provided to the visitor on arrival, provided the letter of invitation is available.

Laos

Official Name	Lao People's Democratic Republic.
Population	Approximately 5.1 million.
Main Cities	Vientiane is the capital.
Government	Communist state.
Language	Lao is the official language. English and French also spoken.
Religion	Buddhist 85%, other 15%.
Literacy Rate	84%
GDP	$5.7 billion. $1,150 per capita.
Currency	New kip (NK). Approximately 960 to one U.S. dollar.
Exports	Electricity, wood products, tin.
Imports	Fuel, foodstuffs, consumer goods.
Local Agent	Highly recommended.
Business Tips	Government ownership and control of all economic activity.
Climate	Tropical. Monsoon season is May to September.
Health	Medical facilities extremely limited. Anti-malaria medication recommended.
Local Holidays	National Day (December 2).
Local Time	9 A.M. EST is 9 P.M. in Laos.
Travel Documents	Passport and visa required. Visa obtained from Laos diplomatic mission abroad.

Latvia

Official Name	Republic of Latvia.
Population	Approximately 2.4 million.
Main Cities	Riga is the capital.
Government	Recently independent state of former U.S.S.R.
Language	Latvian is the official language. Other languages are Russian and Lithuanian.

Religion	Lutheran, Roman Catholic, Russian Orthodox.
Literacy Rate	100%
Currency	Lat. Approximately 0.56 to one U.S. dollar.
Exports	Dairy products, vehicles, machinery, foodstuffs.
Imports	Fuel, electricity, raw materials.
Local Agent	Recommended.
Local Holidays	Independence Day (November 18).
Local Time	9 A.M. EST is 4 P.M. in Latvia.
Travel Documents	Passport only required.

Lebanon

Official Name	Lebanese Republic.
Population	Approximately 3.5 million.
Main Cities	Beirut is the capital. Tripoli is another major center.
Government	Elected president, and Chamber of Deputies divided equally between Christians and Muslims.
Language	Arabic is the official language, with English and French widely spoken in business.
Religion	Islam 70%, Christian 30%.
Literacy Rate	80%
GDP	$13 billion. $3,400 per capita.
Currency	Lebanese Pound (£L). Approximately 1,550 to one U.S. dollar.
Exports	Agricultural products, textiles, metal products.
Imports	Petroleum, machinery, consumer goods.
Local Agent	Essential.
Business Tips	Lebanon is going through a major rebuilding phase following the prolonged civil war.
Climate	Average summer temperature in Beirut is 80 degrees, and 60 degrees in winter. It is colder at higher elevations, and snow is not unusual in the mountains.
Health	Immunization certificate required for yellow fever if travelling from infected area.
Local Holidays	The working week is Monday through Thursday. Muslim holidays are observed, as are Christian holidays such as Easter and Christmas. New Year's Day (January 1), Arab League Anniversary (March 22), Independence Day (November 22).
Local Time	9 A.M. EST is 4 P.M. in Lebanon.
Travel Documents	Passport and visa required.

Liberia

Official Name	Republic of Liberia.
Population	Approximately 2.6 million.
Main Cities	Monrovia is the capital.
Government	Republic with elected president and House of Representatives, but currently undergoing civil war.
Language	English is the official language. Many other local languages spoken.
Religion	Local 70%, Islam 20%, Christian 10%.
Literacy Rate	40%
GDP	$2.4 billion. $1,100 per capita.
Currency	Liberian dollar (L$). Approximately 50 to one U.S. dollar.
Exports	Iron ore, rubber, timber.
Imports	Fuels, machinery, chemicals, foodstuffs.
Local Agent	Highly recommended.
Business Tips	Most businesspeople have fled the country because of the civil war.
Climate	Hot, humid, and rainy summers. Dry winters with hot days and cool nights.
Health	Medical facilities are basic. Immunizations for yellow fever and cholera are recommended, as well as anti-malaria medication.
Local Holidays	Independence Day (July 26).
Local Time	9 A.M. EST is 3 P.M. in Liberia.
Travel Documents	Passport and visa required. Visa obtained from Liberian diplomatic mission abroad.

Libya

Official Name	Socialist People's Libyan Arab Great Jamahiriya.
Population	Approximately 5.6 million.
Main Cities	Tripoli is the capital. Benghazi is also a major center.
Government	The General People's Congress has the ruling power, with the General People's Committee exercising the power and electing the head of state.
Language	Arabic is the official language. Berber, French, and English also spoken.
Religion	Islam 97%, other 3%.
Literacy Rate	64%
Crime Rate	890 total offenses per 100,000 persons, 2.26 murders per 100,000 persons, 208 thefts per 100,000 persons.

GDP	$35 billion. $6,570 per capita.
Currency	Libyan dinar (LD). Approximately 0.3 to one U.S. dollar.
Exports	Petroleum, natural gas.
Imports	Machinery, foodstuffs.
Local Agent	Highly recommended.
Climate	Coastal areas have summer temperatures up to 105, and winter temperatures around 80 during the day and around 40 at night. Desert temperatures are very hot in the day (120) and cool to cold at night.
Health	Require certificates for yellow fever and cholera immunizations if arriving from an infected area. Immunizations against cholera, typhoid, and polio are recommended, as well as medication against malaria.
Local Holidays	The Muslim weekend (Thursday and Friday), Muslim holidays, and the month of Ramadan are observed.
Local Time	9 A.M. EST is 3 P.M. in Libya.
Travel Documents	Passport and visa required. All visitors must register on arrival.

Lithuania

Official Name	Republic of Lithuania.
Population	Approximately 3.8 million.
Main Cities	Vilnius is the capital. Klaipeda is an ice-free port.
Government	Recently independent state of former U.S.S.R. Republic with elected president and parliament (Seimas).
Language	Lithuanian is the official language. Polish and Russian are also spoken.
Religion	Roman Catholic, Lutheran, and others.
Literacy Rate	100%
Currency	Lita. Approximately 4 to one U.S. dollar.
Exports	Electronics, foodstuffs, chemicals.
Imports	Fuel, machinery.
Local Agent	Recommended.
Climate	Moderate winters.
Local Holidays	Independence Day (February 16).
Local Time	9 A.M. EST is 4 P.M. in Lithuania.
Travel Documents	Passport only required.

Madagascar

Official Name	Republic of Madagascar.
Population	Approximately 13 million.
Main Cities	Antananarivo is the capital.
Government	Republic with elected president and Popular National Assembly.
Language	French and Malagasy are the official languages.
Religion	Local 52%, Christian 41%, Islam 7%.
Literacy Rate	80%
GDP	$12 billion. $880 per capita.
Currency	Malagasy franc (FMG). Approximately 4,000 to one U.S. dollar.
Exports	Coffee, vanilla, sugar, cloves.
Imports	Petroleum, machinery, foodstuffs, consumer goods.
Local Agent	Highly recommend.
Climate	Tropical.
Health	Immunizations against yellow fever and cholera are recommended, as well as anti-malaria medication.
Local Holidays	National Day (June 26), Assumption Day (August 15), All Saint's Day (November 1).
Local Time	9 A.M. EST is 5 P.M. in Madagascar.
Travel Documents	Passport and visa required.

Malaysia

Official Name	Malaysia.
Population	Approximately 19 million.
Main Cities	Kuala Lumpur is the capital. Other major cities on the Malaysia Peninsula are Penang, Ipoh, Malacca, and Johore Baru. On the Island of Borneo, the major cities are Kota Kinabalu in Sabah and Kuching in Sarawak.
Government	Constitutional monarchy with elected House of Representatives.
Language	Malay is the official language, but English is widely spoken.
Religion	The official religion is Islam. Other religions include Buddhism, Confucianism, Taoism, and Hinduism.
Local Customs	Muslim customs are predominant, such as the rule against passing food with the left-hand and forbidden items such as pork and alcohol.
Literacy Rate	78%

Crime Rate	566 total offenses per 100,000 persons, 2.04 murders per 100,000 persons, 442 thefts per 100,000 persons.
GDP	$215 billion. $10,750 per capita.
Currency	Ringgit (M$). Approximately 2.55 to one U.S. dollar.
Exports	Integrated circuits, clothing, rubber, electronic components, petroleum.
Imports	Industrialized products, paper, foodstuffs, consumer goods.
Regulations	Import duties are prevalent, but free trade zones allow duty-free imports if they will be exported with Malaysian value added.
Local Agent	To do business with the government, the local agent should be a Bumi Putra or indigenous person.
Business Tips	Joint ventures with local companies are popular with the government. Countertrade is popular.
Health	A valid International Certificate of Vaccination against cholera is required, plus yellow fever if arriving from an infected area. Tetanus, polio, and typhoid immunizations are also recommended. Anti-malaria medication is also recommend.
Business Hours	8:30 A.M. to 1 P.M., then 2 P.M. to 4:30 P.M. Monday through Friday. Parts of the country observe the Muslim weekend of Thursday and Friday.
Climate	Hot and humid, with average daytime temperatures about 85 degrees and 75 degrees at night.
Clothing	Lightweight shirt, tie, and trousers are appropriate for most business meetings. Suits should be worn when visiting senior officials.
Local Holidays	Muslim holidays, New Year's Day (January 1), Chinese New Year (February), Labor Day (May 1), Malaysian National Day (August 31), Christmas Day (December 25).
Local Time	9 A.M. EST is 10 P.M. in Malaysia.
Travel Documents	Passport and visitor's pass, issued at the port of entry, good for stay up to 3 months.

Mexico

Official Name	United Mexican States.
Population	Approximately 98 million.
Main Cities	Mexico City is the capital and center of commerce. Other main cities are Guadalajara and Monterrey.
Government	A federal republic, with an elected presidential term of six years, and a congress consisting of a Chamber of Deputies and a Chamber of Senators. There are 31 states and one federal district.
Language	Spanish is the main language although, many businesspeople speak English.
Religion	Predominately Roman Catholic.

Literacy Rate	90%
Crime Rate	108 total offenses per 100,000 persons, 7.34 murders per 100,000 persons, 28.05 thefts per 100,000 persons.
GDP	$777 billion. $8,100 per capita.
Currency	New peso (Mex$). Approximately 7.8 to one U.S. dollar.
Exports	Petroleum, agricultural products, electronic components.
Imports	Industrialized products.
Regulations	Prior to the North America Free Trade Agreement, import permits were required for most categories of goods, but this requirement is changing.
Local Agent	Highly recommended for both marketing purposes and to assist in the documentation requirements.
Health	No special requirements, but the thin and polluted air of Mexico City may cause heart or respiratory problems. For travel in rural tropical areas, anti-malaria medication is recommended.
Business Hours	9 A.M. to 1 P.M., then 2 P.M. to 5 P.M. or 6 P.M.
Climate	The climate varies from tropical along the coasts to cooler but mild in the central plateau. For example, the average temperature in Mexico City in January is 54 degrees and in June it is 64 degrees.
Clothing	In Mexico City, Monterrey, and Guadalajara, business suits are worn. In the south and in tourist areas such as Acapulco, sports shirts are the norm.
Local Holidays	Christian holidays, Independence Day (September 16).
Local Time	9 A.M. EST is 8 A.M. in Mexico City.
Travel Documents	A passport and tourist card, which can be issued by a travel agent or the airlines.

Monaco

Official Name	Principality of Monaco.
Population	Approximately 31,000.
Main Cities	Monaco is the capital.
Government	Constitutional monarchy, with elected National Assembly.
Language	French is the official language, but English and Italian are widely spoken.
Religion	Roman Catholic 95%, other 5%.
Crime Rate	4,068 total offenses per 100,000 persons, 1,953 thefts per 100,000 persons.
GDP	$800 million. $25,000 per capita.
Currency	French franc (F). Approximately 5.4 to the U.S. dollar.

Local Agent	Highly recommended.
Business Tips	There are no income taxes in Monaco.
Climate	Mediterranean, with hot, dry summers and mild, wet winters.
Local Holidays	Christian holidays, National Day (November 19).
Local Time	9 A.M. EST is 3 P.M. in Monaco.
Travel Documents	Passport only required for visit up to 2 months.

Mongolia

Official Name	Mongolia.
Population	Approximately 2.4 million.
Main Cities	Ulan Batar is the capital.
Government	Republic with elected president and State Great Hural.
Language	Mongol.
Religion	Buddhist 96%, Islam 4%.
GDP	$5.1 billion. $2,060 per capita.
Currency	Tughrik (Tug). Approximately 710 to one U.S. dollar.
Exports	Raw materials, animal products.
Imports	Machinery, foodstuffs.
Local Agent	Highly recommended.
Business Tips	Mongolia has the largest number of livestock per person in the world.
Climate	Cool summers, and very cold winters.
Local Holidays	National Day (July 11).
Local Time	9 A.M. EST is 10 P.M. in Mongolia.
Travel Documents	Passport and visa required.

Morocco

Official Name	Kingdom of Morocco.
Population	Approximately 30 million.
Main Cities	Rabat is the capital. Casablanca is the largest city. Other centers are Fes, Marrakech, and Meknes.
Government	Constitutional monarchy, with elected parliament.
Language	Arabic is the official language, but French is used in government and business.

Religion	Islam 99%, Christian and other 1%.
Literacy Rate	50%
GDP	$97 million. $3,260 per capita.
Currency	Moroccan dirham (DH). Approximately 9.02 to one U.S. dollar.
Exports	Raw material, foodstuffs, semi-processed goods, consumer goods.
Imports	Raw material, equipment, foodstuffs, consumer goods.
Local Agent	Highly recommended.
Business Tips	Business is conducted in French, English is rarely used.
Climate	Temperatures in coastal areas are about 50 degrees in January and 70 degrees in August. In the interior, temperatures vary from 30 degrees in February to 110 degrees in August.
Clothing	Lightweight suits in summer, heavier suits and raincoats in winter.
Health	Immunizations are advisable for typhoid, cholera, tetanus, and polio, as well as medication to prevent malaria.
Local Holidays	During the month of Ramadan, government and businesses work reduced hours. New Year's Day (January 1), National Holiday (January 11), Coronation Day (March 3), Labor Day (May 1), National Holiday (May 23), King's Birthday (July 9), National Holiday (August 14), Green March Day (November 6), Independence Day (November 18).
Local Time	9 A.M. EST is 2 P.M. in Morocco.
Travel Documents	Valid passport only required for up to 90-day visit.

Mozambique

Official Name	Republic of Mozambique.
Population	Approximately 18 million.
Main Cities	Maputo is the capital.
Government	Transitioning from a communist state.
Language	Portuguese is the official language. Many local languages spoken.
Religion	Local 60%, Christian 30%, Islam 10%.
Literacy Rate	33%
GDP	$12 billion. $670 per capita.
Currency	Metical (Mt). Approximately 11,450 to one U.S. dollar.
Exports	Shrimp, nuts, sugar.
Imports	Petroleum, foodstuffs, clothing, machinery.
Local Agent	Highly recommended.
Climate	Tropical.

Health	Medical facilities are basic. Immunizations against typhoid, tetanus, and hepatitis are recommended, as well as anti-malaria medication.
Local Holidays	New Year's Day (January 1), Mozambican Heroes Day (February 3), Mozambican Women's Day (April 7), Workers Day (May 1), Independence Day (June 25), Lusaka Agreement Day (September 7), Family Day (December 25).
Local Time	9 A.M. EST is 4 P.M. in Mozambique.
Travel Documents	Passport and visa required. Visa good for 30 days, obtained at Mozambique diplomatic mission abroad.

Nepal

Official Name	Kingdom of Nepal.
Population	Approximately 23 million.
Main Cities	Kathmandu is the capital.
Government	Elected House of Representatives.
Language	Nepali is the official language. Many other languages spoken.
Religion	Hindu 90%, Buddhist 5%, Islam 3%, other 2%.
Literacy Rate	26%
GDP	$26 billion. $1,200 per capita.
Currency	Nepalese rupee (NR). Approximately 57 to one U.S. dollar.
Exports	Carpets, clothing, textiles.
Imports	Petroleum, fertilizers, machinery.
Local Agent	Highly recommended.
Climate	Cool summers and severe winters in the north, warm summers and mild winters in the south.
Health	Immunizations against typhus, hepatitis, polio, yellow fever, and meningitis are recommended, as well as anti-malaria medication.
Local Holidays	King's Birthday (December 28).
Local Time	9 A.M. EST is 7:45 P.M. in Nepal.
Travel Documents	Passport and visa required. A tourist visa for stays up to 15 days are issued at the airport.

Netherlands

Official Name	Kingdom of the Netherlands.
Population	Approximately 15.3 million.

Main Cities	Amsterdam is the capital. Other major centers are Rotterdam, The Hague, Utrecht, Eindhoven, and Arnhem.
Government	Constitutional monarchy, with elected First Chamber and Second Chamber.
Language	Dutch, but most of the people speak English.
Religion	Roman Catholic 36%, Protestant 27%, other 37%.
Literacy Rate	99%
GDP	$315 billion. $20,454 per capita.
Currency	Netherlands guilder, gulden, or florin (f.). Approximately 1.80 to one U.S. dollar.
Exports	Industrialized products, electronics.
Imports	Raw materials, petroleum, chemicals, foodstuffs.
Regulations	There are bans on many foods with additives. Many other foodstuffs are under import controls.
Local Agent	Dutch firms prefer to deal directly with manufacturers on large volume sales, but agents are recommended for products with numerous smaller sales.
Business Tips	Avoid visits during the holiday months of July and August.
Climate	Cool summers average about 68 degrees, and mild winters average about 35 degrees.
Clothing	Usual business wear.
Local Holidays	Christian holidays, New Year's Day (January 1), Queen's Birthday (April 30).
Local Time	9 A.M. EST is 3 P.M. in the Netherlands.
Travel Documents	Passport only required for stay up to 90 days.

New Zealand

Official Name	New Zealand.
Population	Approximately 4 million.
Main Cities	Wellington is the capital, but Auckland is the main industrial city and the largest in the country. Christchurch is also a major center.
Government	Similar to that of the United Kingdom.
Language	English is the official language. Maori also spoken.
Religion	Mainly Christian.
Literacy Rate	99%
GDP	$66 billion. $18,500 per capita.
Currency	New Zealand dollar (NZ$). Approximately 1.42 to the U.S. dollar.
Exports	Sheep and cattle products, pulp, paper.
Imports	Fuel, industrialized products, consumer goods.

Regulations	Strict regulations apply to the importation of animal and plant products.
Local Agent	Agents based in Aukland are recommended, unless for government customers when a Wellington agent may be more appropriate. Many New Zealanders resent Australia-based agents.
Business Tips	Avoid business trips during the summer holidays of December and January.
Health	No special precautions needed.
Business Hours	8:30 P.M. to 5 P.M., Monday through Friday.
Climate	Similar to the northwest coast of the United States.
Clothing	Usual business wear.
Local Holidays	Christian holidays, ANZAC Day (April 25), Queen's Birthday (June 4), Labor Day (October 22).
Local Time	9 A.M. EST is 3 P.M. the next day in New Zealand.
Travel Documents	Passport only required for stay up to 3 months.

Nicaragua

Official Name	Republic of Nicaragua.
Population	Approximately 4 million.
Main Cities	Managua is the capital.
Government	Republic with elected president and National Assembly.
Language	Spanish is the official language.
Religion	Roman Catholic 95%, Protestant 5%.
Literacy Rate	57%
GDP	$7.7 billion. $1,800 per capita.
Currency	Cordoba (C$). Approximately 8.63 to one U.S. dollar.
Exports	Coffee, cotton, sugar, bananas.
Imports	Petroleum, machinery, clothing, foodstuffs.
Local Agent	Highly recommended.
Business Tips	Much of the economy is under government control.
Climate	Tropical along the coast, cooler in the highlands.
Health	Anti-malaria medication is recommended.
Local Holidays	Christian holidays, New Year's Day (January 1), Labor Day (May 1), Revolution Day (July 19), Independence Day (September 15).
Local Time	9 A.M. EST is 8 A.M. in Nicaragua.
Travel Documents	Passport only required.

Nigeria

Official Name	Federal Republic of Nigeria.
Population	Approximately 107 million.
Main Cities	Lagos is the capital and commercial center. Other major centers are Ibadan, Kano, and Kaduna.
Government	Military dictatorship.
Language	English is the official and business language. Many other languages are spoken in the country.
Religion	Islam 50%, Christian 40%, local 10%.
Literacy Rate	51%
GDP	$144 billion. $1,380 per capita.
Currency	Naira (N). Approximately 22 to one U.S. dollar.
Exports	Petroleum.
Imports	Industrialized products, foodstuffs.
Regulations	Import regulations are very confusing, and government bureaucracy is very inefficient at sorting them out.
Local Agent	Many local agents claim special influence because of relatives; however, foreign-owned trading companies handle most of the import business.
Business Tips	Bribery and government corruption is rampant.
Health	Must have an International Certificate of Immunization against yellow fever. Anti-malaria medication is highly recommended.
Business Hours	8 A.M. to 12:30 P.M., then 2 P.M. to 4:30 P.M., Monday through Friday.
Climate	Hot and humid, temperature range is 70 to 90 degrees.
Local Holidays	Muslim and Christian holidays, New Year's Day (January 1), Worker's Day (May 1), National Day (October 1).
Local Time	9 A.M. EST is 3 P.M. in Nigeria.
Travel Documents	Passport and visa required. Visa obtained from Nigerian diplomatic mission abroad.

North Korea

Official Name	Democratic People's Republic of Korea.
Population	Approximately 24 million.
Main Cities	P'yongyang is the capital.
Government	Communist state ruled by leader of Korean Workers' Party.
Language	Korean.
Religion	Buddhism, Confucianism, and some Christianity.

Literacy Rate	99%
GDP	$22 billion. $1,000 per capita.
Currency	North Korean won (Wn). Approximately 2.1 to one U.S. dollar.
Exports	Raw materials, fish products, machinery, military equipment.
Imports	Petroleum, machinery, foodstuffs, consumer goods.
Local Agent	Highly recommended.
Business Tips	More than 90% of the economy is socialized, and state-owned industry produces almost all of the manufactured goods.
Climate	Warm and wet summers. Cold winters with snow.
Local Holidays	National Liberation Day (August 15), DPRK Foundation Day (September 9).
Local Time	9 A.M. EST is 11 P.M. in North Korea.
Travel Documents	U.S. citizens require Treasure Board license to travel in North Korea. Visa is obtained from North Korean diplomatic mission abroad.

Norway

Official Name	Kingdom of Norway.
Population	Approximately 4.3 million.
Main Cities	Oslo is the capital. Other centers are Bergen, Trontheim, and Stavanger.
Government	Constitutional monarchy, with a Parliament elected for a four-year term.
Language	Norwegian, but English is widely spoken.
Religion	Lutheran 88%, other 12%.
Literacy Rate	99%
Crime Rate	5,220 total offenses per 100,000 persons, 1.99 murders per 100,000 persons, 3,936 thefts per 100,000 persons.
GDP	$114 billion. $26,200 per capita.
Currency	Norwegian kroner (NKr). Approximately 6.44 to one U.S. dollar.
Exports	Petroleum, machinery, fish products.
Imports	Machinery, chemicals, raw materials, foodstuffs.
Regulations	A number of state-owned companies have monopolies on trade in certain products such as grain, liquor, fishing equipment, drugs.
Local Agent	Local Norwegian agent essential.
Business Hours	8 A.M. to 3:30 P.M. Monday through Friday.
Climate	Moderate climate due to Gulf Stream. Temperatures range from 0 in winter to 85 degrees in summer.
Clothing	Usual business dress.

Local Holidays	Christian holidays, New Year's Day (January 1), Labor Day (May 1), Constitution Day (May 17).
Local Time	9 A.M. EST is 3 P.M. in Norway.
Travel Documents	Passport only required for stay up to 3 months.

Oman

Official Name	Sultanate of Oman.
Population	Approximately 2 million.
Main Cities	Muscat is the capital.
Government	Absolute monarchy ruled by a sultan, with an advisory council.
Language	Arabic, but English is widely spoken in business.
Religion	Islam.
Local Customs	Muslim customs are predominant, in which alcohol and pork are forbidden. Food and other items should be taken and passed with the right hand, never with the left hand.
GDP	$21 billion. $9,500 per capita.
Currency	Omani rial (RO). Approximately 0.38 to one U.S. dollar.
Exports	Petroleum, natural gas.
Imports	Industrialized products, foodstuffs, automobiles.
Local Agent	Agent required by law, and they must be a national.
Business Tips	Business depends heavily on frequent personal contact. Avoid visits during the month of Ramadan.
Health	Immunizations against typhoid, tetanus, polio, hepatitis, and meningococcal meningitis are recommended. In addition, anti-malaria medication is recommended.
Business Hours	8 A.M. to 12:30 P.M., then 4 P.M. to 7 P.M., Saturday through Wednesday.
Climate	Hot and humid in summer, milder in winter.
Clothing	Lightweight business clothes.
Local Holidays	The Muslim weekend (Thursday and Friday), Muslim holidays, and the month of Ramadan are observed. National Day (November 18), Sultan's Birthday (November 19).
Local Time	9 A.M. EST is 6 P.M. in Oman.
Travel Documents	Passport and visa are required, obtainable only by a letter of invitation from a national sponsor. It is best to have the sponsor arrange for the visa and then send it to you.

Pakistan

Official Name	Islamic Republic of Pakistan.
Population	Approximately 132 million.
Main Cities	Islamabad is the capital, but Karachi is the largest city. Other centers are Lahore, Faisalbad, Rawalpindi, and Hyderabad.
Government	Republic with elected National Assembly and Senate that elect the president.
Language	Official language is Urdu. English is widely spoken in business and government.
Religion	Islam 97%, other 3%.
Literacy Rate	35%
GDP	$296 billion. $2,300 per capita.
Currency	Pakistani rupee (PRs). Approximately 40 to one U.S. dollar.
Exports	Cotton, clothing and textiles, rice.
Imports	Petroleum, machinery, consumer goods.
Local Agent	Essential.
Climate	Climate varies from mountains to desert. Average temperatures are 60 degrees in winter and 100 in summer but can rise up to 120 in some areas. Monsoon season is July to September.
Health	Anti-malaria medication is recommended. Must have immunization certificate for cholera and yellow fever if arriving from an infected area.
Local Holidays	The Muslim weekend (Thursday and Friday), Muslim holidays, and the month of Ramadan are observed. Pakistan Day (March 23), Independence Day (August 14).
Local Time	9 A.M. EST is 7 P.M. in Pakistan.
Travel Documents	Passport and visa required. Requirements vary, check with nearest Pakistani diplomatic mission.

Panama

Official Name	Republic of Panama.
Population	Approximately 2.6 million.
Main Cities	Panama city is the capital.
Government	Republic with elected president and Legislative Assembly.
Language	Spanish is the official language, but English is widely spoken.
Religion	Roman Catholic 85%, Protestant 15%.
Literacy Rate	88%
Crime Rate	703 total offenses per 100,000 persons, 6.12 murders per 100,000 persons, 406 thefts per 100,000 persons.

GDP	$14 billion. $5,300 per capita.
Currency	Balboas (B). Fixed at 1 to one U.S. dollar.
Exports	Bananas, shrimp, clothing.
Imports	Petroleum, foodstuffs, consumer goods.
Local Agent	Highly recommended.
Climate	Hot and humid.
Health	Immunizations against hepatitis, polio, typhoid, tetanus, and yellow fever, as well as anti-malaria medication are recommended.
Local Holidays	Christian holidays, New Year's Day (January 1), Labor Day (May 1), Revolution Day (October 11), Independence Day (November 3).
Local Time	9 A.M. EST is 9 A.M. in Panama.
Travel Documents	Passport and tourist card, issued by airline, only required for stay up to 30 days.

Papau New Guinea

Official Name	Independent State of Papua New Guinea.
Population	Approximately 4.5 million.
Main Cities	Port Moresby is the capital.
Government	Parliamentary democracy with elected National Assembly.
Language	Many different languages spoken. English spoken by most businesspeople.
Religion	Local 34%, Roman Catholic 22%, Protestant 44%.
Literacy Rate	52%
Crime Rate	948 total offenses per 100,000 persons, 9.82 murders per 100,000 persons, 201 thefts per 100,000 persons.
GDP	$11 billion. $2,400 per capita.
Currency	Kina (K). Approximately 0.75 to one U.S. dollar.
Exports	Raw materials, timber, coffee, cocoa, lobster.
Imports	Fuels, machinery, foodstuffs, consumer goods.
Local Agent	Recommended.
Climate	Tropical climate. Monsoon seasons are from December to March and from May to October.
Health	Anti-malaria medication, including for chloroquine-resistant strains, is recommended.
Local Holidays	Independence Day (September 16).
Local Time	9 A.M. EST is midnight in Papua New Guinea.
Travel Documents	Passport only required for stay up to 30 days.

Paraguay

Official Name	Republic of Paraguay.
Population	Approximately 5.6 million.
Main Cities	Asuncion is the capital.
Government	Republic with elected president, Chamber of Senators, and Chamber of Deputies.
Language	Spanish is the official language.
Religion	Predominantly Roman Catholic.
Literacy Rate	90%
GDP	$18 billion. $3,200 per capita.
Currency	Guarani (G). Approximately 2,140 to one U.S. dollar.
Exports	Cotton, soybeans, timber.
Imports	Fuels, industrialized products.
Local Agent	Highly recommended.
Climate	Average summer temperatures are about 85 degrees, and average winter temperatures are about 50 degrees.
Health	Anti-malaria medication is recommended.
Local Holidays	Christian holidays, New Year's Day (January 1), Heroes Day (March 1), Labor Day (May 1), Constitution Day (August 25), Victory of Boqueron Day (September 29).
Local Time	9 A.M. EST is 10 A.M. in Paraguay.
Travel Documents	Passport only required for stay up to 90 days.

Peru

Official Name	Republic of Peru.
Population	Approximately 26 million.
Main Cities	Lima is the capital and commercial center.
Government	Republic with elected president and Democratic Constituent Congress.
Language	Spanish and Quechua are the official languages, but Spanish is the language of business.
Religion	Roman Catholic is major religion.
Local Customs	Local crime can be a problem.
Literacy Rate	85%
GDP	$92 billion. $3,800 per capita.

Currency	Nuevo sol (S/.). Approximately 2.6 to one U.S. dollar.
Exports	Copper, silver, fishmeal, coffee, petroleum products.
Imports	Industrialized products, foodstuffs, consumer goods.
Regulations	Many agricultural imports require import permits.
Local Agent	Most government business is done through agents.
Business Tips	Punctuality is not widely practiced.
Health	Immunization against smallpox and yellow fever is recommended, plus anti-malaria medication.
Business Hours	Business hours vary with the seasons. In summer, government hours are only 5 hours per day.
Climate	On the coast, the average maximum temperature in February (midsummer) is 83 degrees, and the average minimum temperature in August (midwinter) is 56 degrees. The highlands are cooler and the jungle is hotter.
Clothing	Lightweight clothing in summer and medium-weight in winter.
Local Holidays	Christian holidays, New Year's Day (January 1), Labor Day (May 12), Independence Day (July 28).
Local Time	9 A.M. EST is 9 A.M. in Peru.
Travel Documents	Passport allows 90 day visit.

Philippines

Official Name	Republic of the Philippines.
Population	Approximately 76 million.
Main Cities	Manila is the capital and major business center.
Government	Based on the U.S. system.
Language	Main language is Tagalog, but English is the language of business.
Religion	Roman Catholic 83%, Protestant 9%, Islam 5%, other 3%.
Literacy Rate	90%
Crime Rate	316 total offenses per 100,000 persons, 36.87 murders per 100,000 persons, 81 thefts per 100,000 persons.
GDP	$194 billion. $2,600 per capita.
Currency	Philippine peso (P). Approximately 26 to one U.S. dollar.
Exports	Electronics, textiles, clothing.
Imports	Petroleum, industrialized products, consumer goods.
Regulations	Tariffs are high, and many products are subject to import controls.
Local Agent	Highly recommended, based in Manila.
Business Tips	Allow flexibility for meeting times.

Health	International Certificate of Vaccination against yellow fever is required if arriving from an infected area. Immunizations against cholera, tetanus, polio and typhoid are strongly recommended, as well as anti-malaria medication.
Business Hours	8 A.M. to 5 P.M. Monday through Friday.
Climate	Tropical with average temperatures over 80 degrees.
Clothing	Open-necked shirt is standard business dress.
Local Holidays	Christian holidays, Independence Day (June 12).
Local Time	9 A.M. EST is 9 P.M. in the Philippines.
Travel Documents	Passport allows 21-day visit.

Poland

Official Name	Republic of Poland.
Population	Approximately 39 million.
Main Cities	Warsaw is the capital.
Government	Democratic state with elected president and Senate.
Language	Polish.
Religion	Roman Catholic 95%, other Christian 5%.
Literacy Rate	98%
GDP	$246 billion. $6,400 per capita.
Currency	Zlotych (Zl). Approximately 2.82 to one U.S. dollar.
Exports	Machinery, raw materials, foodstuffs.
Imports	Machinery, fuels.
Local Agent	Recommended.
Climate	Mild summers and cold, harsh winters.
Local Holidays	Christian holidays, Constitution Day (May 3).
Local Time	9 A.M. EST is 3 P.M. in Poland.
Travel Documents	Passport only required for stay up to 90 days.

Portugal

Official Name	Portuguese Republic.
Population	Approximately 10 million.
Main Cities	Lisbon is the capital. Other major centers are Porto, Setubal, Coimbra, and Braga.

Government	Republic with elected president and Assembly of the Republic.
Language	Portuguese, with Spanish widely spoken.
Religion	Roman Catholic 97%, other 3%.
Literacy Rate	85%
Crime Rate	712 total offenses per 100,000 persons, 4.5 murders per 100,000 persons, 403 thefts per 100,000 persons.
GDP	$122 billion. $12,400 per capita.
Currency	Portugese escudo (Esc). Approximately 160 to the U.S. dollar.
Exports	Textiles, machinery, cork, wine.
Imports	Petroleum, machinery, raw materials.
Local Agent	Highly recommended.
Climate	Average January temperature is 50 degrees, and average July temperature is 70 degrees.
Clothing	Usual business wear.
Local Holidays	Christian holidays, Republic Day (October 5), Restoration of Independence (December 1).
Local Time	9 A.M. EST is 2 P.M. in Portugal.
Travel Documents	Passport only required for stays up to 60 days.

Puerto Rico

Official Name	Commonwealth of Puerto Rico.
Population	Approximately 3.8 million.
Main Cities	San Juan is the capital and commercial center.
Government	Puerto Rico is somewhat like any U.S. state, in that it has an elected Senate and Legislature that control lawmaking. Puerto Ricans are citizens of the U.S. and have all rights, privileges, and obligations of any other citizen, with the exception that they may not vote in a U.S. presidential election unless they move to the mainland.
Language	Spanish and English are the two official languages.
Religion	Roman Catholic is predominant.
Literacy Rate	89%
GDP	$32 billion. $8,200 per capita.
Currency	U.S. dollar.
Exports	Electronics, clothing, rum.
Imports	Petroleum, foodstuffs.
Regulations	Puerto Rico comes under the U.S. Federal Customs System.

Local Agent	Puerto Rican law stipulates that an agent agreement cannot be terminated without just cause.
Climate	Tropical climate with average winter temperatures of about 73 degrees, and average summer temperatures of about 80 degrees.
Clothing	Lightweight suits year round.
Local Holidays	Mainland U.S. holidays plus Three Kings Day (January 6), De Hostos' Birthday (January 11), Emancipation Day (March 22), De Diego's Birthday (April 16), Munoz Rivera's Birthday (July 17), Constitution Day (July 25), Discovery Day November 19).
Local Time	9 A.M. EST is 10 A.M. in Puerto Rico.
Travel Documents	Non-U.S. citizens require a valid passport.

Qatar

Official Name	State of Qatar.
Population	Approximately 670,000.
Main Cities	Doha is the capital.
Government	Governed by a ruling family.
Language	Official language is Arabic, but English is widely spoken in business.
Religion	Islam.
Local Customs	Muslim customs are predominant, in which alcohol and pork are forbidden. Food and other items should be taken and passed with the right hand.
Literacy Rate	76%
Crime Rate	248 total offenses per 100,000 persons, 3.5 murders per 100,000 persons, 119 thefts per 100,000 persons.
GDP	$12 billion. $21,300 per capita.
Currency	Qatar riyal (QR). Approximately 3.6 to one U.S. dollar.
Exports	Petroleum.
Imports	Industrialized products, foodstuffs, automobiles.
Local Agent	Agent required by law, and they must be a national.
Business Tips	Business depends heavily on frequent personal contact. Avoid visits during the month of Ramadan.
Health	Immunizations against typhoid, tetanus, polio, and meningococcal meningitis are recommended.
Business Hours	8 A.M. to 12:30 P.M., then 4 P.M. to 7 P.M., Saturday through Wednesday.
Climate	Hot and humid in summer (110 degrees), milder in winter.
Clothing	Lightweight business clothes.

Local Holidays	The Muslim weekend (Thursday and Friday), Muslim holidays, and the month of Ramadan are observed. Independence Day (September 3).
Local Time	9 A.M. EST is 5 P.M. in Qatar.
Travel Documents	Passport and visa are required, obtainable from a Qatar diplomatic mission abroad with a letter of invitation from a national sponsor.

Romania

Official Name	Romania.
Population	Approximately 23 million.
Main Cities	Bucharest is the capital.
Government	Republic with elected president, Senate, and House of Deputies.
Language	Romanian, Hungarian, and German.
Religion	Christian 82%, other 18%.
Literacy Rate	98%
GDP	$113 billion. $5,200 per capita.
Currency	Leu (L). Approximately 5,970 to one U.S. dollar.
Exports	Machinery, fuels, consumer goods, agricultural products.
Imports	Fuels, machinery, consumer goods.
Local Agent	Highly recommended.
Climate	Warm summers, cold winters with snow.
Health	Immunizations against polio and hepatitis recommended.
Local Holidays	New Year's Day (January 1), Labor Day (May 1), Liberation Day (August 23).
Local Time	9 A.M. EST is 4 P.M. in Romania.
Travel Documents	Passport and visa required. Transit visa for 72 hours obtained at border, tourist visa for up to 6 months obtained from Romanian diplomatic missions abroad.

Russia

Official Name	Russian Federation.
Population	Approximately 147 million.
Main Cities	Moscow is the capital.
Government	Elected president and Congress of People's Deputies that elects the Supreme Soviet.
Language	Russian, as well as many other languages.

Religion	Christian, Islam, and others.
Literacy Rate	100%
Currency	Ruble (R). Approximately 5,727 to one U.S. dollar, but fluctuates widely.
Exports	Petroleum, natural gas, wood products, machinery.
Imports	Machinery, foodstuffs, consumer goods.
Regulations	New capitalist regulations being developed.
Local Agent	A local partner is recommended, to work with constantly changing bureaucratic requirements.
Business Tips	Business infrastructure is transitioning from communist to capitalist concepts. Slow moving bureaucracy still in place.
Climate	Ranges from subarctic in Siberia, to warm summers in the southern areas.
Local Holidays	Independence Day (June 12).
Local Time	9 A.M. EST is 4 P.M. in Moscow.
Travel Documents	Passport and visa required.

Rwanda

Official Name	Rwandese Republic.
Population	Approximately 8 million.
Main Cities	Kigali is the capital.
Government	Currently being defined in the aftermath of a civil war.
Language	Kinyarwanda and French are the official languages.
Religion	Roman Catholic 65%, Protestant 9%, Islam 1%, local and other 25%.
Literacy Rate	50%
Crime Rate	640 total offenses per 100,000 persons, 141 murders per 100,000 persons, 133 thefts per 100,000 persons.
GDP	$3.8 billion. $400 per capita.
Currency	Rwandan franc (RF). Approximately 310 to one U.S. dollar.
Exports	Coffee, tea, tin.
Imports	Machinery, foodstuffs, petroleum.
Local Agent	Highly recommended.
Climate	Temperate climate, with occasional frost and snow in the mountains.
Health	Anti-malaria medication is recommended.
Local Time	9 A.M. EST is 4 P.M. in Rwanda.
Travel Documents	Passport and visa required.

Saudi Arabia

Official Name	Kingdom of Saudi Arabia.
Population	Approximately 20 million.
Main Cities	Riyadh is the capital. Other major centers are Jeddah, Dhahran, Dammam, and Al Khobar. Mecca and Medina are sacred cities restricted to only Moslems.
Government	Monarchy, based on Islamic law.
Language	Official language is Arabic, but English spoken by many businesspeople.
Religion	Islam. No other religions are allowed to be practiced.
Literacy Rate	62%
Crime Rate	201 total offenses per 100,000 persons, 1.08 murders per 100,000 persons, 70 thefts per 100,000 persons.
GDP	$205 billion. $10,600 per capita.
Local Customs	Moslem customs are strictly adhered to. Pork is strictly forbidden, and alcohol is against the law. Photographs should not be taken without permission. Women are not allowed to drive cars.
Currency	Saudi riyal (SR). Approximately 3.75 to one U.S. dollar.
Exports	Petroleum.
Imports	Industrialized products, automobiles, foodstuffs, consumer goods.
Regulations	All commercial sales within the country must be handled by Saudi nationals. Government contracts over one million riyals (approx. $260,000 U.S.) require bids from at least three firms.
Local Agent	Essential, and by law it must be a Saudi. Switching agents is very difficult.
Business Tips	Avoid visits during the month of Ramadan.
Health	Immunizations against typhoid, tetanus, polio, and meningococcal meningitis are recommended. Anti-malaria medication is recommended if traveling in the south and west.
Business Hours	8 A.M. to 1 P.M., then 5 P.M. to 8 P.M., Saturday through Wednesday.
Climate	In summer coastal areas are hot and humid, and the temperatures in the interior areas can be up to 120 degrees. In winter, the temperatures are milder.
Clothing	Lightweight business dress. Western women should dress conservatively and may be required to wear veils.
Local Holidays	The Muslim weekend (Thursday and Friday), Muslim holidays, and the month of Ramadan are strictly observed.
Local Time	9 A.M. EST is 5 P.M. in Saudi Arabia.
Travel Documents	Visa is required, obtainable only by a letter of invitation from a Saudi sponsor. Visa is obtained from Saudi Arabian diplomatic missions abroad, and the procedure can be complicated and time consuming. The visa is good for one entry only, within two months of issue, and is usually good for only one month.

Singapore

Official Name	Republic of Singapore.
Population	Approximately 3.4 million.
Main Cities	Singapore is a city state.
Government	Republic with elected president and Parliament.
Language	There are four official languages: Malay, Chinese (Mandarin), Tamil, and English. English is the predominant language of business.
Religion	Buddhist, Islam, Christian, Hindu, Sikh, Taoist, Confucianist.
Local Customs	Singapore is squeaky clean. There is a $500 fine for littering.
Literacy Rate	88%
Crime Rate	1,733 total offenses per 100,000 persons, 2.04 murders per 100,000 persons, 1,067 thefts per 100,000 persons.
GDP	$72 billion. $21,200 per capita.
Currency	Singapore dollar (S$). Approximately 1.47 to one U.S. dollar.
Exports	Electronic goods, textiles, consumer goods.
Imports	Paper, raw materials, foodstuffs, petroleum.
Regulations	Completely free trade system.
Local Agent	Highly recommended, particularly for government business.
Health	International Certificate of Vaccination against yellow fever and cholera if arriving from an infected area. Immunization against cholera, tetanus, and polio is recommended. Anti-malaria medication is also recommended.
Business Hours	8 A.M. or 9 A.M. to 5 P.M., Monday through Friday.
Climate	Hot and humid, with daytime temperatures in the high 80 degrees and night temperatures in the high 70 degrees.
Clothing	Trousers, shirt, and tie are standard business dress. Be prepared for frequent changes of clothing due to the heat and humidity.
Local Holidays	National Day (August 9).
Local Time	9 A.M. EST is 10 P.M. in Singapore.
Travel Documents	Passport allows a two-week visit pass on arrival, which can be renewed.

Slovakia

Official Name	Slovak Republic. (Part of the former Czechoslovakia.)
Population	Approximately 5.3 million.
Main Cities	Bratislava is the capital.

Government	Parliamentary democracy with elected National Council that elects the president.
Language	Slovak is the official language. Hungarian is also spoken.
Religion	Roman Catholic 60%, Protestant 8%, Orthodox 4%, other 28%.
GDP	$43 billion. $8,000 per capita.
Currency	Koruna (Kc). Approximately 31 to one U.S. dollar.
Exports	Machinery, raw materials, agricultural products.
Imports	Machinery, raw materials, agricultural products.
Local Agent	Recommended.
Climate	Cool summers, cold winters.
Local Holidays	Slovak National Uprising Day (August 29).
Local Time	9 A.M. EST is 4 P.M. in Slovakia.
Travel Documents	Passport only required.

Slovenia

Official Name	Republic of Slovenia. (Part of the former Yugoslavia.)
Population	Approximately 2 million.
Main Cities	Ljubljana is the capital.
Government	Elected president and State Assembly.
Language	Slovenian is the main language. Serbo-Croatian is also spoken.
Religion	Roman Catholic 96%, Islam 1%, other 3%.
GDP	$24 billion. $12,300 per capita.
Currency	Tolar (SIT). Approximately 141 to one U.S. dollar.
Exports	Machinery, manufactured goods, chemicals, foodstuffs.
Imports	Machinery, manufactured goods, raw materials, foodstuffs.
Local Agent	Recommended.
Business Tips	Slovenia was the most prosperous of the Yugoslav republics and has strong ties to Western Europe.
Climate	Mediterranean climate on the coast, with mild summers and cold winters inland.
Local Holidays	Statehood Day (June 25).
Local Time	9 A.M. EST is 3 P.M. in Slovenia.
Travel Documents	Passport only required.

Somalia

Official Name	Somalia.
Population	Approximately 6.6 million.
Main Cities	Mogadishu is the capital.
Government	Recovering from civil war.
Language	Somali and Arabic are official languages. English and Italian are often used in business.
Religion	Islam.
Literacy Rate	24%
GDP	$3.6 billion. $500 per capita.
Currency	Somali shilling (SoSh). Approximately 4,100 to one U.S. dollar.
Exports	Bananas, animal products.
Imports	Petroleum, foodstuffs.
Local Agent	Highly recommended.
Climate	Hot and humid. Average temperatures are about 85 degrees but can reach 110.
Health	Immunizations against cholera, yellow fever, typhoid, and polio recommended, as well as medication against malaria.
Local Holidays	The Muslim weekend (Thursday and Friday), Muslim holidays, and the month of Ramadan are observed. New Year's Day (January 1), Independence Day (June 26), National Day (July 1).
Local Time	9 A.M. EST is 5 P.M. in Somalia.
Travel Documents	Passport and visa required by all visitors.

South Africa

Official Name	Republic of South Africa.
Population	Approximately 43 million.
Main Cities	Pretoria is the administrative capital, Cape Town the legislative capital, and Bloemfontein is the judicial capital.
Government	Democratic republic.
Language	Afrikaans and English are the official languages. Many other languages spoken.
Religion	Christian, Hindu, and Islam.
Literacy Rate	76%
GDP	$227 billion. $5,400 per capita.
Currency	Rand (R). Approximately 4.6 to one U.S. dollar.

Exports	Gold, raw materials, foodstuffs.
Imports	Machinery, petroleum, chemicals, textiles.
Local Agent	Highly recommend.
Climate	Subtropical along the coast, semiarid inland.
Health	Immunization against cholera is recommended.
Local Holidays	Christian holidays, New Year's Day (January 1), Founder's Day (April 6), Republic Day (May 31), Kruger Day (October 10).
Local Time	9 A.M. EST is 4 P.M. in South Africa.
Travel Documents	Passport and visa required. Visa obtained from South African diplomatic mission abroad.

South Korea

Official Name	Republic of Korea (ROK).
Population	Approximately 45 million.
Main Cities	Seoul is the capital. Other major centers are Inchon and Pusan.
Government	Republic, with elected president and National Assembly.
Language	Korean, but many businesspeople speak English.
Religion	Christianity 48%, Buddhism 47%, other 5%.
Literacy Rate	96%
Crime Rate	2,229 total offenses per 100,000 persons, 1.3 murders per 100,000 persons, 229 thefts per 100,000 persons.
GDP	$647 billion. $14,200 per capita.
Currency	South Korean Won (W). Approximately 850 to one U.S. dollar.
Exports	Electronic products, automobiles, clothing, consumer goods.
Imports	Fuel, foodstuffs, raw materials.
Regulations	Import licenses are required for most products, and heavy tariffs exist to protect local industry.
Local Agent	A good agent is essential.
Business Tips	Involving local companies in production is an important consideration.
Climate	Similar to the northeastern United States, with summer temperatures averaging about 70 degrees.
Clothing	Business suits are common.
Local Holidays	New Years Day (January 1), National Day (August 15), Foundation Day (October 3), Hangul Day (October 9).
Local Time	9 A.M. EST is 11 P.M. in South Korea.
Travel Documents	Passport only required for stays up to 15 days.

Spain

Official Name	Kingdom of Spain.
Population	Approximately 39 million.
Main Cities	Madrid is the capital. Other major centers are Barcelona, Bilbao, and Valencia.
Government	Parliamentary monarchy, with elected Senate and Congress of Deputies.
Language	Spanish is the official language, and some businesspeople speak English.
Religion	Predominantly Roman Catholic.
Literacy Rate	95%
Crime Rate	2,519 total offenses per 100,000 persons, 2.28 murders per 100,000 persons, 1,948 thefts per 100,000 persons.
GDP	$593 billion. $15,300 per capita.
Currency	Peseta (Pta). Approximately 134 to one U.S. dollar.
Exports	Foodstuffs, metal products, chemicals.
Imports	Petroleum, raw material, machinery.
Local Agent	Highly recommended.
Climate	In the north, winters are cool and damp, with average summer temperature of about 64 degrees. The central plain has dry winters with average January temperature about 40 degrees, and hot summers with average July temperature of about 78 degrees. In the south, winters are mild with average January temperature of about 50 degrees, and summers are hot with average July temperature about 80 degrees.
Health	Immunization against typhoid, typhus, and hepatitis is recommended.
Clothing	Usual business wear.
Local Holidays	Christian holidays, National Day (October 12).
Local Time	9 A.M. EST is 3 P.M. in Spain.
Travel Documents	Passport only required for stay up to 6 months.

Sri Lanka

Official Name	Democratic Socialist Republic of Sri Lanka.
Population	Approximately 18 million.
Main Cities	Colombo is the financial, commercial, and administrative capital and is also the largest port.
Government	Parliamentary democracy based on the UK system.
Language	Sinhalese and Tamil are the official languages. English is widely used in business.
Religion	Buddhist 70%, Hindu 16%, Islam 7%, Christian 7%.

Literacy Rate	85%
Crime Rate	509 total offenses per 100,000 persons, 30.54 murders per 100,000 persons, 179 thefts per 100,000 persons.
GDP	$70 billion. $3,760 per capita.
Currency	Sri Lankan rupee (SLRes). Approximately 57 to one U.S. dollar.
Exports	Tea, clothing and textiles, rubber, agricultural products.
Imports	Petroleum, machinery, foodstuffs.
Local Agent	Highly recommended.
Business Tips	Business approach is cautious and slow paced.
Climate	Tropical climate, with temperatures varying with elevation. Temperatures in Colombo vary from 75 to 93 by day and 70 to 80 at night.
Clothing	Shirt and tie for general business. Lightweight suits for formal calls.
Health	Immunization against cholera and hepatitis, also anti-malaria medication is recommended.
Local Holidays	All full moon days are public holidays. National Day (February 4), Sinhala and Tamil New Year Day (April 14), May Day (May 1), National Hero's Day (May 22), Deepavail Festival Day (November 13), Christmas Day (December 25).
Local Time	9 A.M. EST is 7:30 P.M. in Sri Lanka.
Travel Documents	Valid passport only required for tourists for a stay up to one month. Visa required for business purposes, obtained at Sri Lankan diplomatic offices abroad.

Sudan

Official Name	Republic of Sudan.
Population	Approximately 33 million.
Main Cities	Khartoum is the capital.
Government	Ruled by a Revolutionary Command Council as a result of military takeover in 1989.
Language	Arabic is the official language. Several local languages spoken.
Religion	Islam 70%, local 25%, Christian 5%.
Literacy Rate	27%
GDP	$27 billion. $860 per capita.
Currency	Dinar. Approximately 1,500 to one U.S. dollar.
Exports	Cotton and cotton products.
Imports	Petroleum, manufactured goods, chemicals, foodstuffs.
Local Agent	Highly recommended.

Climate	Hot and dry. Temperatures in Khartoum are about 105 in summer and 80 in winter.
Health	Immunizations recommend for yellow fever, cholera, typhoid, and polio, as well as medication against malaria.
Local Holidays	The Muslim weekend (Thursday and Friday), Muslim holidays, and the month of Ramadan are observed. Independence Day (January 1), Unity Day (March 3), Uprising Day (April 6).
Local Time	9 A.M. EST is 4 P.M. in Sudan.
Travel Documents	Passport and visa required by all. Must register with police within three days of arrival. Special permits required to travel outside of Khartoum.

Sweden

Official Name	Kingdom of Sweden.
Population	Approximately 8.9 million.
Main Cities	Stockholm is the capital. Other major centers are Goteborg and Malmo.
Government	Constitutional monarchy, with a Parliament elected for a three-year term.
Language	Swedish, but English is widely spoken.
Religion	Predominantly Lutheran.
Literacy Rate	99%
Crime Rate	12,837 total offenses per 100,000 persons, 7.2 murders per 100,000 persons, 7,630 thefts per 100,000 persons.
GDP	$184 billion. $20,200 per capita.
Currency	Swedish krona (SKr). Approximately 7.0 to one U.S. dollar.
Exports	Iron, steel, lumber, pulp and paper, vehicles, electrical equipment.
Imports	Petroleum, machinery, foodstuffs, textiles, chemicals.
Regulations	Most products do not require import licenses.
Local Agent	Recommended.
Business Tips	Avoid visiting in July which is summer vacation month.
Business Hours	8 A.M. to 5 P.M. Monday through Friday.
Climate	Cold and dry in the north, milder and wetter in the south. Stockholm average summer temperature is about 62 degrees, and average winter temperature about 28 degrees.
Clothing	Usual business wear.
Local Holidays	Christian holidays, New Year's Day (January 1), Labor Day (May 1).
Local Time	9 A.M. EST is 3 P.M. in Sweden.
Travel Documents	Passport only required for visits under 90 days.

Switzerland

Official Name	Swiss Confederation.
Population	Approximately 7 million.
Main Cities	Berne is the capital. Zurich is the largest city. Other major centers are Basle, Geneva, Lausanne, and Lucerne.
Government	Legislature has an elected National Council and a Council of States representing the cantons or provinces. The president is nominated for a one-year term.
Language	The three official languages are German (65%), French (18%) and Italian (12%). English is widely spoken.
Religion	Roman Catholic 48%, Protestant 45%, other 7%.
Local Customs	People are very industrious, with few labor disputes.
Literacy Rate	99%
Crime Rate	4,988 total offenses per 100,000 persons, 2.25 murders per 100,000 persons, 4,337 thefts per 100,000 persons.
GDP	$161 billion. $22,600 per capita.
Currency	Swiss franc (SwF). Approximately 1.40 to one U.S. dollar.
Exports	Machinery, machine tools, precision instruments, textiles, watches.
Imports	Petroleum, raw material, foodstuffs.
Regulations	Agriculture is highly subsidized, and food imports are highly taxed.
Local Agent	Agents are required for most products.
Business Tips	The Swiss are very punctual and expect others to be as well.
Business Hours	8 A.M. to 6 P.M. Monday through Friday.
Climate	Climate varies with altitude. Average winter temperature is about 34 degrees, and average summer temperature is about 65 degrees.
Clothing	Usual business wear.
Local Holidays	Christian holidays, New Year's Day (January 1), National Day (August 1).
Local Time	9 A.M. EST is 3 P.M. in Switzerland.
Travel Documents	Passport only for visits under 90 days.

Syria

Official Name	Syrian Arab Republic.
Population	Approximately 16 million.
Main Cities	Damascus is the capital.
Government	Socialist republic with elected president and People's Assembly.

Language	Arabic is the official language. English and French sometimes spoken in business.
Religion	Islam 90%, Christian 10%.
Literacy Rate	64%
Crime Rate	46 offenses per 100,000 persons, 1.87 murders per 100,000 persons, 32 thefts per 100,000 persons.
GDP	$98 billion. $6,300 per capita.
Currency	Syrian pound (£S). Approximately 42 to one U.S. dollar.
Exports	Petroleum, agricultural products.
Imports	Machinery, foodstuffs, consumer goods.
Local Agent	Highly recommended.
Climate	Coastal areas have hot summers (90 degrees) and cool winters (50 degrees). Much hotter inland.
Health	Cholera immunizations are recommend, as well as medication against malaria.
Local Holidays	Muslim weekly holiday of Friday, Muslim holidays, and the month of Ramadan are observed. Main Christian holidays are also observed. New Year's Day (January 1), Revolution Day (March 8), Beginning of October War (October 6), National Day (November 16).
Local Time	9 A.M. EST is 5 P.M. in Syria.
Travel Documents	Passport and visa required. Journalists must report to authorities within 24 hours of arrival, others must report if they intend to stay longer than 15 days.

Taiwan

Official Name	Republic of China or Taiwan.
Population	Approximately 21 million.
Main Cities	Taipei is the capital. Other main centers are Kaohsiung, Taichung, and Taitung.
Government	The elected president is also the head of the Kuomintang, the ruling political party that defines the country's policy. The policy is applied by the Executive Yuan, which consists of the various government ministries. The National Assembly, in which only about a third are elected, is largely symbolic.
Language	Mandarin Chinese is official language, but English is widely spoken.
Religion	Buddhist, Taoist, Confucian.
Local Customs	"Face" is the prestige and respect one has in the eyes of others, and losing, gaining, or giving face is very important.
Literacy Rate	90%
GDP	$315 billion. $14,700 per capita.
Currency	New Taiwan dollar (NT$). Approximately 27 to one U.S. dollar.
Exports	Machinery, electronic products, textiles, consumer goods.

Imports	Petroleum, coal, raw materials, foodstuffs.
Regulations	Imports are strictly controlled, and all imports over $1,000 U.S. must have an import license.
Local Agent	Agents as commonly known are not allowed in Taiwan. Instead foreign companies use a public agency like Central Trust of China which is a state owned trading company, a private trading company or distributor, or business services consultants.
Business Tips	Exchanging business favors is an important part of business life.
Health	International Certificate of Vaccination against cholera if arriving from an infected area.
Business Hours	9 A.M. to 5 P.M., Monday through Friday. 9 A.M. to noon on Saturday.
Climate	Hot and humid summers with temperatures between 80 and 95 degrees. Mild but humid winters.
Clothing	Business suits, and nothing too colorful.
Local Holidays	Founding of the Republic of China (January 1–2), Chinese New Year (variable), Youth Day (March 29), Tomb-Sweeping Day (April 5), Dragon Boat Festival (June 8).
Local Time	9 A.M. EST is 10 P.M. in Taiwan.
Travel Documents	Passport and visa required for stay up to 60 days.

Tanzania

Official Name	United Republic of Tanzania.
Population	Approximately 27 million.
Main Cities	Dar es Salaam is the capital.
Government	Republic with elected president and National Assembly.
Language	Swahili and English are the official languages.
Religion	Christian 40%, Islam 33%, local 27%.
Literacy Rate	46%
Crime Rate	1,124 total offenses per 100,000 persons, 7.27 murders per 100,000 persons, 324 thefts per 100,000 persons.
GDP	$19 billion. $650 per capita.
Currency	Tanzanian shilling (TSh). Approximately 597 to one U.S. dollar.
Exports	Coffee, cotton, tobacco, tea, nuts.
Imports	Manufactured goods, petroleum, foodstuffs.
Local Agent	Highly recommended.
Climate	Tropical along the coast to temperate inland.
Health	Anti-malaria medication is recommended.

Local Holidays	Christian and Muslim holidays, Zanzibar Revolutionary Day (January 12), Union Day (April 26), International Workers Day (May 1), Peasants Day (July 7), Independence Day (December 9).
Local Time	9 A.M. EST is 5 P.M. in Tanzania.
Travel Documents	Passport and visa required. Obtain visa at Tanzanian diplomatic mission abroad.

Thailand

Official Name	Kingdom of Thailand.
Population	Approximately 59 million.
Main Cities	Bangkok is the government and commercial center and the major port. Chiang Mai, Khorat, Hat Yai, and Songkhla are other main cities.
Government	Constitutional monarchy with elected government and Prime Minister appointed by the king.
Language	Thai, but English widely used commercially.
Religion	90% Buddhist. Muslim minority in the south.
Local Customs	High respect for religion and the monarchy. Good manners and patience very important. Pointing the sole of the foot at people or Buddha is an insult.
Literacy Rate	93%
Crime Rate	343 total offenses per 100,000 persons, 11.1 murders per 100,000 persons, 89 thefts per 100,000 persons.
GDP	$456 billion. $7,700 per capita.
Currency	Baht (B). Approximately 26 to one U.S. dollar.
Exports	Rice, sugar, teak, tin, timber, rubber.
Imports	Industrialized products, fuels, base metals, fertilizer, consumer goods.
Regulations	Most goods may enter Thailand without an import license. The export of some products, such as silk and silverware, is controlled to preserve quality standards. Some products such as teak logs and Buddha images are banned from export.
Local Agent	Must have an effective local agent because of the complexities of the Thai market and bureaucracy.
Business Tips	Avoid travel in October when widespread flooding occurs. Allow flexibility in meeting deadlines, because of the slower paced approach to business and often the heavy traffic during business hours.
Health	International Certificate of Vaccination against cholera and yellow fever may be required. Immunization against hepatitis and anti-malaria medication recommended.
Business Hours	8 A.M. to 5 P.M. Monday to Friday, 8 A.M. to noon Saturday.
Climate	Hot and humid. Daytime temperatures average over 90 degrees, and nighttime temperatures around 80 degrees. Rainy season has occasional showers June to August, heavy downpours September and October.

Clothing	Lightweight trousers, shirt, and tie are standard business dress. Business suits are usually worn only on calls to senior officials.
Local Holidays	New Year's Day (January 1), Chinese New Year (3 days in January or February), Chakri Memorial Day (April 6), Songkran festival (April 13), Coronation Day (May 5), Plowing Ceremony (May 7), Queen's Birthday (August 12), Chulalongkorn Day (October 23), King's Birthday (December 5), Constitution Day (December 10), Christmas Day (December 25).
Local Time	9 A.M. EST is 9 P.M. same day in Bangkok.
Travel Documents	Passport allows 15-day visit, tourist visa for up to 30 days.

Trinidad and Tobago

Official Name	Republic of Trinidad and Tobago.
Population	Approximately 1.1 million.
Government	A republic with an elected House of Representatives, a Senate nominated by the House of Representatives, and the President appointed by the House of Representatives and the Senate.
Language	English is the official and commercial language.
Religion	Roman Catholic 32%, Hindu 24%, Protestant 28%, Islam 6%, other 10%.
Literacy Rate	95%
Crime Rate	4,232 total offenses per 100,000 persons, 9.91 murders per 100,000 persons, 2,807 thefts per 100,000 persons.
GDP	$17 billion. $13,500 per capita.
Currency	Trinidad and Tobago dollar (TT$). Approximately 6.1 to one U.S. dollar.
Exports	Petroleum.
Imports	Industrialized products, foodstuffs, consumer goods.
Regulations	A large number of items require an import license.
Local Agent	Local agent is advisable, and the agreement must be registered with the government.
Business Tips	Avoid the winter tourist season and Carnival in February.
Health	An International Certificate of Vaccination against cholera and yellow fever may be required, depending on previous travel.
Business Hours	8 A.M. to 12 noon, then 1 P.M. to 4 P.M.
Climate	Trinidad is tropical and hot with average daytime temperature of about 85 degrees and about 10 degrees cooler at night. Tobago is slightly cooler and less humid.
Clothing	Lightweight business suits are usually worn.
Local Holidays	Independence Day (August 31).

Local Time	9 A.M. EST is 10 A.M. in Trinidad and Tobago.
Travel Documents	Passport only required for stay up to 2 months.

Tunisia

Official Name	Republic of Tunisia.
Population	Approximately 9.2 million.
Main Cities	Tunis is the capital.
Government	Republic with elected president and National Assembly.
Language	Arabic is the official language, but French is widely spoken and the major commercial language.
Religion	Islam 98%, other 2%.
Literacy Rate	65%
GDP	$43 billion. $4,800 per capita.
Currency	Tunisian dinar (TD). Approximately 1 to one U.S. dollar.
Exports	Petroleum, agricultural products.
Imports	Industrial goods, foodstuffs, consumer goods.
Local Agent	Recommended.
Climate	North coast has Mediterranean climate, with average summer temperature in Tunis of about 85 degrees and 55 in winter. Inland areas are hot and humid.
Health	Vaccination certificate for yellow fever required if arriving from an infected area.
Local Holidays	The Muslim weekly holiday of Friday, and the Christian holiday of Sunday are observed, as are Muslim holidays. New Year's Day (January 1), Independence Day (March 20), Labor Day (May 1), Republic Day (July 25).
Local Time	9 A.M. EST is 3 P.M. in Tunisia.
Travel Documents	Passport and visa required.

Turkey

Official Name	Republic of Turkey.
Population	Approximately 64 million.
Main Cities	Ankara is the capital. Other major centers are Istanbul, Izmir, Antalya, Mersin, Samsun, and Bursa.
Government	Elected Grand National Assembly.
Language	Turkish is the official language, but English is widely used in business.

Religion	Almost totally Islam.
Literacy Rate	81%
Crime Rate	110 total offenses per 100,000 persons, 1.45 murders per 100,000 persons, 68 thefts per 100,000 persons.
GDP	$379 billion. $6,100 per capita.
Currency	Turkish lira (TL). Approximately 110,000 to one U.S. dollar.
Exports	Manufactured goods, foodstuffs, raw materials.
Imports	Industrialized products, fuel.
Regulations	Import licensing and quotas restrict many products from entry into the country.
Local Agent	Highly recommended, to understand and work the tendering system.
Business Tips	Local agent must get early notice of impending tenders to ensure a bidding opportunity and, if possible, influence the specifications.
Health	Immunization against cholera as well as medications against malaria are advisable.
Business Hours	9 A.M. to 6 P.M., Monday through Friday.
Climate	Climate varies with location. Coastal areas are hot and humid in summer and milder in winter. In the mountains of the interior, winters can be severe.
Local Holidays	Muslim holidays and the month of Ramadan are observed. New Year's Day (January 1), National Day (April 23), Victory Day (August 30), Republic Day (October 28–29).
Local Time	9 A.M. EST is 4 P.M. in Turkey.
Travel Documents	Passport only required for stay up to 3 months.

Uganda

Official Name	Republic of Uganda.
Population	Approximately 21 million.
Main Cities	Kampala is the capital.
Government	Republic with elected National Resistance Council.
Language	English is the official language. Many local languages spoken.
Religion	Roman Catholic 33%, Protestant 33%, Islam 16%, local 18%.
Literacy Rate	48%
GDP	$17 billion. $900 per capita.
Currency	Ugandan shilling (U.S.h). Approximately 1,030 to one U.S. dollar.
Exports	Coffee.
Imports	Petroleum, machinery, textiles, foodstuffs.
Local Agent	Highly recommended.

Climate	Tropical to semiarid.
Health	Anti-malaria medication is recommended.
Local Holidays	Independence Day (October 9).
Local Time	9 A.M. EST is 5 P.M. in Uganda.
Travel Documents	Passport and visa required. Obtain visa at Uganda diplomatic mission abroad.

Ukraine

Official Name	Ukraine.
Population	Approximately 50 million.
Main Cities	Kiev is the capital.
Government	Republic with an elected president and Supreme Council.
Language	Ukrainian, Russian, Romanian, Polish.
Religion	Mainly Ukrainian Orthodox.
Literacy Rate	100%
Currency	Hryrhia. Approximately 1.86 to one U.S. dollar.
Exports	Electric power, raw material, grain, foodstuffs.
Imports	Machinery, textiles, chemicals.
Local Agent	Recommended.
Climate	Summers are hot in the south and warm elsewhere. Winters are cool in the south and cold elsewhere.
Local Holidays	Independence Day (August 24).
Local Time	9 A.M. EST is 4 P.M. in the Ukraine.
Travel Documents	Passport only required.

United Arab Emirates

Official Name	United Arab Emirates.
Population	Approximately 2.3 million.
Main Cities	Abu Dhabi is the capital. Other major centers are Dubai, Sharjah and Al-Ain.
Government	Made up of seven emirates: Abu Dhabi, Dubai, Sharjah, Fujairah, Umm al-Qaiwain, Ras Al Khaimah, and Ajman. The Supreme Council is made up of the hereditary rulers of the seven emirates, who elect the president. A Federal National Council is appointed by the rulers.
Language	Official language is Arabic, but English is widely spoken in business.

Religion	Islam 96%, other 4%.
Local Customs	Muslim customs are predominant, in which alcohol and pork are forbidden. Food and other items should be taken and passed with the right hand.
Literacy Rate	68%
Crime Rate	1,496 total offenses per 100,000 persons, 1.8 murders per 100,000 persons, 206 thefts per 100,000 persons.
GDP	$73 billion. $23,800 per capita.
Currency	Emirian dirham (Dh). Approximately 3.7 to one U.S. dollar.
Exports	Petroleum, natural gas.
Imports	Industrialized products, foodstuffs, automobiles, consumer products.
Local Agent	Agent required by law, and they must be a national.
Business Tips	Business depends heavily on frequent personal contact. Avoid visits during the month of Ramadan.
Health	Immunizations against cholera, typhoid, tetanus, polio, and meningococcal meningitis are recommended. AIDS test required for those taking up residence.
Business Hours	8 A.M. to 12:30 P.M., then 4 P.M. to 7 P.M., Saturday through Wednesday.
Climate	Hot and humid in summer with temperatures up to 115 degrees. Milder in winter.
Clothing	Lightweight business clothes.
Local Holidays	The Muslim weekend (Thursday and Friday), Muslim holidays and the month of Ramadan are observed. New Year's Day (January 1), National Day (December 2).
Local Time	9 A.M. EST is 6 P.M. in the UAE.
Travel Documents	Passport and visa required, obtainable only by a letter of invitation from a national sponsor. The visa can be provided to the visitor upon their arrival by the sponsor.

United Kingdom

Official Name	United Kingdom of Great Britain and Northern Ireland.
Population	Approximately 60 million. Ethnic divisions are English 81%, Scottish 10%, Irish 2.5%, other 6.5%.
Main Cities	London is the capital. Several other major industrial centers.
Government	Constitutional monarchy, with elected House of Commons and appointed House of Lords.
Language	English.
Religion	Anglican 45%, Roman Catholic 15%, other 40%.
Literacy Rate	99%
Crime Rate	7,396 total offenses per 100,000 persons, 1.97 murders per 100,000 persons, 5,534 thefts per 100,000 persons.

GDP	$1.19 trillion. $20,400 per capita.
Currency	British pound (£). Approximately 0.60 to one U.S. dollar.
Exports	Manufactured goods, machinery, chemicals.
Imports	Consumer goods, machinery, foodstuffs.
Local Agent	May be useful in early stages.
Climate	Temperate, with frequent overcast.
Clothing	Standard business dress.
Local Holidays	Christian holidays, New Year's Day (January 1), May Day (May 1), Queen's Birthday (second Saturday in June), various local holidays.
Local Time	9 A.M. EST is 2 P.M. in the United Kingdom.
Travel Documents	Passport only required for stay up to 6 months.

United States of America

Official Name	United States of America.
Population	Approximately 268 million.
Main Cities	Washington is the capital city. Many other major financial and industrial centers.
Government	Federal republic, with elected president, upper house (Senate), and lower house (House of Representatives). Consists of 50 states, one district, and several dependent areas.
Language	English, some Spanish.
Religion	Protestant 56%, Roman Catholic 28%, other 16%.
Literacy Rate	97%
Crime Rate	5,664 total offenses per 100,000 persons, 8.4 murders per 100,000 persons, 5,248 thefts per 100,000 persons.
GDP	$7.61 trillion. $28,600 per capita.
Currency	U.S. dollar ($).
Exports	Consumer goods, capital goods, automobiles, industrial supplies, raw materials, agricultural products.
Imports	Consumer goods, petroleum products, machinery, automobiles, raw materials, food.
Climate	Mainly temperate. Tropical in Hawaii and Florida and arctic in Alaska.
Clothing	Standard business dress.
Local Holidays	Christian holidays, New Year's Day (January 1), Martin Luther King Day (January 20), Presidents' Day (February), Memorial Day (last Monday in May), Independence Day (July 4), Labor Day (first Monday in September), Columbus Day (October 13), Veteran's Day (November 11), Thanksgiving Day (fourth Thursday in November).
Travel Documents	Passport only required for visits up to 6 months.

Uruguay

Official Name	Oriental Republic of Uruguay.
Population	Approximately 3.1 million.
Main Cities	Montevideo is the capital.
Government	Republic.
Language	Official language is Spanish.
Religion	Roman Catholic 66%, other 34%.
Literacy Rate	96%
Crime Rate	1,027 total offenses per 100,000 persons, 3.06 murders per 100,000 persons, 814 thefts per 100,000 persons.
GDP	$26 billion. $8,000 per capita.
Currency	New Uruguayan peso ($Ur). Approximately 8.6 to one U.S. dollar.
Exports	Textiles, meat, leather.
Imports	Petroleum, industrialized products.
Regulations	Import permits not required, but all imports must be registered.
Local Agent	Recommended.
Climate	Dry and temperate with summer temperatures around 80 degrees and winter temperatures around 45 degrees.
Health	Uruguay has the highest health standards in Latin America.
Local Holidays	New Year's Day (January 1), Epiphany (January 6), Carnival Week (prior to Lent), Holy Week (variable), Labor Day (May 1), Constitution Day (July 18), Independence Day (August 25), Christmas (December 25).
Local Time	9 A.M. EST is 10 A.M. in Uruguay.
Travel Documents	Passport only required for stay up to 3 months.

Venezuela

Official Name	Republic of Venezuela.
Population	Approximately 22 million.
Main Cities	Caracas in the capital. Other major centers are La Guaira, Puerto Cabello, and Cumana.
Government	Federal republic with elected president, Senate, and House of Representatives. Consists of 22 states and one federal district.
Language	Spanish is the official language, many businesspeople speak English.
Religion	Roman Catholic 96%, other 4%.
Literacy Rate	88%

Crime Rate	1,158 total offenses per 100,000 persons, 9.11 murders per 100,000 persons, 867 thefts per 100,000 persons.
GDP	$197 billion. $9,000 per capita.
Currency	Bolivar (Bs). Approximately 480 to one U.S. dollar.
Exports	Petroleum, raw materials.
Imports	Industrialized products, raw materials, foodstuffs.
Regulations	Import quotas on many items, many others are restricted to importation only by the government.
Local Agent	Highly recommended.
Climate	Climate varies with altitude. The coastal areas are hot and humid, but the climate moderates in the interior mountains.
Health	Health conditions are good. Malaria medication is highly recommended.
Local Holidays	New Year's Day (January 1), Carnival (variable), Easter (variable), Declaration of Independence (April 19), Labor Day (May 1), Independence Day (July 5), Simon Bolivar's Birthday (July 24), Christmas (December 24–25).
Local Time	9 A.M. EST is 10 A.M. in Venezuela.
Travel Documents	Passport only required for tourist stay up to 60 days. Business visa required for carrying on business. A business visa requires letter of guarantee (stating purpose of visit, contacts, length of stay) and proof of transportation out of the country.

Vietnam

Official Name	Socialist Republic of Vietnam.
Population	Approximately 75 million.
Main Cities	Hanoi is the capital. Ho Chi Minh City is another center.
Government	Communist state.
Language	Vietnamese is the official language. Other languages spoken include English and French.
Religion	Buddhist, Taoist, Christian, Islam, other.
Literacy Rate	88%
GDP	$109 billion. $1,470 per capita.
Currency	New dong (D). Approximately 11,100 to one U.S. dollar.
Exports	Raw materials, agricultural products, seafood.
Imports	Petroleum, industrialized equipment, foodstuffs, textiles.
Local Agent	Highly recommended.
Climate	Tropical in the south. Warm summers and cool winters in central lowlands and mountains. Hot summers and dry winters in north.
Health	Anti-malaria medication is recommended.

Local Holidays	Independence Day (September 2).
Local Time	9 A.M. EST is 9 P.M. in Vietnam.
Travel Documents	U.S. citizens require Treasury Board license to visit Vietnam.

Yemen

Official Name	Republic of Yemen.
Population	Approximately 15 million.
Main Cities	Capital is Sana'a, and Aden is another major center.
Government	In 1990 the Yemen Arab Republic and the People's Democratic Republic of Yemen joined to become the Republic of Yemen. In 1994 a civil war erupted, the outcome of which is not determined at the time of this writing.
Language	Official language is Arabic.
Religion	Primarily Islam.
Literacy Rate	38%
GDP	$39 billion. $2,900 per capita.
Currency	Yemeni riyal (YR). Approximately 12 to one U.S. dollar.
Exports	Petroleum, agricultural products.
Imports	Machinery, foodstuffs, consumer goods.
Local Agent	Highly recommended.
Climate	The coastal area is hot and humid. The higher altitudes in the interior are warm in summer and cold in winter.
Health	Immunization against cholera and yellow fever recommended, as well as medication against malaria.
Local Holidays	The Muslim weekend (Thursday and Friday), Muslim holidays, and the month of Ramadan are observed. Labor Day (May 1), National Unity Day (May 22), National Day (September 26), National Day (October 14).
Local Time	9 A.M. EST is 5 P.M. in Yemen.
Travel Documents	Passport and visa required. Exit visa is required for stays longer than seven days.

Zaire

Official Name	Democratic Republic of the Congo.
Population	Approximately 41 million.
Main Cities	Kinshasa is the capital.
Government	Republic with elected president and Legislative Council.

Language	Many local languages. French is spoken by many businesspeople.
Religion	Roman Catholic 50%, Protestant 20%, Islam 10%, other 20%.
Literacy Rate	72%
GDP	$9.2 billion. $235 per capita.
Currency	Zaire (Z). Approximately 2,000,000 to one U.S. dollar.
Exports	Coffee, copper, other minerals.
Imports	Fuels, machinery, foodstuffs.
Local Agent	Highly recommended.
Climate	Varies from hot and humid to warm and wet.
Health	Immunization against typhoid and yellow fever, as well as anti-malaria medication are recommended.
Local Holidays	New Year's Day (January 1), Day of Martyrs (January 4), Labor Day (May 1), New Constitution Day (June 24), Independence Day (June 30), Parent's Day (August 1), President's Birthday (October 14), Armed Forces Day (November 17), Anniversary of the New Regime (November 24).
Local Time	9 A.M. EST is 3 P.M. in Zaire.
Travel Documents	Passport and visa required. Visa obtained from Zaire diplomatic mission abroad.

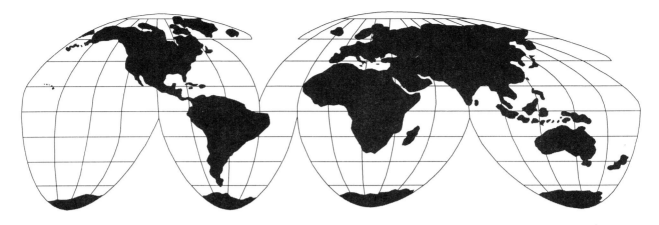

International Marketing Terms

Ad valorem (a/v, a.v., *or* AV)
According to the value. Usually a percentage of the value used for customs duties.

Advising bank
The bank that informs the exporter of the terms and conditions of the letter of credit that the purchaser has stipulated for payment.

After date (a/d)
Payment is due a specific number of days after presentation of the draft.

Agent
A person or company that is the foreign representative of an exporter. There are several types of agents, the most common being the commission agent and the distributor.

Air consignment note
Air cargo shipping document used by international air cargo carriers. The term is used interchangeably with air waybill.

Air waybill

Shipping document used by international air cargo carriers that lists the goods being shipped and the destination. The term is used interchangeably with air consignment note.

All risks

Insurance coverage on all risks of physical damage or loss from any external cause, although there may be some exclusions.

Alongside

Goods are placed on the dock alongside the ship for loading.

At sight

Payment of a negotiable document is to be made on presentation of the document.

Bank draft

A check drawn by a bank on another bank.

Barratry

Fraudulent, criminal, or wrongful act of the ship's captain or crew that causes loss or damage to the ship or cargo.

Barter

Payment for goods with other goods.

Bill of entry

The detailed statement of the nature and value of the goods in a consignment, used for customs purposes.

Bill of lading

The ship receipt for goods taken on board a vessel for transit to a stated destination. It describes the conditions under which the goods are accepted by the carrier and details the nature and quantity of the goods.

Bonded warehouse

A facility authorized by customs authorities for the duty-free storage of goods until their removal.

Carnet (pronounced car-nay)

An international customs document that allows the temporary export and import of goods without further customs documentation or the payment of duty.

Certificate of origin

A document certifying the place of manufacture of the goods.

C.&F. or C&F
Cost of the goods and freight.

C.&I. or C&I
Cost of goods and insurance.

C.I.F. or CIF
Cost of the goods, insurance, and freight.

c.o.d.
Cash on delivery.

Consignee
The receiver of the goods.

Consignor
The sender of the goods.

Counterfoil
Portion of carnet given to customs to match a voucher.

Cranage
Cost of using the wharf cranes.

Credit risk insurance
Insurance covering non-payment for goods delivered.

Customs broker
A person or company authorized to clear goods through customs on behalf of others.

Demurrage
Excess time taken for unloading or loading a vessel.

Destuff
Unpack a shipping container.

Dock receipt
Receipt from the port authority for the goods received prior to loading.

Draft
A document directing the drawee to pay the stated amount to a payee at a specified date.

Dumping
Exporting goods to a country at prices lower than in the exporter's country.

Duty

A tax on imports into a country.

Ex works

The seller has no responsibility beyond his own premises.

Export license

A government document allowing the exporter to export designated goods to a designated destination.

Force majeure

An insurance term indicating that the insurance company will not be responsible for the results of conditions that are beyond their control, such as war and earthquakes.

Free alongside ship (f.a.s. or FAS)

The cost of the goods plus all charges associated with delivering them alongside the ship at a named port.

Free in and out (f.i.o. or FIO)

The charterer of the vessel is responsible for the cost of loading and unloading the goods onto and off the vessel.

Free on board (f.o.b. *or* FOB)

The cost of the goods plus all charges associated with delivering them to a named port and placing them on a vessel.

Free port

A location to which goods may be delivered duty free while awaiting re-export or sale.

Free trade agreement

Trade agreement between Canada and the United States that was superseded by the North American Free Trade Agreement.

Free trade zone

An area designated by a country where goods may be stored or used in manufacture and re-exported without duty being paid.

Freight forwarder

A company that handles most of the aspects of shipping goods, including arranging for the shipping and the required documentation.

GATT

General Agreement on Tariffs and Trade, adopted by most trading nations.

Gross weight

Total weight of goods and packing material.

IATA

International Air Transport Association. A trade association of international air transport airlines.

Import license

An official government document required in some countries to allow the importation of designated goods.

Incoterms

International trade terms as defined by the International Chamber of Commerce.

Irrevocable, confirmed letter of credit

The purchaser's bank confirms the credit in the LC and undertakes to make the required payments to the exporter provided the terms and conditions of the LC are complied with. See letter of credit.

Irrevocable letter of credit

The purchaser's bank undertakes that the LC cannot be canceled or amended before the expiration date without the express consent of all parties concerned. See letter of credit.

Letter of credit

An agreement between the exporter, the exporter's bank, the purchaser's bank, and the purchaser on the terms for payment for and delivery of goods and services. Of the several types of LC, the most common are: revocable letter of credit, irrevocable letter of credit, and irrevocable, confirmed letter of credit.

Licensing

A business arrangement in which one company gives another company permission to manufacture its product for a specified payment.

Marine insurance

Insurance covering the loss or damage of goods at sea that cannot be recovered from the vessel owners.

Net weight

Weight of goods only, without packing or container.

North American Free Trade Agreement

Trade agreement between Canada, Mexico, and the United States implemented in 1994.

On consignment

Goods provided to the consignee by the consignor for sale, with payment to be made when sold.

Open account

A business arrangement in which goods are shipped to a foreign agent or purchaser without payment guarantee.

Pro forma invoice

An invoice with approximate weights and values, sent in advance of shipment, that enables the buyer to obtain an import permit and other documentation.

Quota

The quantity of goods that a country will allow to be imported before additional duty or restrictions are imposed.

Revocable letter of credit

This LC may be canceled or amended at any time after it is issued, without the consent of and without notice to the exporter or his bank. See letter of credit.

Ship's manifest

The document listing the ship's cargo.

Sight draft

A draft payable on presentation.

Stuff

Pack a shipping container.

Tare weight

The weight of the goods' packing material or container, without the goods.

Transshipment

Shipment of goods through another country.

Voucher

Portion of carnet retained by customs when temporarily exporting goods.

Wharfage

Fee for the use of a wharf.

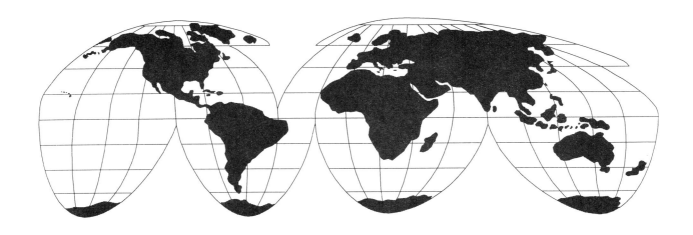

Index

ESTABLISH A FRAMEWORK
FOR EXCELLENCE
WITH THE OASIS PRESS ®

BOOKS & SOFTWARE
Celebrating 25 Years

THE OASIS PRESS*

PSI RESEARCH

P.O. BOX 3727

CENTRAL POINT, OR

97502·0032

Fastbreaking changes in technology and the global marketplace continue to create unprecedented opportunities for businesses through the '90s and into the new millennium. However with these opportunities will also come many new challenges. Today, more than ever, businesses, especially small businesses, need to excel in all areas of operation to complete and succeed in an ever-changing world.

The Successful Business Library takes you through the '90s and beyond, helping you solve the day-to-day problems you face now, and prepares you for the unexpected problems you may be facing down the road. With any of our products, you will receive up-to-date and practical business solutions, which are easy to use and easy to understand. No jargon or theories, just solid, nuts-and-bolts information.

Whether you are an entrepreneur going into business for the first time or an experienced consultant trying to keep up with the latest rules and regulations, The Successful Business Library provides you with the step-by-step guidance, and action-oriented plans you need to succeed in today's world. As an added benefit, PSI Research/The Oasis Press® unconditionally guarantees your satisfaction with the purchase of any book or software application in our catalog.

More than a marketplace for our products, we actually provide something that many business Web sites tend to overlook... useful information!

It's no mystery that the World Wide Web is a great way for businesses to promote their products, however most commercial sites stop there. We have always viewed our site's goals a little differently. For starters, we have applied our 25 years of experience providing hands-on information to small businesses directly to our Web site. We offer current information to help you start your own business, guidelines to keep it up and running, useful federal and state-specific information (including addresses and phone numbers to contact these resources), and a forum for business owners to communicate and network with others on the Internet. We would like to invite you to check out our Web site and discover the information that can assist you and your small business venture.

ALL MAJOR CREDIT CARDS ACCEPTED

CALL TO PLACE AN ORDER
— or —
TO RECEIVE A FREE CATALOG **1-800-228-2275**

International Orders (541) 479-9464   *Fax Orders* (541) 476-1479
Web site http://www.psi-research.com   *Email* sales@psi-research.com

PSI Research P.O. Box 3727 Central Point, Oregon 97502 U.S.A.

The Oasis Press Online
http://www.psi-research.com

NEW FROM THE OASIS PRESS

Let *SmartStart* pave your way through today's complex business environment.

You may be like more than 35 million other Americans — you dream of owning a business. In fact, there has never been a better time to start a small business. According to a recent research study by the Entrepreneurial Research Consortium, one out of three U.S. households has someone who is involved in a small business startup. With statistics like these, the odds seem to be in your favor... until you start dealing with the many regulations, laws, and financial requirements placed on 21st century business owners.

SmartStart Your (State*) Business goes a step beyond other business how-to books and provides you with:

✗ Each book is state specific, with information and resources that are unique. This gives you an advantage over other general business start-up books that have no way of providing current local information you will need;

✗ Quick reference to the most current mailing and Internet addresses and telephone numbers for the federal, state, local, and private agencies that will help get your business up and running;

✗ State population statistics, income and consumption rates, major industry trends, and overall business incentives to give you a better picture of doing business in your state; and

✗ Logical checklists, sample forms, and a complete sample business plan to assist you with the numerous start-up details.

SmartStart is your roadmap to avoid legal and financial pitfalls and direct you through the bureaucratic red tape that often entangles fledgling entrepreneurs. This is your all-in-one resource tool that will give you a jump start on planning for your business.

SmartStart Your (State) Business
$19.95, paperback

*When ordering, be sure to tell us which state you are interested in receiving

Order direct from The Oasis Press®

You can order any Successful Business Library title directly from The Oasis Press®. We would be happy to hear from you and assist you in finding the right titles for your small business needs at:

1-800-228-2275

Because *SmartStart* is a new state-specific series, new states are being released every month, please call to confirm a state's scheduled release date — or check with your favorite bookstore.

From The Leading Publisher of Small Business Information
Books that save you time and money.

Prepares a business to enter the export market. Clearly explains the basics, then articulates specific requirements for export licensing, preparation of documents, payment methods, packaging, and shipping. Includes advice on evaluating foreign representatives, planning international marketing strategies, and discovering official U.S. policy for various countries and regional sources.

Export Now   **Pages: 152**
Paperback: $24.95   ISBN: 1-55571-167-7
Binder: $39.95   ISBN: 1-55571-192-8

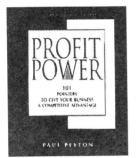

This useful guide discusses techniques for developing a solid foundation on which to build a successful business. Includes many real-world pointers that any business can implement into its day-to-day operations. Contains 30 checklists, evaluations, figures, and charts that will give you the power to drive your business' profits in the right direction.

Profit Power   **Pages: 272**
Paperback: $19.95   ISBN: 1-55571-374-2

Explains how you can conduct your own market research. Shows how to set objectives, determine which techniques to use, create a schedule, and monitor expenses. Encompasses primary research (trade shows, telephone interviews, mail surverys), plus secondary research utilizing available information in print.

Know Your Market   **Pages: 240**
Paperback: $19.95   ISBN: 1-55571-333-5
Binder: $39.95   ISBN: 1-55571-341-6

Surviving Success presents a program for those who wish to lead their companies from promising startup to industry dominance. Meet the challenges of business growth and transition with new insights. Learn from success stories. Be prepared to take proactive steps into your company's next growth transition.

Surviving Success   **Pages: 230**
Paperback: $19.95   ISBN: 1-55571-446-3

ALL MAJOR CREDIT CARDS ACCEPTED

CALL TO PLACE AN ORDER
— or —
TO RECEIVE A FREE CATALOG   1-800-228-2275

International Orders (541) 479-9464   Fax Orders (541) 476-1479
Web site http://www.psi-research.com   Email sales@psi-research.com

PSI Research   P.O. Box 3727   Central Point, Oregon   97502   U.S.A.

From The Leading Publisher of Small Business Information
Books that save you time and money.

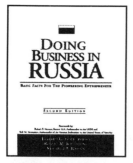

Explores and explains the strategies, atmosphere, and nuances involved with conducting a successful business in Russia's new market economy. This sourcebook provides an overview of the current economic situation, the best investment opportunities, commercial development incentives, and the framework for in-depth coverage of specific topics.

Doing Business in Russia, 2nd Edition   **Pages: 240**
Paperback: $19.95   **ISBN: 1-55571-375-0**

Cuts through the hype and shows why it is essential to first establish a solid image and communicative environment with your key audiences on the Internet. Examines all of the Internet tools available, not just the World Wide Web — and the significance of public relations and the Internet. Covers methods and considerations for international and multi-lingual marketing efforts with the Internet.

Connecting Online   **Pages: 475**
Paperback: $21.95   **ISBN: 1-55571-403-X**

Pursuing a high-tech business has never been more opportune, however the competition in the industry is downright grueling. Author Richard Manweller brings a smart, in-depth strategy with motivational meaning. It will show you how to tailor your strategy to gain investor's attention.

Funding High-Tech Ventures   **Pages: 160**
Paperback: $21.95   **ISBN: 1-55571-405-6**

Author Luigi Salvaneschi clearly shows how studying eight specific liberal arts principles can help nurture your own leadership skills within — and make you an asset for the business world of the 21st century. Each chapter leads you through his new concept in management thinking and tells how it applies to both the business world and your own personal life. Includes exercises to explore at home, work, and while traveling.

Renaissance 2000   **Pages: 345**
Paperback: $22.95   **ISBN: 1-55571-412-9**

ALL MAJOR CREDIT CARDS ACCEPTED

CALL TO PLACE AN ORDER
— or —
TO RECEIVE A FREE CATALOG   **1-800-228-2275**

International Orders (541) 479-9464   *Fax Orders* (541) 476-1479
Web site http://www.psi-research.com   *Email* sales@psi-research.com

PSI Research   P.O. Box 3727   Central Point, Oregon   97502   U.S.A.

The Oasis Press® Order Form

07/98

Call, Mail, Email, or Fax Your Order to: PSI Research, P.O. Box 3727, Central Point, OR 97502
Email: sales@psi-research.com   Website: http://www.psi-research.com
Order Phone USA & Canada: +1 800 228-2275   Inquiries & International Orders: +1 541 479-9464   Fax: +1 541 476-1479

TITLE	✔ BINDER	✔ PAPERBACK	QUANTITY	COST
Advertising Without An Agency		❏ $19.95		
Bottom Line Basics	❏ $39.95	❏ $19.95		
BusinessBasics: A Microbusiness Startup Guide		❏ $17.95		
The Business Environmental Handbook	❏ $39.95	❏ $19.95		
Business Owner's Guide to Accounting & Bookkeeping		❏ $19.95		
Buyer's Guide to Business Insurance	❏ $39.95	❏ $19.95		
California Corporation Formation Package	❏ $39.95	❏ $29.95		
Collection Techniques for a Small Business	❏ $39.95	❏ $19.95		
A Company Policy and Personnel Workbook	❏ $49.95	❏ $29.95		
Company Relocation Handbook	❏ $39.95	❏ $19.95		
CompControl: The Secrets of Reducing Worker's Compensation Costs	❏ $39.95	❏ $19.95		
Complete Book of Business Forms		❏ $19.95		
Connecting Online: Creating a Successful Image on the Internet		❏ $21.95		
Customer Engineering: Cutting Edge Selling Strategies	❏ $39.95	❏ $19.95		
Develop & Market Your Creative Ideas		❏ $15.95		
Developing International Markets		❏ $19.95		
Doing Business in Russia		❏ $19.95		
Draw The Line: A Sexual Harassment Free Workplace		❏ $17.95		
Entrepreneurial Decisionmaking		❏ $19.95		
The Essential Corporation Handbook		❏ $21.95		
the Essential Limited Liability Company Handbook	❏ $39.95	❏ $21.95		
Export Now: A Guide for Small Business	❏ $39.95	❏ $24.95		
Financial Decisionmaking: A Guide for the Non-Accountant		❏ $19.95		
Financial Management Techniques for Small Business	❏ $39.95	❏ $19.95		
Financing Your Small Business		❏ $19.95		
Franchise Bible: How to Buy a Franchise or Franchise Your Own Business	❏ $39.95	❏ $24.95		
Friendship Marketing: Growing Your Business by Cultivating Strategic Relationships		❏ $18.95		
Funding High-Tech Ventures		❏ $21.95		
Home Business Made Easy		❏ $19.95		
Information Breakthrough		❏ $22.95		
The Insider's Guide to Small Business Loans	❏ $29.95	❏ $19.95		
InstaCorp – Incorporate In Any State (Book & Software)		❏ $29.95		
Joysticks, Blinking Lights and Thrills		❏ $18.95		
Keeping Score: An Inside Look at Sports Marketing		❏ $18.95		
Know Your Market: How to Do Low-Cost Market Research	❏ $39.95	❏ $19.95		
The Leader's Guide		❏ $19.95		
Legal Expense Defense: How to Control Your Business' Legal Costs and Problems	❏ $39.95	❏ $19.95		
Location, Location, Location: How to Select the Best Site for Your Business		❏ $19.95		
Mail Order Legal Guide	❏ $45.00	❏ $29.95		
Managing People: A Practical Guide		❏ $21.95		
Marketing for the New Millennium: Applying New Techniques		❏ $19.95		
Marketing Mastery: Your Seven Step Guide to Success	❏ $39.95	❏ $19.95		
The Money Connection: Where and How to Apply for Business Loans and Venture Capital	❏ $39.95	❏ $24.95		
Moonlighting: Earn a Second Income at Home		❏ $15.95		
People Investment	❏ $39.95	❏ $19.95		
Power Marketing for Small Business	❏ $39.95	❏ $19.95		
Profit Power: 101 Pointers to Give Your Business a Competitive Edge		❏ $19.95		
Proposal Development: How to Respond and Win the Bid	❏ $39.95	❏ $21.95		
Raising Capital		❏ $19.95		
Renaissance 2000: Liberal Arts Essentials for Tomorrow's Leaders		❏ $22.95		
Retail in Detail: How to Start and Manage a Small Retail Business		❏ $15.95		
Secrets to High Ticket Selling		❏ $19.95		
Secrets to Buying and Selling a Business		❏ $24.95		
Secure Your Future: Financial Planning at Any Age	❏ $39.95	❏ $19.95		
The Small Business Insider's Guide to Bankers		❏ $18.95		
SmartStart Your (State) Business... series		❏ $19.95		
PLEASE SPECIFY WHICH STATE(S) YOU WANT:				
Smile Training Isn't Enough: The Three Secrets to Excellent Customer Service		❏ $19.95		
Start Your Business (Available as a book and disk package)		❏ $ 9.95 (without disk)		

BOOK SUB-TOTAL (Additional titles on other side)

TITLE	✔ BINDER	✔ PAPERBACK	QUANTITY	COST
Starting and Operating a Business in...series *Includes FEDERAL section PLUS ONE STATE section*	❏ $34.95	❏ $27.95		
PLEASE SPECIFY WHICH STATE(S) YOU WANT:				
STATE SECTION ONLY (BINDER NOT INCLUDED) SPECIFY STATE(S):	❏ $8.95			
FEDERAL SECTION ONLY (BINDER NOT INCLUDED)	❏ $12.95			
U.S. EDITION (FEDERAL SECTION – 50 STATES AND WASHINGTON DC IN 11-BINDER SET)	❏ $295.95			
Successful Business Plan: Secrets & Strategies	❏ $49.95	❏ $27.95		
Successful Network Marketing for The 21st Century		❏ $15.95		
Surviving Success		❏ $19.95		
TargetSmart! Database Marketing for the Small Business		❏ $19.95		
Top Tax Saving Ideas for Today's Small Business		❏ $16.95		
Twenty-One Sales in a Sale: What Sales Are You Missing?		❏ $19.95		
Which Business? Help in Selecting Your New Venture		❏ $18.95		
Write Your Own Business Contracts	❏ $39.95	❏ $24.95		
BOOK SUB-TOTAL (Be sure to figure your amount from the previous side)				

OASIS SOFTWARE   Please specify which computer operating system you use (DOS, MacOS, or Windows)

TITLE	✔ Windows	✔ MacOS	Price	QUANTITY	COST
California Corporation Formation Package ASCII Software	❏	❏	$ 39.95		
Company Policy & Personnel Software Text Files	❏	❏	$ 49.95		
Financial Management Techniques (Full Standalone)	❏		$ 99.95		
Financial Templates	❏	❏	$ 69.95		
The Insurance Assistant Software (Full Standalone)	❏		$ 29.95		
Start Your Business (Software for Windows™)	❏		$ 19.95		
Successful Business Plan (Software for Windows™)	❏		$ 99.95		
Successful Business Plan Templates	❏	❏	$ 69.95		
The Survey Genie - Customer Edition (Full Standalone)	❏ $199.95 (WIN)	❏ $149.95 (DOS)			
The Survey Genie - Employee Edition (Full Standalone)	❏ $199.95 (WIN)	❏ $149.95 (DOS)			
SOFTWARE SUB-TOTAL					

BOOK & DISK PACKAGES   Please specify which computer operating system you use (DOS, MacOS, or Windows)

TITLE	✔ Windows	✔ MacOS	✔ Binder	✔ Paperback	QUANTITY	COST
The Buyer's Guide to Business Insurance w/ Insurance Assistant	❏		❏ $ 59.95	❏ $ 39.95		
California Corporation Formation Binder Book & ASCII Software	❏	❏	❏ $ 69.95	❏ $ 59.95		
Company Policy & Personnel Book & Software Text Files	❏	❏	❏ $ 89.95	❏ $ 69.95		
Financial Management Techniques Book & Software	❏		❏ $129.95	❏ $ 119.95		
Start Your Business Paperback & Software (Software for Windows™)	❏			❏ $ 24.95		
Successful Business Plan Book & Software for Windows™	❏		❏ $125.95	❏ $109.95		
Successful Business Plan Book & Software Templates	❏	❏	❏ $109.95	❏ $ 89.95		
BOOK & DISK PACKAGE SUB-TOTAL						

AUDIO CASSETTES

Power Marketing Tools For Small Business	❏ $ 49.95	
The Secrets To Buying & Selling A Business	❏ $ 49.95	
AUDIO CASSETTES SUB-TOTAL		

Sold To: **Please give street address**

NAME:

Title:

Company:

Street Address:

City/State/Zip:

Daytime Phone: Email:

Ship To: **If different than above, please give alternate street address**

NAME:

Title:

Company:

Street Address:

City/State/Zip:

Daytime Phone:

Your Grand Total

SUB-TOTALS (from other side)	$
SUB-TOTALS (from this side)	$
SHIPPING (see chart below)	$
TOTAL ORDER	$

If your purchase is:	Shipping costs within the USA:
$0 - $25	$5.00
$25.01 - $50	$6.00
$50.01 - $100	$7.00
$100.01 - $175	$9.00
$175.01 - $250	$13.00
$250.01 - $500	$18.00
$500.01+	4% of total merchandise

07/98

Payment Information: **Rush service is available, call for details.**
International and Canadian Orders: Please call for quote on shipping.

❏ CHECK Enclosed payable to PSI Research   Charge: ❏ VISA   ❏ MASTERCARD   ❏ AMEX   ❏ DISCOVER

Card Number: Expires:

Signature: Name On Card:

Please answer these questions to let us know how our products are working for you, and what we could do to serve you better.

Developing International Markets

Rate this product's overall quality of information:
☐ Excellent
☐ Good
☐ Fair
☐ Poor

Rate the quality of printed materials:
☐ Excellent
☐ Good
☐ Fair
☐ Poor

Rate the format:
☐ Excellent
☐ Good
☐ Fair
☐ Poor

Did the product provide what you needed?
☐ Yes ☐ No

If not, what should be added?
_____
_____
_____
_____
_____
_____
_____
_____
_____
_____

This product is:
☐ Clear and easy to follow
☐ Too complicated
☐ Too elementary

Were the worksheets easy to use?
☐ Yes ☐ No ☐ N/A

Should we include?
☐ More worksheets
☐ Fewer worksheets
☐ No worksheets

How do you feel about the price?
☐ Lower than expected
☐ About right
☐ Too expensive

How many employees are in your company?
☐ Under 10 employees
☐ 10 - 50 employees
☐ 51 - 99 employees
☐ 100 - 250 employees
☐ Over 250 employees

How many people in the city your company is in?
☐ 50,000 - 100,000
☐ 100,000 - 500,000
☐ 500,000 - 1,000,000
☐ Over 1,000,000
☐ Rural (Under 50,000)

What is your type of business?
☐ Retail
☐ Service
☐ Government
☐ Manufacturing
☐ Distributor
☐ Education

What types of products or services do you sell?
_____
_____

What is your position in the company?
(please check one)
☐ Owner
☐ Administrative
☐ Sales/Marketing
☐ Finance
☐ Human Resources
☐ Production
☐ Operations
☐ Computer/MIS

How did you learn about this product?
☐ Recommended by a friend
☐ Used in a seminar or class
☐ Have used other PSI products
☐ Received a mailing
☐ Saw in bookstore
☐ Saw in library
☐ Saw review in:
  ☐ Newspaper
  ☐ Magazine
  ☐ Radio/TV

Where did you buy this product?
☐ Catalog
☐ Bookstore
☐ Office supply
☐ Consultant

Would you purchase other business tools from us?
☐ Yes ☐ No

If so, which products interest you?
☐ EXECARDS® Communications Cards
☐ Books for business
☐ Software

Would you recommend this product to a friend?
☐ Yes ☐ No

Do you use a personal computer?
☐ Yes ☐ No

If yes, which?
☐ Macintosh
☐ PC Compatible
☐ Other

Check all the ways you use computers?
☐ Word processing
☐ Accounting
☐ Spreadsheet
☐ Inventory
☐ Order processing
☐ Design/Graphics
☐ General Data Base
☐ Customer Information
☐ Scheduling
☐ Internet

May we call you to follow up on your comments?
☐ Yes ☐ No

May we add your name to our mailing list? ☐ Yes ☐ No

If you'd like us to send associates or friends a catalog, just list names and addresses on back.

Is there anything we should do to improve our products?
_____

Just fill in your name and address here, fold (see back) and mail.

Name _____

Title _____

Company _____

Phone _____

Address _____

City/State/Zip _____

Email Address (Home) _____ (Business) _____

PSI Research creates this family of fine products to help you more easily and effectively manage your business activities:

The Oasis Press
PSI Successful Business Library

PSI Successful Business Software
EXECARDS Communication Tools

07/98

If you have friends or associates who might appreciate receiving our catalogs, please list here. Thanks!

Name_____   Name_____

Title_____   Title_____

Company_____   Company_____

Phone_____   Phone_____

Address_____   Address_____

Address_____   Address_____

FOLD HERE FIRST

NO POSTAGE
NECESSARY
IF MAILED
IN THE
UNITED STATES

BUSINESS REPLY MAIL
FIRST CLASS MAIL PERMIT NO. 002 MERLIN, OREGON

POSTAGE WILL BE PAID BY ADDRESSEE

PSI Research
PO BOX 1414
Merlin OR 97532-9900

FOLD HERE SECOND, THEN TAPE TOGETHER

✂
Please cut
along this
vertical line,
fold twice,
tape together
and mail.

184198